Flowers Can Even Bloom in Schools

Selected Readings in Educational Psychology

Marcia H. Perlstein /Foreword by Herbert R. Kohl

Westinghouse Learning Press
Division of Westinghouse Learning Corporation

Flowers Can Even Bloom in Schools
Selected Readings in Educational Psychology

Text set in 10 point Times Roman, with
display lines in Optima and Souvenir Light,
by Reeder Typesetting, Fremont, California

Design and cover by Joseph di Chiarro,
Palo Alto, California

Cover photo by Elihu Blotnick/BBM Associates,
Berkeley, California

Development and production by
Westinghouse Learning Press,
Sunnyvale, California

Printed and bound by R. R. Donnelley
& Sons

ISBN 0-88250-401-0

Library of Congress
Catalog Card Number: 74-4713

Copyright © 1974
by Westinghouse Learning Corporation

Westinghouse Learning Press
Sunnyvale, California 94086

Division of Westinghouse Learning Corporation
New York, New York 10017

Printed in the United States of America

1 2 3 4 5 6 7 8 9 10 77 76 75 74

1/18/79 Berhens Tylor 6.00

I'd like to thank each author who has written an article for this book. Every one of you has had a profound influence on my personal and professional development. This book is my opportunity to share your influence, support, challenge, acceptance, and motivation with teachers and paraprofessionals across the nation. I want to thank you especially for being people whom I can trust, care about, and learn from. Mildred McClosky, Jane Zahn, and Clark Robinson, as my very special teachers and friends, you gave me more of a sense of what a teacher–person may become than an infinite number of articles would have. Mary Kohler, Joan Levinson, Judy Bebelaar, Tom Shaheen, Eugene Howard, Herbert Kohl, Anna Einfeld, and Hank Giarretto, you all added scope to my professional and personal growth. The entire Opportunity II family, my students and colleagues, constantly provide encouragement. Thanks to all of you.

Bibliographic assistance was provided by Linda Whipperman, Helen Jacobsen and Teresa Milazzo.

My sincere appreciation goes to the many teachers in my classroom beyond the walls of my school building. These include former school board members Laurel Glass, Zuretti Goosby, Howard Nemerovski, and Claire Lilienthal. Community leader Julia Commer has often shared her vision and energy with me. Peter Sandmann and Ken Hecht as advocates for youth were available whenever needed. Peter Kleinbard, John Lichtenstein, Carol and Gregory Abbey, Claire and Don Rothenberg, Ruth Chance, Phil and Ellen Siegelman, Herb McClosky, Ruth Collins, Deborah Paterakis, Bert Edises, Katherine and Greg Castillo, Vern and Madeline Houston, Diane Scott, Bernadette and Luigi Corsiglia, John and Carol Liu-Klein, Terry and Joellen Murphy, Judy and Don Flory, and Dotty and Frank Barnett were involved in an infinite number of discussions where the concepts discussed in this book were developed.

And finally, thanks to my East Coast family, both actual and extended. You show me constantly that three thousand miles is a distance merely in geography and not in spirit.

Acknowledgments

In memory of

Colleen

who sadly forgot

and in appreciation of

Jane

and her affirmation of life

and is dedicated to

**MY NEAREST AND DEAREST
FRIENDS AND FAMILY**

who helped me answer the question
that Colleen raised

I'LL ALWAYS REMEMBER

I didn't learn much in teachers' college that was useful to me as a classroom teacher. The books assigned in the classes were written by educational researchers and other experts whose theories missed the everyday reality of classroom life. Our professors were, for the most part, the people who wrote the books. Some of them could have been excellent teachers a decade or so ago, but in the university they were out of touch with young people.

Almost everything presented to us prospective teachers was positive. We were shown the most modern curriculum, told how to handle behavior and discipline problems, given lessons on classroom control and maintenance, and assured that if we followed the rules and prescriptions laid down for us we would be perfect teachers—that is, untroubled pure adults who would be both examples for and leaders of the young.

Despite a year and a summer of classes and student teaching, on the first day that I had my own class I realized how unprepared I was. The students scared me; the curriculum that seemed so good at teachers' college bored the class; my anger, which was not supposed to show, came out. The students, who were mostly black and Puerto Rican, looked upon me as an enemy, not a model, and followed my suggestions and commands only occasionally, and usually then under protest.

I did not expect to be a failure with my students and was crushed. Nothing had prepared me for the process of developing trust, respect, and good feeling between student and teacher. Nor had anyone told me how long five hours in a classroom can seem, how much time must be filled up when students and teachers are not living in consonance. I had no sense of the process of translating ideas into effective programs nor of the amount of improvisations and the number of mistakes that go into learning how to be a good teacher.

One thing missing from my education was the voice of classroom teachers talking simply and honestly about their problems and about how they managed to thrive, survive, or get wiped out. I needed to know as much about failures as about successes, about the daily grind of being a teacher as well as the rewards. This book provides just that. It is full of the voices of people who have worked with young people and are willing to talk honestly about their successes and failures, about the specific, unpredictable personal things that develop in the classroom or the schoolyard or the lunchroom that are often as crucial as the ideas the adults hold or the goals they set for their students. There are essays by classroom teachers, principals, paraprofessionals, and teacher trainers in this book, and even some words from a superintendent of schools

Foreword

who fought to change the system and got wiped out. Most of these authors are practitioners as well, and they have seen new programs grow, occasionally thrive, more frequently fail. They know about struggle in specific terms and not merely philosophically or rhetorically.

There is one particularly valuable aspect of this book—the commitment to the development of the basic skills of reading and math, even in nontraditional programs. Reading and math are survival skills in our culture, and no program that is committed to aiding young people grow can ignore this. Many people have felt that the acquisition of basic skills is inconsistent with open or child-centered or nonauthoritarian education. Not so—there are many different ways to learn to read and calculate, and the contributors to this book believe these skills can be developed without humiliating or punishing or manipulating young people.

Structure is another problem in the debate between traditional and alternative educational philosophy. Often alternative education is equated with non-structured, formless, chaotic learning situations. Again, not so. It is a mistake to believe that there is only one way to structure human relationships—the authoritarian way. There are many democratic ways to function, many ways that self-regulating structures grow and modify themselves according to people's needs. Several essays in this book deal directly with the issue of non-traditional structure and illustrate how structure can work to nurture people's growth instead of to control them.

The emphasis in the book is practical, and the articles are sometimes painfully intimate. From these pages emerges a sense of people doing work or recovering from enormous commitments of energy and love that ended in frustration or disappointment. There is some theory too—some tentative approaches to putting together a viable analysis of educational change, drawing on work that has already been done.

This is a good, gritty, strong, useful book for people who want to get a sense of what it is really like living with young people at least five hours a day, five days a week, for most of the year. Parents as well as professionals can benefit from reading it to understand the energy, compassion, and patience needed to work effectively with the young, and, at the same time, defend oneself from an unresponsive and often hostile institution. Teaching well is not merely working well with students but also working toward changing repressive school systems and learning how to survive oneself.

Of course no book can make effective teachers. This one makes no such absurd or romantic pretense. It merely provides the prospective teacher with other people's experiences and perceptions in the hope that we can learn something of value from each other and do not have to repeat the same mistakes endlessly. Considering the general academic literature available to future teachers, this is no small accomplishment.

Herbert R. Kohl

Contents

3

About Learning and How It Happens

4

New Options

Experiential Learning

Beliefs into Action

a golden key
to open all doors
for all
at any time
full of earthy energy
with warmth and honesty
that's the perfect teacher
a realistic
listening
friend

Kathy Mackin

Dear Reader,

I invite you to travel through the following pages in your own way, to consider the issues raised—some issues regrettably old and still unsolved, others more recent, with tentative solutions signifying that more can happen. Consider how some schools and systems persist in staying stuck, holding rigidly and tenaciously to unverified dogma. Consider how many attempts to change fail because of overreaction and sloppy, hasty planning.

Somewhere between these two poles lie the projects, classrooms, schools, and ideas highlighted in this book. These programs represent a thoughtful, new thrust and are like flowers scattered across the country. Young people in Rabun Gap, Georgia, and in San Francisco, California, have something in common—they are delighting in education, feeling good about themselves, and forming lasting, significant relationships with adults and with each other. These students are simultaneously developing serious academic skills and realizing the infinite possibilities for exploration in the world outside themselves.

But effective new programs are still in the minority. Excitement about what *can be* in a few isolated instances cannot hide *what is*. But we can still explore the models that let us know that classrooms of the present can move beyond their current boundaries. In order to move from what is, we need to expand our notions of what can be. The samples in this book reflect beginnings, attempts that constantly undergo intensive scrutiny and modification. Not all programs need be the same as these, but the principles will be the same— variations on the theme of young people growing and experiencing joy in their own beings, in their own potentials, and in their own competencies.

Two major themes run throughout the book. The first is that any educational psychological theories worth concentrating on can be applied, perhaps with necessary modification, to any classroom, at any grade level, in any setting. Educational principles stand only when they can be translated into practices. The second theme is balance. Effective programs can simultaneously utilize innovation and tradition. Educators need not adhere rigidly to either status quo or latest fad. Changes must be carefully planned, using sound principles of educational psychology.

The four major sections of this book move progressively outward, starting with techniques to help teachers look at themselves and view their own behavior, continuing with some difficult questions on educational value orientations, pausing to examine psychological components of positive learning situations, and finally moving to descriptions of programs that embody all the principles developed in the earlier sections.

Introduction

We are addressing this book to anyone interested in education. You may be a teacher of few or many years, following any one of many philosophies. You may be a paraprofessional at the beginning of your education courses, a teacher trainee at any point toward certification, or a veteran teacher, continuously exploring major educational issues. But a teacher is not alone in educating a young person. You may be a parent or a member of the community, with resources to offer and a desire to participate in educating youth. Even though in this book our setting is the classroom, we invite anyone interested in education to stop awhile and try to understand the teacher's perspective and maybe even take part in the educational process.

We want to share with you what we have learned from what we've tried to do. We've tried to write, to teach, to found new programs. We are authors, teachers, trainers of teachers, and superintendents of schools. We all speak from our own learnings; most of us are day to day or often in the classroom. There we learn, we formulate our theories, we test them through experience and then reformulate and test and think again. We try to balance thought and action; we think and practice our thoughts. We recommend this process to you. We share with you our own experiential learning and some models we have tried for students. We want to meet you and to enter your classrooms with you and to generate some interchange. We'd love to have you get in touch with us and let us know how you react and what you think and how it works in practice.

Marcia Perlstein

Marcia H. Perlstein

Both old and new teachers go through a continuous process of personal growth. Most of us see ourselves as people first—people who happen to have chosen the role of teacher. Our attempts to understand our behavior and apply our understanding to the classroom are significant for us as well as for the many students with whom we try to connect. The articles that follow are written by educators who have grappled with their humanity and their efficacy with others. They have taught at a variety of levels in a number of different situations. None pretends to have ended the process of becoming; all have some suggestions about the kinds of qualities and danger signals to watch for in themselves as well as in others and to overcome or accentuate to help the students realize their potentials.

1 The Beings Teachers Can Become

The Interpersonal Relationship in the Facilitation of Learning
Carl R. Rogers

Carl R. Rogers, now Resident Fellow at the Center for Studies of the Person in La Jolla, California, developed the concept of client-centered therapy, an idea he has broadened and developed in more than eleven major publications dealing with various kinds of psychological relationships.

Hanging Up the Students
Herbert R. Kohl

Herbert R. Kohl, author of *36 Children* and *The Open Classroom,* has been a vocal proponent of the need for finding new ways to approach education.

Looking at Ourselves: Communication with Students
Jane C. Zahn

Chairman of the Department of Interdisciplinary Studies in Education at California State University, San Francisco, Jane Zahn has participated in numerous projects and conferences dealing with communications and effecting attitude change at all levels of education.

The Difficult but Necessary Art of Introspection
Marcia H. Perlstein

Marcia Perlstein has been vitally involved in seeking new designs for education, not only in her work with the Opportunity High Schools in San Francisco, but in workshops, conferences, and training courses all over the country.

Looking Inward: Some Techniques

The articles in this section attempt to stimulate careful view of self and the application of the insights thus attained to relationships with students. The view inward can be made a conscious process, and although each of us has to vary approaches according to personal style and students' needs, some general principles can aid us in looking inward.

In "The Interpersonal Relationship in the Facilitation of Learning," Carl Rogers goes far beyond the usual cliches of the humanistic-psychology movement in exploring how teachers can promote learning. Herbert Kohl, in "Hanging Up the Students," looks at some of the inadvertent, but often critical, mistakes we make when we try to play our roles as teachers while remembering we are persons too. In "Looking at Ourselves: Communication with Students," Jane Zahn shows positive ways to give students information about themselves. She helps teachers understand their own attitudes and possible defenses in order to present feedback most effectively. I close this section with "The Difficult but Necessary Art of Introspection" by discussing some of the mechanisms I use for reviewing my own role in classroom interactions.

In all these approaches, careful consideration is given to the conceptual base upon which these techniques are built as well as to personal application of these important principles.

I wish to begin . . . with a statement that may seem surprising to some and perhaps offensive to others. It is simply this : Teaching, in my estimation, is a vastly overrated function.

Having made such a statement, I scurry to the dictionary to see if I really mean what I say. Teaching means "to instruct." Personally I am not much interested in instructing another in what he should know or think. "To impart knowledge or skill." My reaction is, why not be more efficient, using a book or programmed learning? "To make to know." Here my hackles rise. I have no wish to make anyone know something. "To show, guide, direct." As I see it, too many people have been shown, guided, directed. So I come to the conclusion that I do mean what I said. Teaching is, for me, a relatively unimportant and vastly overvalued activity.

But there is more in my attitude than this. I have a negative reaction to teaching. Why? I think it is because it raises all the wrong questions. As soon as we focus on teaching, the question arises, what shall we teach? What, from our superior vantage point, does the other person need to know? I wonder if, in this modern world, we are justified in the presumption that we are wise about the future and the young are foolish. Are we really sure . . . what they should know? Then there is the ridiculous question of coverage. What shall the course cover? This notion of coverage is based on the assumption that what is taught is what is learned; what is presented is what is assimilated. I know of no assumption so obviously untrue. One does not need research to provide evidence that this is false. One needs only to talk with a few students.

But I ask myself, "Am I so prejudiced against teaching that I find no situation in which it is worthwhile?" I immediately think of my experiences in Australia, not so long ago. I became interested in the Australian aborigine. Here is a group which for more than twenty thousand years has managed to live and exist in a desolate environment in which modern man would perish within a few days. The secret of the aborigine's survival has been teaching. He has passed on to the young every shred of knowledge about how to find water, about how to track game, about how to kill the kangaroo, about how to find his way through the trackless desert. Such knowledge is conveyed to the young as being the way

Reprinted from *Freedom to Learn* by permission of the author and the publisher, Charles E. Merrill Publishing Company.

The Interpersonal Relationship in the Facilitation of Learning

Carl R. Rogers

to behave, and any innovation is frowned upon. It is clear that teaching has provided him the way to survive in a hostile and relatively unchanging environment.

Now I am closer to the nub of the question which excites me. Teaching and the imparting of knowledge make sense in an unchanging environment. This is why it has been an unquestioned function for centuries. But if there is one truth about modern man, it is that he lives in an environment which is continually changing. . . .

We are, in my view, faced with an entirely new situation in education where the goal of education, if we are to survive, is the facilitation of change and learning. The only man who is educated is the man who has learned how to learn; the man who has learned how to adapt and change; the man who has realized that no knowledge is secure, that only the process of seeking knowledge gives a basis for security. Changingness, a reliance on process rather than upon static knowledge, is the only thing that makes any sense as a goal for education in the modern world.

So now with some relief I turn to an activity, a purpose, which really warms me—the facilitation of learning. When I have been able to transform a group— and here I mean all the members of a group, myself included—into a community of learners, then the excitement has been almost beyond belief. To free curiosity; to permit individuals to go charging off in new directions dictated by their own interests; to unleash the sense of inquiry; to open everything to questioning and exploration; to recognize that everything is in process of change— here is an experience I can never forget. I cannot always achieve it in groups with which I am associated, but when it is partially or largely achieved then it becomes a never-to-be-forgotten group experience. Out of such a context arise true students, real learners, creative scientists and scholars and practitioners, the kinds of individuals who can live in a delicate but ever-changing balance between what is presently known and the flowing, moving, altering problems and facts of the future.

Here then is a goal to which I can give myself wholeheartedly. I see the facilitation of learning as the aim of education, the way in which we might develop the learning man, the way in which we can learn to live as individuals in process. I see the facilitation of learning as the function that may hold constructive, tentative, changing, process answers to some of the deepest perplexities which beset man today. . . .

We know—and I will briefly describe some of the evidence—that the initiation of such learning rests not upon the teaching skills of the leader, not upon his scholarly knowledge of the field, not upon his curricular planning, not upon his use of audiovisual aids, not upon the programmed learning he utilizes, not upon his lectures and presentations, not upon an abundance of books, though each of these might at one time or another be utilized as an important resource. No, the facilitation of significant learning rests upon certain attitudinal qualities which exist in the personal relationship between the facilitator and the learner.

We came upon such findings first in the field of psychotherapy, but increasingly there is evidence which shows that these findings apply in the classroom as well. We find it easier to think that the intensive relationship between therapist and client might possess these qualities, but we are also finding that they may exist in the countless interpersonal interactions (as many as a thousand per day, as Jackson [1966] has shown) between the teacher and her pupils.

What are these qualities, these attitudes, which facilitate learning? Let me describe them very briefly, drawing illustrations from the teaching field.

Realness in the Facilitator of Learning

Perhaps the most basic of these essential attitudes is realness or genuineness. When the facilitator is a real person, being what he is, entering into a relationship with the learner without presenting a front or facade, he is much more likely to be effective. This means that the feelings which he is experiencing are available to him, available to his awareness, that he is able to live these feelings, be them, and able to communicate them if appropriate. It means that he comes into a direct personal encounter with the learner, meeting him on a person-to-person basis. It means that he is being himself, not denying himself.

Seen from this point of view it is suggested that the teacher can be a real person in his relationship with his students. He can be enthusiastic, he can be bored, he can be interested in students, he can be angry, he can be sensitive and sympathetic. Because he accepts these feelings as his own he has no need to impose them on his students. He can like or dislike a student product without implying that it is objectively good or bad or that the student is good or bad. He is simply expressing a feeling for the product, a feeling which exists within himself. Thus, he is a person to his students, not a faceless embodiment of a curricular requirement nor a sterile tube through which knowledge is passed from one generation to the next.

It is obvious that this attitudinal set, found to be effective in psychotherapy, is sharply in contrast with the tendency of most teachers to show themselves to their pupils simply as roles. It is quite customary for teachers rather consciously to put on the mask, the role, the facade, of being a teacher, and to wear this facade all day, removing it only when they have left the school at night.

But not all teachers are like this. Take Sylvia Ashton-Warner, who took resistant, supposedly slow-learning primary-school Maori children in New Zealand and let them develop their own reading vocabulary. Each child could request one word—whatever word he wished—each day, and she would print it on a card and give it to him. *Kiss, ghost, bomb, tiger, fight, love, daddy*—these are samples. Soon they were building sentences, which they could also keep. *He'll get a licking. Pussy's frightened.* The children simply never forgot these self-initiated learnings. But it is not my purpose to tell you of her methods. I want instead to give you a glimpse of her attitude, of the passionate realness which must have been as evident to her tiny pupils as to her readers. An editor asked her some questions and she responded: "A few cool facts you asked me for . . . I don't know that there's a cool fact in me, or anything else cool for that matter, on this particular subject. I've got only hot long faces on the matter of Creative Teaching, scorching both the page and me." [Ashton-Warner, 1963]

Here is no sterile facade. Here is a vital *person,* with convictions, with feelings. It is her transparent realness which was, I am sure, one of the elements that made her an exciting facilitator of learning. She doesn't fit into some neat educational formula. She *is,* and students grow by being in contact with someone who really and openly *is.*

Take another very different person, Barbara Shiel, whose exciting work in facilitating learning in sixth graders has been described earlier. [Rogers, 1969] She gave her pupils a great deal of responsible freedom . . . . Here is an example of the way she shared herself with her pupils—not just sharing feelings of sweetness and light, but anger and frustration. She had made art materials freely available, and students often used these in creative ways, but the room frequently looked like a picture of chaos. Here is her report of her feelings and what she did with them.

I find it maddening to live with the mess—with a capital M! No one seems to care except me. Finally, one day I told the children . . . that I am a neat, orderly person by nature and that the mess was driving me to distraction. Did they have a solution? It was suggested there were some volunteers who could clean up. . . . I said it didn't seem fair to me to have the same people clean up all the time for others—but it would solve it for me. "Well, some people like to clean," they replied. So that's the way it is. [Shiel, 1966]

I hope this example puts some lively meaning into the phrases I used earlier, that the facilitator is able to live these feelings, be them, and able to communicate them if appropriate. I have chosen an example of negative feelings, because I think it is more difficult for most of us to visualize what this would mean. In this instance, Miss Shiel is taking the risk of being transparent in her angry frustrations about the mess. And what happens? The same thing which, in my experience, nearly always happens. These young people accept and respect her feelings, take them into account, and work out a novel solution which none of us, I believe, would have suggested. Miss Shiel wisely comments, "I used to get upset and feel guilty when I became angry. I finally realized the children could accept *my* feelings too. And it is important for them to know when they've 'pushed me.' *I have my limits, too."* [Shiel, 1966]

Just to show that positive feelings, when they are real, are equally effective, let me quote briefly a college student's reaction, in a different course: "Your sense of humor in the class was cheering; we all felt relaxed because you showed us your human self, not a mechanical teacher image. I feel as if I have more understanding and faith in my teachers now. . . . I feel closer to the students too." Another says: "You conducted the class on a personal level and therefore in my mind I was able to formulate a picture of you as a person and not as merely a walking textbook." Another student in the same course: "It wasn't as if there was a teacher in the class, but rather someone whom we could trust and identify as a 'sharer.' You were so perceptive and sensitive to our thoughts, and this made it all the more 'authentic' for me. It was an 'authentic' experience, not just a class." [Bull, 1966]

I trust I am making it clear that to be real is not always easy, nor is it achieved all at once, but it is basic to the person who wants to become that revolutionary individual, a facilitator of learning.

Prizing, Acceptance, Trust

There is another attitude which stands out in those who are successful in facilitating learning. I have observed this attitude. I have experienced it. Yet, it is hard to know what term to put to it so I shall use several. I think of it as prizing the learner, prizing his feelings, his opinions, his person. It is a caring for the learner, but a nonpossessive caring. It is an acceptance of this other individual as a separate person, having worth in his own right. It is a basic trust—a belief that this other person is somehow fundamentally trustworthy. Whether we call it prizing, acceptance, trust, or by some other term, it shows up in a variety of observable ways. The facilitator who has a considerable degree of this attitude can be fully acceptant of the fear and hesitation of the student as he approaches a new problem as well as acceptant of the pupil's satisfaction in achievement. Such a teacher can accept the student's occasional apathy, his erratic desires to explore byroads of knowledge, as well as his disciplined efforts to achieve major goals. He can accept personal feelings which both disturb and promote learning—rivalry with a sibling, hatred of authority, concern about personal adequacy. What we are describing is a prizing of the learner as an imperfect human being with many feelings, many potentialities. The facilitator's prizing or acceptance of the learner is an operational expression of his essential confidence and trust in the capacity of the human organism.

I would like to give some examples of this attitude from the classroom situation. Here any teacher statements would be properly suspect, since many of us would like to feel we hold such attitudes and might have a biased perception of our qualities. But let me indicate how this attitude of prizing, of accepting, of trusting, appears to the student who is fortunate enough to experience it.

Here is a statement from a college student in a class with Dr. Morey Appell:

Your way of being with us is a revelation to me. In your class I feel important, mature, and capable of doing things on my own. I want to think for myself, and this need cannot be accomplished through textbooks and lectures alone, but through living. I think you see me as a person with real feelings and needs, an individual. What I say and do are significant expressions from me, and you recognize this. [Appell, 1959]

One of Miss Shiel's sixth-graders expresses much more briefly her misspelled appreciation of this attitude: "You are a wounderful teacher period! ! !" [Shiel, 1966]

College students in a class with Dr. Patricia Bull describe not only these prizing, trusting attitudes, but the effect these have had on their other interactions.

I feel that I can say things to you that I can't say to other professors. . . . Never before have I been so aware of the other students or their personalities. I have never had so much interaction in a college classroom with my classmates. The climate of the classroom has had a very profound effect on me . . . the free atmosphere for discussion affected me . . . the general atmosphere of a particular session affected me. There have been many times when I have carried the discussion out of the class with me and thought about it for a long time.

I still feel close to you, as though there were some tacit understanding between us, almost a conspiracy. This adds to the in-class participation on my part because I feel that at least one person in the group will react, even when I am not sure of the others. It does not matter really whether your reaction is positive or negative, it just IS. Thank you. [Bull, 1966] . . .

As you might expect, college students are often suspicious that these seeming attitudes are phony. One of Dr. Bull's students writes:

Rather than observe my classmates for the first few weeks, I concentrated my observations on you, Dr. Bull. I tried to figure out your motivations and purposes. I was convinced that you were a hypocrite . . . . I did change my opinion, however. You are not a hypocrite, by any means. . . . I do wish the course could continue. "Let each become all he is capable of being." [Bull, 1966]

I am sure these examples are more than enough to show that the facilitator who cares, who prizes, who trusts the learner, creates a climate for learning so different from the ordinary classroom that any resemblance is "purely coincidental."

A further element that establishes a climate for self-initiated, experiential learning is empathic understanding. When the teacher has the ability to understand the student's reactions from the inside, has a sensitive awareness of the way the process of education and learning seems *to the student,* then again the likelihood of significant learning is increased.

This kind of understanding is sharply different from the usual evaluative understanding, which follows the pattern of "I understand what is wrong with you." When there is a sensitive empathy, however, the reaction in the learner follows something of this pattern: "At last someone understands how it feels and seems to be *me* without wanting to analyze me or judge me. Now I can blossom and grow and learn."

This attitude of standing in the other's shoes, of viewing the world through the student's eyes, is almost unheard of in the classroom. One could listen to thousands of ordinary classroom interactions without coming across one instance of clearly communicated, sensitively accurate, empathic understanding. But it has a tremendously releasing effect when it occurs.

Let me take an illustration from Virginia Axline, dealing with a second-grade boy. Jay, age seven, has been aggressive, a troublemaker, slow of speech and learning. Because of his "cussing" he was taken to the principal, who paddled him, unknown to Miss Axline. During a free work period, he fashioned a man of clay, very carefully, down to a hat and a handkerchief in his pocket. "Who is that?" asked Miss Axline. "Dunno," replied Jay. "Maybe it is the principal. He has handkerchief in his pocket like that." Jay glared at the clay figure. "Yes," he said. Then he began to tear the head off and looked up and smiled. Miss Axline said, "You sometimes feel like twisting his head off, don't you? You get so mad at him." Jay tore off one arm, another, then beat the figure to a pulp with his fists. Another boy, with the perception of the young, explained, "Jay is mad at Mr. X because he licked him this noon." "Then you must feel lots better now," Miss Axline commented. Jay grinned and began to rebuild Mr. X. [Adapted from Axline, 1944]

The other examples I have cited also indicate how deeply appreciative students feel when they are simply *understood*—not evaluated, not judged, simply understood from their own point of view, not the teacher's. If any teacher set himself the task of endeavoring to make one nonevaluative, acceptant, empathic response per day to a student's demonstrated or verbalized feeling, I believe he would discover the potency of this currently almost nonexistent kind of understanding.

I remember sitting at home some Sunday evenings sipping wine and talking to my wife about books, music, politics—about anything but children and school. And I remember thinking before going to bed how nice it would be to stay home and make love all the next day, or to go to the park and walk around, or read an adult book for a change. The next morning I usually felt slightly angry and resentful on the way to school, and in my fantasies I fled from the school or destroyed it.

I also remember other Sundays, working like mad to prepare for Monday, putting together all kinds of materials for the students, impatient for the week to start, angry at the students when the week started because they weren't as enthusiastic about what I prepared for them as I was.

I'm teaching again right now, a kindergarten and first grade for the first time, and I've been thinking about the ways in which my and other adults' feelings and attitudes affect our work with children in the classroom.

It is a great strain to deny our feelings and to be constant over five hours every day, five days a week. The easiest modes to fall into consist of praising students who obey us and blaming or tearing down those who don't. I remember screaming at students for being bad, when I really just wished they would let me alone. I also remember praising students when they did just what I wanted, when I knew that they weren't learning anything other than how to please me and cash in later on my positive feelings toward them. I wasn't a mean or nasty or evil person. It was just that the pressure of being with students so much got to me occasionally, and when I began teaching I didn't know how to tell them that. I was feeling my way as a teacher. I looked to the other teachers for models; they were yelling, screaming, praising, or retreating to the toilet or teachers' lunchroom, and I fell into that pattern for a while. As soon as I got my bearings and developed some trust with the students, I could be much more natural, but that took me two years of learning how to teach, while being paid and credentialed as a fully qualified teacher.

These situations took place nine and ten years ago. Now there are a number of nontraditional teaching situations where teachers do not have to feel unnatural and suppressed most of the time. In open classrooms, free schools, and

Hanging Up the Students

Herbert R. Kohl

other alternative learning situations emphasis is frequently put upon teachers being open and natural with their students. Teachers learn to spend time on so-called affective learning and are often less inhibited about telling their students how they feel as well as about encouraging the students to express feelings. Learning then becomes possible even within the context of a generally permissive school or school system, particularly if learning is seen as understanding new and often frightening things and opening up difficult and unresolved questions. There are dangers in being too open, however, or in using openness with the students to involve them with our own personal adult problems. There is a thin line between being open in the service of our students and being open in the service of our own needs. Often we find out too late that some students are sucked into our lives without our really intending it.

I know teachers who, lusting for love, have offered love to students who took the offer more seriously and on a different level than intended. I know others who convinced young people that they, the teachers, would be around for years and years to give support, only to move away emotionally when their own lives became more settled or interesting.

Openness, naturalness, and closeness are all necessary with young people, especially if a person is serious about remaking this culture and society in a humane and just way. Rather than abandon these virtues because they are difficult and dangerous, I think it is important to be aware of some of the problems they present and continually to examine, define, and redefine in concrete terms the nature and quality of relationships with individuals and groups of students. I find it important to be hard on myself in order to avoid hanging up my students with my own hang-ups.

There are no guidelines to sanity and responsibility. I can only suggest some things I have seen, mention some mistakes I have made and observed, and make some tentative suggestions.

Love

There is danger in needing to have all our students love, or pretend to love, us. Love is a bonus in personal relationships. The most we can expect is respect, which cannot be forced but can only be developed through our acts. Love is a very loose term that often passes in so-called hip culture for agreement in style and in common opposition to some loosely defined notion of "straight" living. I know a number of hip and politically radical young white teachers whose first words to their ghetto-trapped students were "I love you all." One young man said to me, "That teacher said he loved me and he didn't even know me. The dude must be out of his mind."

In my teaching career I have come to love a small number of my students and have tried to minimize that love in the classroom by being fair to everyone. I have obligations to try to set up a sensible, open, and caring learning environment for all of my students and not to pretend to love all of them or to act in special ways toward the ones I really love. Of course, the special feelings teachers have for some students can never be fully suppressed. The students know who the teacher's pets are even if the terminology and ideology pretend that there are no pets. Personal preferences are more likely to be accepted if we are just to everyone. In any case, fairness is not so difficult and ambitious as loving everyone is.

I happen to like mischievous, wild, and independent people. Quiet is not my mode. I respect the calm and inner depth of silent people but get seduced by the loud, stylish troublemakers. These preferences sneak out in my relationships with students, and I have had to learn to give my time and concern to all of the young people I work with, not just to those who give me pleasure. All teachers have to face their own personal affinities and at the same time hold them in check so that they do not destroy, deny, or deceive students who do not strike some responsive note in their souls.

Another danger teachers face is wanting their students to understand them. **Understanding** Some people make themselves the curriculum, talk all the time about their marital problems, financial woes, or therapy. They focus on themselves and forget about the students, while thinking it is open and groovy to be so honest with their students.

Young people love to hear stories about the lives of their elders. My own children often ask me to tell a story about when I was young, about my friends, about my life before them, about meetings and work. And stories are wonderful to tell and wonderful to hear. But stories are different from confessions. Perhaps I am uptight and old-fashioned in believing that part of my life has to remain private and not at all understood by anyone except, perhaps, myself— but I do believe it. I believe further that young people ought not to be subjected to the problems of all of the adults they happen to be thrust with in unnatural settings, such as school. Young people need much more to understand themselves, each other, their parents, their community. The teacher might be understood too, but school is not the world, the teacher is not the only model of adult life, and the main goal of even the best schooling is to enable young people to get out of school able to do something they value and can give to others.

A subtle variant of wanting to be understood is wanting to be pitied. Some **Pity** adults want young people to feel sorry for them, to recognize their weaknesses, and to be kind to them. Most teachers who take this stance with their students get wiped out quickly in schools where the students come from poor families. In middle-class schools, however, mutual self-pity is a fashionable mode of existence, and teachers who assume this mode can become popular with students who need desperately to feel stronger and wiser than some adults. But pity often leads to scorn, and teachers who adopt this mode are likely to find themselves rejected and mocked in private by their students. If you feel sorry for yourself, you really shouldn't be a teacher and put that sad defeat on anyone else.

A number of teachers want to politicize their students. I do too. I've tried over **Politics** and over and have found that the more dogmatic I get about my politics, the less the students pay attention to me. On the other hand the more opportunity the students have to discover how political stances are developed and to experience political action, the more willing they are to take a position.

I have experienced a number of silly disappointments because I wanted my students to become radical. I wanted young people of fourteen, fifteen, sixteen, and seventeen to develop the political attitudes I developed, after ten years of struggle, without going through anything themselves. I failed to realize or remember that their priorities and perspectives were not the same as mine. They needed to learn how to make love, how to live away from home, how to determine which adults to respect and believe, how to deal with money. I could not provide any shortcut to social commitment, and they did not want to take any risk that did not make sense to them. The students I am talking about were in an alternative secondary school in Berkeley. They were hip in the sense that they had long hair, smoked dope, wore fine leather boots, played good music. They had the money and space to indulge themselves in being hip but didn't know anything about being radical in the sense of caring about the lives of people who did not have the luxury of being so easily hip. I know no certain way to get white middle-class students to care about a world beyond themselves. But my anger and impatience and my radical stance did not help much because in an important way it excluded the students and made light of their needs as they perceived them. A number of teachers who work with students from poor families fall into similar traps. They want their students to become militant, while all the students want to do is get some money and a job that will free them of poverty.

Some students do become politically aware in high school. For most others political awareness and radical commitment emerge, if at all, from experiences at work and on the street, not from school. That doesn't mean that teachers should not help their students become aware of radical alternatives to the institutions and modes of life common in this society. Rather, it means that, though awareness can be facilitated by a teacher, commitment cannot be manufactured in the classroom.

Moods Small things in a teacher's private life tend to mess up things in classrooms—things like hangovers, fits of depression or elation, spring fever, occasional boredom, weariness of being with young people so much, and so forth. Slight discomfort can easily be turned into an excuse to stay away from school, to develop imaginary maladies, or to create rationalizations about the need for teachers, as well as students, to have choices—and, therefore, the right of the teacher to choose to be absent a good deal.

I have found that often it is better to force myself to go in and tell the students how I feel than to stay away. On some days, of course, it is impossible to be around anyone, and therefore I have to be absent. But it is possible to function with a little bit of pain, and it is important for teachers not to pamper themselves or become chronic complainers. If teaching becomes a draining burden, we should prepare ourselves for other work.

Another hang-up some teachers have is the need to be a martyr. Some people hate teaching, hate schools, act as if they are fed up with the students all the time, and yet feel that the reason they are hanging in is to save the students. Often the students do not feel they are being saved and do not like being reminded constantly of how much the teacher is sacrificing to save them.

I have taught for eleven years, though never more than three years in a row or three years at one place. I can take young people and schools in three-year doses. After that time I get restless and need to do something else. A useful guideline I have followed is that whenever, over a period of a month, I feel no joy at seeing my students, drag myself to school every day, and long to stay home or run away, it is time for me to leave the next year.

Often large crises in our lives have to affect our work with young people. Love affairs break up, friends die, a new political obscenity develops, some insane violence comes to haunt one's life. These occasions have to change the rhythm of life—death or the end of an affair have to be mourned; political anguish is real and necessary if we are to remain human. I have found that in moments of crisis I can share my feelings with young people and that they understand and care about what I go through. My personal pain has often led young people to talk about their pain, about what they see other adults experiencing, and about what they themselves experience. The important thing is not to turn personal pain into an excuse for rejecting or abandoning students.

It is extremely difficult to develop that combination of consistency, strength, and openness that seems to enable a teacher to work effectively with young people. There are many hang-ups that all of us have as adults and many temptations to bring all of them into the classroom. This is especially true of adults who work in open settings, where the expression and display of feeling is part of the fabric of life. We have to become tough with ourselves and realize that teaching in an open setting does not give us license to play out our fantasies or fulfill all of our needs through the lives of young people. Our roles as teachers should be to turn our students on to themselves, to each other, and to all the things there are to learn about in the world.

Martyrdom

Crises

Teaching takes place through communication. Good teachers understand the effects of their communications—not that successful teaching requires a mastery of the intricacies of communication theory; most teachers lack the time and opportunity to analyze fully the communication patterns in even one class a day. To make such an analysis complete, information has to be gleaned not only from students but from friends and colleagues as well. This is obviously beyond the scope of the ordinary classroom situation, but still teachers need to communicate as well as they can. They need to make the best interpretations and the wisest decisions possible in the classroom. To do this, they must examine their communication with students, and they must understand the principles of feedback.

Feedback is a process of learning by getting information from others about our performance. In every classroom and in many outside contacts with students, the teacher gives the student feedback. When the student performs a task correctly, the learning process requires him to know it is the correct performance. When he perfoms a task incorrectly or takes steps that may lead him into harmful or false results, he needs feedback to return to profitable learning paths. When his conduct hinders his own learning or the learning of others, he requires feedback to inform him of the effect of his actions.

As teachers, we want to help students increase their awareness of the impact their actions have on their own development and on others. Wanting to help is not enough. Improper feedback can harm more than it helps. We must look at our own styles and methods of feedback. When we hurt or confuse students, we may mean well, but we show a lack of skill in giving feedback.

Feedback is both verbal and nonverbal. A slumped posture may tell the class we feel discouraged or tired today; a smile may indicate we like what was just said; raising our eyebrows may indicate disbelief. We encourage through nods and smiles; we discourage through shaking our heads or frowning.

It is difficult to understand our nonverbal behavior because we are rarely aware of it. Our gestures, facial expressions, and ways of holding and using our bodies are not recorded as words are. Also, what students read into our nonverbal behavior is often not what we intend. I may frown because I am puzzled

Looking at Ourselves

Communication with Students

Jane C. Zahn

or don't understand; I may also frown because I am listening intently. Usually students interpret a frown as disapproval, which may not be what is meant. I may smile in amused delight, but a student who feels foolish may think I am making fun of his performance. Verbal communication is often misunderstood, but nonverbal communication is even more often misunderstood because we aren't aware of what we are communicating or what our students may be receiving from this kind of communication.

When our communication has seemed to go astray in the classroom, it helps to ask ourselves some questions—either at the time or when we think over the day or prepare for the next class.

Do I give more positive than negative feedback?   No teacher wants to be a villain. Most of us dislike having to give negative feedback to a student, even if it seems necessary to advance his learning. Too often, however, classroom interaction consists of silence when an idea or performance is good or improving, but plenty of verbal and nonverbal feedback when performance is inadequate or mistaken. Yet we know that new habits are more quickly developed and more firmly fixed through reward than through punishment. [Hilgard, 1956] Praise, encouragement, and recognition of progress are vital for effective and lasting learning. Positive feedback need not be false or dishonest. Improvement in even the amount of effort expended can be noticed and commented on approvingly. "I notice that you got five problems right this time" helps learning more than "You got seven problems wrong." Negative feedback is necessary too, but for good teaching we must try to outbalance negative feedback by positive feedback. Good teaching days are those on which we give more positive than negative feedback.

Do I mean to be helpful to the student?   It is easy to convince ourselves that our duty is to be "open" and "honest." As Marcia Perlstein points out in her article "The Difficult but Necessary Art of Introspection," there is a distinction between honesty and bluntness. Honesty is in the service of helpfulness; bluntness, in the service of revenge. If our "honest" response comes from a need to put a disturbing student in his place, the student senses that our feedback arises out of our need, not out of honest concern for him. Of course, sometimes a student feels punished by our actions when, in fact, our actions were genuinely motivated by concern for him; such mistakes do happen. Despite our motivations, however, feedback not perceived as help will be rejected. Its teaching purpose is foiled.

Sometimes we very human teachers have a need to unload. A classroom situation has driven us to a point where we feel we must express ourselves about it or run the risk of the unexpressed feeling hindering learning. Such emotional expression honestly presented might be understood by the class, and the teacher might feel relieved. But if it is offered as though for the students' good, it will never be accepted. Aggressive students are especially alert to the difference between "I'm getting very angry at the noise in this class right now" (a statement about the teacher's needs, acceptable to the class) and "You students are so noisy you are ruining this class" (aggression under the pretense of feedback about behavior, not meant to be helpful, rejected by the class).

The teacher who seems to be self-serving or uncaring will be seen by the student as indifferent to his feelings and needs and won't be trusted to help him. This is also true if the teacher's tone, expression, or choice of words communicates an abstract observation.

Is the student willing and able to accept feedback right now?   At times and in some circumstances anyone finds it hard to accept critical remarks about his products or behavior. An angry or confused student does not need another difficult idea to wrestle with. A student pressured by his peers is not able to accept feedback from the teacher. A lot of laughter in the classroom can take attention from the teacher, and the feedback goes unheard.

If the student asks for feedback in a specific area, he probably really wants an honest response from the teacher and will receive it with an open mind. When a student asks for evaluation of his performance after completing a skill trial, he is probably open to any feedback, as long as he sees the information as intended to help. But if he asks you how he's doing in the class, the request is so general it is hard to respond helpfully; the teacher may have difficulty being certain that the request is sincere.

Is the student able to do something about it?   Feedback about behavior we don't know how to change or can't change is merely frustrating. If a student seems very shy, telling him he is oversensitive won't help. He doesn't know what to do to stop being oversensitive—and he may not even be clear about what is meant by *oversensitive*. If instead he is told specifically about something he can change, he can be helped both to see the effect of his behavior and to make the specific change. For example, a student can stop using words offensive to those in a different ethnic group. If he is told those words are insulting, he can use different ones if he wants to avoid offending others. Whenever we comment on a student's actions, we should ask ourselves if he can do something about the barriers we see to his effective learning. Remember, however, that a student can't do anything about physical defects, speech impairments, or even certain facial expressions.

Am I being specific rather than general?   Generalities aren't very useful for feedback purposes. A student needs specifics—what he said, what he did, how he can perform differently. Suppose I have a student who inhibits other students in the class. If I say, "You are keeping others in the class from learning, Johnny," the statement is general. It doesn't mention specific acts or statements. I could say instead, "Sam started to answer then. You interrupted him. I'd like to hear what Sam has to say and then what you have to say." In this case I have told Johnny what he did that was objectionable and have suggested concrete changes. If I tell a student he talks too much, it isn't as helpful as if I tell him he was talking when I gave the assignment and therefore missed two of the important items. If I tell a student he doesn't express himself clearly, the statement is too general; he doesn't know what he has done that produced unclear communication. On the other hand, if I tell him the specific words he misused or mispronounced, he can correct these to build different speech or writing patterns over a period of time. Giving examples is part of the responsibility of teachers to their students.

Am I talking about dead yesterday or live today?   What happened last week or last month is often already out of mind or distorted by memory. Recent examples communicate much better than ancient ones. Because it is easier in any human interaction to discuss the past rather than the present, we must be careful to emphasize what happened in this class period, not in last week's. It is important to comment on emerging patterns, especially if they are favorable, rather than on those that are dying away.

Am I being judgmental?   When we judge a student by summing up his character, our communication won't help him to learn. "You didn't hand in your homework. You are lazy and irresponsible" is a judgment and won't be heard. "You didn't hand in your homework. I can't give you credit for the assignment" is a description of observed behavior and its consequences. Each statement is painful for the student to hear, but the second statement can help him to learn. *Lazy* and *irresponsible* are labels. Labels of all kinds are either noncommunicative or harmful. Students themselves use labels frequently—labels are quickly learned; they help us avoid describing specific behavior and the complexity of individual differences. We need to be careful not to pick up these habits; we should try to describe rather than judge.

Am I telling too much at once?   It is neither necessary nor desirable to give "complete" feedback to a student. None of us can deal with every aspect of our behavior at one time. The most familiar example of this principle is the advice experts give to those who are trying to stop smoking: concentrate on quitting smoking; do not at the same time try to diet, to budget more carefully, to improve your posture, and to answer all your letters—trying to change too much at once will defeat your efforts to quit smoking. A student too can deal best with one aspect of his performance at a time. At best, encouragement in one area with a suggested improvement in another is the most he can handle successfully.

Am I confusing through pretense?   Pretense communicates to the student. Usually uncertain enough, he is further confused by pretense. One example of pretense is a rhetorical question. "What excuse can you possibly have for such behavior?" is a rhetorical question. The intent of this question is not to find out the reasons for the student's actions, but rather to condemn his behavior and express irritation.

Another example of pretending is to ask a question and then, as a student begins to answer, interrupt. This is pretending; if I ask a question, I am communicating, "Please answer my question." But when I interrupt, I communicate, "I don't want to hear what you have to say; I want to say something instead." The student has been asked to talk and then told not to talk in very rapid succession. He can only conclude that I didn't want him to talk; asking the question was a pretense.

Did I understand what was said? A teacher often answers, not the question that was asked, but one that was not asked. Another frequent observation is a teacher reacting irrelevantly to a response of a student because the student's initial statement wasn't understood correctly. We all mishear. Paraphrasing helps us check our understanding of what was asked. If we restate in our own way what we think a student means, he can say it in a different way if we misunderstood. This process not only clarifies communication but indicates to the student that we want to understand what he is saying. Here is an example of an unchecked communication resulting in misunderstanding:

Student: This is a lousy textbook.
Teacher: I know it isn't very interestingly written, but it has important information in it.

Here is an example of a response that clarifies communication:

Student: I think this is a lousy textbook.
Teacher: Lousy? Do you mean it isn't very interesting?
Student: No, the print is so small I strain my eyes reading it.

Am I seeing this feedback as an opportunity? Honest feedback about ourselves and our behavior is precious. Like students, we learn when we understand the effect our behavior has on others. Friends or colleagues often won't give us needed feedback for fear of harming our relationship with them. When students give us feedback, especially negative feedback, we can try to use the opportunity to learn instead of erecting a wall of excuses. If we try to hear what is said with an open mind and try to understand it, we may learn something to our benefit. To be sure we understand, we can use the same formula I have described for communication with students. We can try to summarize what is said. We can ask for recent examples that describe our behavior rather than judge it. This must be done, however, in a manner that openly invites the helpful information.

After receiving a communication as an opportunity to learn, we can check with other experiences to make sure the criticism is valid. Sometimes a bad effect is true only for a particular student at a particular time. Every student observation is not sufficient reason to change our behavior. But every student observation about us as teachers is worth hearing and making the attempt to understand.

Once we are familiar with these principles of communication and try to apply them, two possible dangers emerge. First, there is the danger of being too cautious. Many teachers are overconcerned about the fragility of their students. For fear of crushing them by telling them what we see them do and how it affects their learning, we hold back and keep silent, hindering their learning even more. By not communicating we can be perceived by students as being uninvolved or uncaring.

Second, there is the danger of watching our own behavior so closely that we lose the spontaneous, open, enthusiastic quality essential to good teaching. If students believe we intend to help, they will generally not hold mistakes against us. But we can ask ourselves these questions when our communication does not seem to be helping the students' learning and when we want to do a good job even better.

Looking at ourselves is not a luxury, it is a necessity. Looking at our actions in terms of intentions and probable effect on others can elevate relationships from mediocrity to meaningfulness. For the very special relationship between teacher and student, the adult needs to develop keen self-examination. Introspection is an art not overtly supported by most education systems. Situations are generally viewed in terms of students' transgressions; administrators automatically support the teacher's view; tenure gives us license to continue doing what we have been doing. Seldom will we be actually forced to look carefully at ourselves. Nothing but a desire to genuinely connect with our students and a deep sense of personal ethics can move us in this direction. The rewards are positive feelings generated by relationships that really work. We may begin by considering our students' needs, but we will benefit ourselves as well.

Often we don't see these values. We excuse our ineffectuality. We point to the state of the universe, the nature of institutions, the experiences that kids bring with them to classrooms, and the myriad additional external forces that affect the delicate relationship between teacher and student as barriers too difficult to overcome. But as teachers we have a choice about how to handle ourselves with students. We have as much control as we responsibly choose to exercise.

A difficult but productive form of introspection began for me with my initial teacher-training experience. In problem-centered seminars of the Graduate Internship Program in Teacher Education at the University of California at Berkeley, we focused on our students—their goals for themselves and our goals for them. We were encouraged to explore how our hang-ups could at times interfere with students' learning. We tried to understand our personal needs and ways they could be met without interfering with and running counter to the needs of our students. We learned some specific techniques to use in this process of introspection.

Replay   Using replay is leaving a situation and recalling it in detail. It is not dwelling obsessively on a situation. We can beat our breasts and wail about our incompetence and the way we mishandled the situation. We can lie awake at night, varying the script but little, and continue to blame ourselves. This process is

The Difficult but Necessary Art of Introspection

Marcia H. Perlstein

convenient but not helpful. As long as we expend our energies on self-recrimination, we need not take responsibility for changing; "I'm sorry" over and over means we do not have to change.

A type of replay I have found productive is to sit down during a fairly non-pressured period and list the types of problems I display in working with students. Then when an upsetting incident occurs in which I'm not satisfied with my own behavior, I place my recollections of it within the context of the categories I've already developed. My list is subject to constant revision; some types of problems can be eliminated when they've been worked through successfully, and others can be added as the need arises. Most important, avoid obsessive replay by planning for actions. I may plan to continue dialogue with the student, allowing for mutual self-disclosure regarding the incident; I may plan direct reference to the incident and my feelings about it to the class, with an opening (but not demand) for possible response; or I may plan a symbolic action that points toward some resolution. For example, suppose a student forgot his homework, and I embarrassed him before the class. The student then defended himself by making a bitter joke, at which the class laughed. During the next few days I notice that the student has become increasingly withdrawn and disinterested. My productive replay may lead me to tell the student privately that I realize I overreacted by embarrassing him before the class, that I feel bad about the situation and have missed his participation during the last few days. I could then ask him what his feelings were. Or I might tell him publicly, in front of the class, that I feel bad about the incident, that I may have put him in a difficult position and wonder if anyone else saw the situation similarly. Or I might change the manner in which homework assignments are handed in by giving students increasing responsibility for keeping their own records. I then explain to the class that I am doing this because I am disturbed because the homework issue caused conflict between me and some of the students and that the intention of the assignments is defeated when this happens.

What we do is not quite as important as doing something. Our choice of action depends on our styles and our students' styles. Any incident important enough for us to think about and recall in detail deserves some sort of follow-through and continued attention with the students. When we deny the importance of critical situations, unresolved feelings build and a seemingly innocuous incident later sets these pent-up feelings in motion. Coping with problems at the moment may seem difficult, but it pays dividends in the long run. Our intuition about what demands immediate attention is a good guide; the problem we take home with us and that continues to bother us bears our most serious consideration. When our introspection process develops successfully, fewer incidents will have to be taken home and mulled over. Solutions that at first we work out introspectively will eventually be available for us to apply again.

We do not always have the luxury of choosing whether or not to return to an incident after a period of thought. Some crises demand immediate attention, although careful review can avert future crises and sometimes help improve relationships after an explosion.

The easiest way to begin dealing with confrontations is by looking at the most dramatic explosions in our classrooms. Some overall patterns can be understood to help us each in viewing our own problems.

First, avoid confrontations at all cost. The losses and complications make simple avoidance a good initial tactic. A full-blown argument between a teacher and a student is not as simple as one between two individuals who are not role-bound. Students don't want to back down in front of their peers; teachers are afraid of looking weak in front of the same group. Getting out gracefully is difficult; it usually becomes a question of who will feel the greater loss of pride.

In examining our roles, we must recognize that although students often provoke confrontations, we have a good deal to do with taking up the challenge. We may say that we were only being honest with the student and felt it necessary to stand our ground. But there is a distinction between honesty and bluntness. Bluntness may accelerate the confrontation. Bluntness is unloading our version of the truth because we need to say it. Bluntness does not consider the effect of these perceptions on the student, the manner in which the information is expressed, or our attitudes and feelings at the time. Honesty may transmit the same information but express it carefully and give its reception primary importance. [See Jane Zahn's article, "Looking at Ourselves: Communication with Students."] When we recall an interaction and try to determine whether we were being honest or blunt, we begin to learn about our individual behavior patterns; we can then apply these insights preventatively, thus avoiding a number of major confrontations.

In dealing with crisis situations, we must also distinguish between style and strategy. All too often we review incidents involving students in terms of the strategy we applied. This view emphasizes our control, our ability to set things up in advance and to program the desired response. We review incidents in terms of our failure to have brought about the results we wanted. This point of view has the subtle implication that we see the student as "the enemy," that battle lines have been drawn, and that the resolution is a matter of the best use of wits and will. But if we review confrontations in terms of our style—the manner in which we come across, our own communications patterns and how they are received—the battleground configuration diminishes.

These distinctions are more than semantic. I am not excusing students, nor am I minimizing the role that they play in confrontations. But we teachers have great control over the roles we play and need to develop some finely sharpened perspectives for looking at ourselves.

Sample List of Categories

Certain responses we make to students belong to patterns we can discover within ourselves. It is important to try to see various specific responses in terms of the general class of behavior to which they belong. The following are some examples of categories we are often apt to fall into.

Responding to Only One Level of a Student's Remark   Very often we respond to the most literal, obvious part of a message, when in fact something more significant was meant. Although we need not always respond immediately and directly to the underlying levels, through careful introspection we can become aware of these underlying messages and plan an appropriate response for another time. [See Terry Borton's article, "Reach, Touch, and Teach," about making the distinction between interests and concerns.]

Students often talk in codes they are unaware of on a conscious level. The perceptive teacher learns to decipher these codes and eventually figures out ways to respond to the student beyond the literal level at the time the message is transmitted. The student who says "This class is boring" is often really saying, "My needs are not being paid attention to." Another code frequently encountered centers around variations of "I can't." The student may really be saying, "Nobody ever made me believe I could, so I won't." The frequent refrain "Do I have to do it?" is often a remonstrance to the teacher: "You haven't demonstrated to me the value this exercise is going to have for me." The days of "Eat your spinach, it's good for you" ought to be over. Teachers must help students understand the value of what is asked of them and help them share responsibility in carrying it out.

Saying Things That Have Racist or Sexist Implications   These are difficult areas to concern ourselves with; we are distressed to think we might have attitudes or approaches with racist or sexist overtones. Such attitudes may be very subtle: we may continually expect a select few students to have all the answers; we may discourage others from trying challenging tasks; when we note academic weakness, we believe that we are reflecting factual information rather than perpetuating prejudicial attitudes. In reality, our third-world students—and, in some subjects, our female students—have often been differentially prepared. The only way to alter these disparities is by expecting productive work from all students and working hard to help all students produce what we expect of them. The literature on self-fulfilling prophecies shows that the teacher's expectations for a student's achievements are the single most salient influence on what the student achieves. Thus we have to be vigilant; we are more likely to give subtle reinforcement to a poor self-image, already badly damaged by cultural forces, than to give negative reinforcement to a relatively secure self-concept.

We can help all students do productive work by getting a good sense of where each student actually is and finding materials that challenge him to progress. Materials should not be degrading in content. We can design classroom activities to serve as "equalizers." These activities draw upon a variety of strengths other than the typically academic and can then be used as springboards for the development of more solid skills. Not all chairpersons of committees need be male, nor all secretaries female. For many types of activities, groups ought to be designed on the basis of interest rather than performance. Students need to be encouraged to help each other. Students ought to be helped to view proficiency in certain areas as a matter of training rather than innate ability; in our classrooms these training processes must be equally accessible to all.

We need to examine carefully whether or not we truly communicate open-ended expectations toward all students. None of us has the corner on truth; none of us can begin to know what each student we touch may become. We need to help students increase their options, flex their own muscles, and develop and experience their strengths. If we begin to expand our own notions of what is possible by looking carefully at how we behave toward our students each day, we will eventually help students behave supportively toward each other. Any prejudicial remark needs to be dealt with gently, but firmly, at the time. A little boy who says innocently that "girls can't do that" needs to be helped to see the implications of his statement. And the little girl needs to be helped to see that she doesn't have to accept "girls can't do that," that she has the strength within herself to make choices. The little boy's words need have no power over her actions.

We cannot be overcautious with issues of racism and sexism. Only constant vigilance will turn the tide. We must call prejudice as we see it—in behavioral, not abstract, terms. The process will eventually be less self-conscious, and we won't have to overcompensate for flagrant abuses that spring from prejudice.

Being Overly Responsive to a Few at the Expense of Others It is impossible to be all things to all people, but it is important to try to reach out to as many students as we can touch. All too often, our classrooms mirror the larger world: the more aggressive persons receive the lion's share of attention. Some students sit silently in corners of classrooms and go through entire days without exchanging a word with their teachers. It is hard to know what is going on in their lives; some may be tuned out, others resigned and apathetic; some may be in turmoil and pain, others comfortably observing the scene. While it is important not to poke and probe, not to force contact from reluctant students, it is also important to set the scene for interaction. We must make ourselves easily accessible to students who may have a hard time reaching out; we must take some risks by gently and gradually reaching out ourselves. During periods of introspection I try to remember any opportunities for small human exchanges that were missed. I recall the girl who quietly stood at my desk while I talked to another and then slipped off before I had a chance to speak with her. I make a mental note to go up to her desk the next day, tell her I'm sorry I missed her the day before, and offer any assistance I can give. I think about things that have happened that may be means of access to certain students—a remark made in class that I have thought more about, a poem or composition turned in, or an incident I wish to comment on.

We can't all be as quick and as tuned in, at a given moment, as we'd like to be, but if we sharpen our tools of introspection and replay, we can begin to rectify these missed moments. Thus, while trying to be as responsive as possible in the present, we have additional opportunities for initiating meaningful interactions in each tomorrow's present.

Being More Concerned with My Own Image Than with Students' Needs

Students commonly refer to this dimension as "ego-tripping." We get carried away by the sounds of our voices and words, our lofty intentions, and a myriad of other considerations that cause us to lose touch with our students. It is often difficult to know when we have overused our role to force our perceptions, our needs, or our views of the world on our students. It is legitimate to present new thoughts and ideas or to share with students an experience that has moved us in the hope that they may be similarly moved. I recall reading a soliloquy of Lady Macbeth's with gusto in order to get some students to consider the possibility that it might be fun to read some Shakespeare, a legitimate presentation of a new idea. But I soon became so involved with the sound of my own voice, my resonance, clarity, and charm, that I forgot my original purpose. By using the classroom as a stage for my own frustrated dramatic aspirations, I entirely lost sight of my students' needs.

Overconcern with our own image may not always be apparent. It involves a careful distinction between overpowering and sharing. We need to check students' responses, make space for their interactions and be ready to step back as they feel freer to move in. Learning ought not to be a passive activity for students, no matter how exciting a teacher thinks he is. It is fine to share excitement and energy with students as long as this sharing is relatively brief and has a built-in opening for their input. Introspection can help us to discover our own excesses in this area.

The self-deconditioning process is often long and slow. It begins with careful replay followed by consciously produced new behaviors. Assumptions about learning need to be reexamined. The teaching-learning process needs to be seen as a shared responsibility rather than a situation for the teacher to have center stage.

In systematizing our introspections, each of us needs to develop appropriate questions to ask ourselves. A teacher is as imperfect a human being as all others, but the teacher–person who takes introspection seriously has an exciting and rewarding life.

Identity

Critical examination is a necessary concomitant of good teaching. The teacher's introspections and the actions made on these may influence students only indirectly, but in a basic way they have significant impact upon the adult. Classrooms are not places for unresolved adults to work out their indentity problems, but adults who are constantly cognizant of the needs of their students can simultaneously learn a good deal about themselves and undergo a subtle transformation in identity.

The simplest yet most profound definition of identity comes from the existentialists—"We are what we do." If we see ourselves differently from the way we are behaving, our task is then to change our behavior to make it more congruent with our intentions. As teachers who are engaged in constant introspection, we can view our actions carefully through the microscopes of our ever-developing identities and continue shaping and defining who we are through what we choose to do next.

The Self-Actualization of Educators: An Introduction to Psychosynthesis
Henry Giarretto and Anna Einfeld

Hank Giarretto is currently Project Director of a child sexual-abuse program. In addition to his work in psychosynthesis, he has been a research specialist in medical technology, including computers in medicine and biometrics.

As marriage, family, and child counselor, Anna Einfeld is at the Center for Human Communication, Los Gatos, California. She is consulting and teaching in conjoint family therapy, child-abuse problems, and management training, as well as training psychosynthesis groups.

Do As I Do: Modeling in Teacher Preparation
Raymond J. Roberts

Raymond Roberts combines his activities as Associate Professor of Secondary Education at California State University, San Francisco, with consulting in alternative education and educational environments.

Helping Teachers Change
Thomas A. Shaheen

Thomas A. Shaheen has served as superintendent of six school districts, most recently in San Francisco, and is presently engaged in writing two books, one on citizen participation in education and the other on school administration.

Facilitating Change in Teachers

Henry Giarretto and Anna Einfeld describe in detail the rationale for the in-service personal growth workshops which they conduct for educators. Although they utilize a number of techniques from many schools of thought, they emphasize psychosynthesis in particular. Raymond Roberts describes ways in which he attempts to model the behaviors he tries to help his student teachers develop. He illustrates his suggestions with anecdotes drawn from his experiences in the field with his neophyte teachers. Finally, Thomas Shaheen talks about the difficulties teachers experience in trying to change the status quo.

The dehumanizing effect of mass-production teaching has led many educators to turn with hope to the principles and techniques of individualized and humanistic education. The leaders of this movement are the humanistic psychologists Carl Rogers and Abraham Maslow. Somewhat less well known, but in our opinion equally important, is Roberto Assagioli, whose book *Psychosynthesis* is the best attempt to date to formulate a comprehensive theory and practice of humanistic psychology. [Assagioli, 1965]

The essence of the humanistic approach to education has been expressed by Maslow:

It is my strong impression that this is the way in which much of the world of education could function. If we want to be helpers, counselors, teachers, guiders, or psychotherapists, what we must do is to accept the person and help him learn what kind of person he is already. What is his style, what are his aptitudes, what is he good for, not good for, what can we build upon, what are his good raw materials, his good potentialities? We would be nonthreatening and would supply an atmosphere of acceptance of the child's nature which reduces fear, anxiety, and defense to the minimum possible. Above all we would care for the child, that is, enjoy him and his growth and self-actualization. [Maslow, 1968]

The Psychosynthesis Research Foundation, whose mandate stems from the work of Assagioli, expands Maslow's prescription by defining the main criteria for a complete education program. The program has two goals: (1) harmonious development of all aspects of the student, his physical, emotional, imaginative, intellectual, ethical, social, and intuitive aspects, and (2) the organic synthesis of these parts into a self-conscious personality. [Psychosynthesis Research Foundation, 1972]

These concepts are intriguing to many educators and others in the helping professions. The literature in humanistic education has grown, but the major impact on education has resulted from the personal experiences of professional helpers in the basic encounter/growth/human-potential groups conducted by

---

The Self-Actualization of Educators

An Introduction to Psychosynthesis

Henry Giarretto and Anna Einfeld

Esalen Institute, the National Training Laboratories, and similar centers that have sprouted throughout the country. Many were deeply impressed by their own group experiences and were eager to spread the word. Education became a key target of the new crusaders. They descended on the schools to teach the teachers the techniques of group encounter, effective communication, sensitivity training, sensory awakening, Gestalt awareness, and psychodrama.

This phase of the humanistic movement was not without its critics. Kurt W. Back, for example, deplores the lack of professional responsibility of encounter-group leaders to group members. He proposes social controls and the development of a code of ethics. [Back, 1972] Other critics voiced objections ranging from invasion of privacy to the charge that group members were subjected to stresses that precipitated psychotic breaks.

Despite these detractions it seems likely that the humanist movement will continue to burgeon and will eventually become a major force in education. An encouraging development in the past three or four years is the move toward such self-exploration methods as meditation, fantasy, and journal keeping, together with a waning interest in head-on encounter groups.

In American psychology a tendency remains for destructive competition. Many seem to think they have the answer for everyone and try to reduce to rubble all preceding concepts and persuasions. Even some of those who call themselves growth psychologists fail to see that the growth movement is itself in growth. Energy spent disparaging the work of others is better spent in reviewing and improving one's own efforts. In this way we keep faith in a key injunction of humanistic psychology, which is to become aware of and be responsible for our own world views.

About three years ago we did some soul searching concerning our effectiveness as educational consultants. We decided to make some changes.

1. We would not concentrate primarily on training teachers in the use of the techniques of humanistic education. Many teachers applied the techniques with some curiosity as to results but without true conviction and confidence. Conviction was missing if the teacher had not personally experienced and assimilated the method. Confidence was missing if the teacher was not given a unifying theory.

2. Promotion of a specific technique often led to indiscriminate use. Teachers assumed that a certain method was appropriate for all students. But while exercises for developing the imagination might be indicated for some students, for others the emphasis should be on training in dealing with the outer world. Rogers' method of effective listening as popularized by Ginott [1969] and Gordon [1970] was often seen by sensitive students as manipulation and one-sided communication. The student was given ample feedback of his own messages but little feedback on just where the teacher stood in the exchange. He was denied the mutually nourishing benefits that result from communications in which both parties are actively listening and responding.

3. Many teachers did not know that certain techniques had to be complemented or balanced by others. There is undeniable value in such affective methods as psychodrama and Gestalt eliciting and surfacing feelings and developing self-awareness. But these must be balanced by will-training techniques for deferring and controlling the expression of feelings and for managing behavior. Educators would better appreciate the humanistic approach if they could experience a variety of techniques in the context of a cognitive structure. A technique should be selected to match the personality dynamics of the individual student.

4. Finally, we decided that in our work with schools we would relate to each teacher more as *person* and less in terms of *teacher*. The teacher has been blamed for the rebellion, poor performance, hostile behavior, and increasing truancy and drop-out rates of students. The teacher undergoes a constant pressure to become a better teacher. Expert after expert presents his bag of tricks. The youth cult focuses concern on students only. But teachers are also victims of our bankrupt educational system. A programmer–computer relationship is a mutually dehumanizing process. The different teacher–student relationship urged by Maslow cannot take place unless we show concern not only for the self-actualization of the student but of the teacher as well. If as teachers, guiders, or psychologists we wish to develop the understanding needed to accept, care for, and enjoy the student and his growth, we must also learn to understand and have regard for our own growth. Paraphrasing Maslow's statement, we must ask: What is *my* style, what are *my* aptitudes, what are *my* good materials and potentialities? And above all we must care for our own growth and self-actualization. We made this the new central message of our work with educators.

To implement our aims, we prepared a thirty-hour course. Material for the course was based on our past work and on the literature of humanistic psychology. In particular, we drew on the approach of psychosynthesis developed by Assagioli.

Psychosynthesis designates Assagioli's conception of the human psyche. [Assagioli, 1965] He has constantly expanded both the theory and the practice of his approach in numerous papers and books. He finds the following similarities between psychosynthesis and existentialist and humanistic views: (1) the method of starting from within, experiencing self-identity; (2) the concept of personal growth; (3) the importance of the meaning which a person makes of his life; (4) the key notion of responsibility and ability to decide among alternatives; (5) the emphasis on present and future rather than regrets or yearnings for the past; and (6) the recognition of each individual's uniqueness. [Assagioli, 1965] These differences are mainly differences in emphasis. Assagioli emphasizes (1) the will as an essential function of self; (2) self-awareness experienced independently of immediate I-consciousness of the various parts of ourselves; (3) a positive view of the human condition (life can be exciting, joyous); (4) systematic use of active techniques which follow an individuated plan for self-actualization or psychosynthesis; (5) assumption of the higher self and of a superconscious, manifested by the spiritual drives such as creative imagination, intuition, aspiration, and genius. [Assagioli, 1965]

As we practice self-awareness and at the same time disidentify ourselves from the body states, feelings, thoughts, roles, and attitudes with which we formerly identified, our real selves become increasingly distinct. We are now ready, according to Assagioli, to build a new personality around the newly found unifying center, the self. To begin this process, we must have a clear image of the new personality we wish to develop and what we must do to achieve our goal.

We do not mean to imply that when a person disidentifies, desensitizes, and dehypnotizes his real self from transient body, feeling, and mind states, he must reject or extinguish these experiences. Rather, he should assimilate and integrate them into his growth process. Experiences that formerly immobilized him in pain or anxiety can be regarded as points of departure for growth. Moreover, an individual need not restrict himself to a dispassionate or even pugnacious life-style. Instead he can aspire to an optimistic life-posture that doesn't simply cope or adapt with situations but enters into them with zest and exuberance.

Assagioli distinguishes between two levels of psychosynthesis: personal and spiritual. In personal psychosynthesis man learns and optimizes the ability of directing, transforming, and sublimating the fundamental psychological energies and bringing them into harmony with the awakening self. These basic energies are associated with the primitive drives and with the thoughts and feelings that are stirred by our normal physical environment. Spiritual psychosynthesis suggests an upward leap toward integration of the psychic energies radiating from our higher urges, the esthetic, mystical, moral, and creative.

Our thirty-hour course does not guarantee self-actualization. It does indicate, however, some of the pathways a person may take to direct himself toward self-actualization. Its principal aims are to foster self-awareness, self-management, and personal psychosynthesis—not as successive phases, but as parallel objectives. By experiential exercises, occasionally supplemented by discussions, we strive to encourage integration at both affective and cognitive levels. We try to attend to all three areas of our principal aims during each session. Certain exercises are pointed especially at self-awareness or self-management, but invariably they nurture both areas. In general, all exercises are concerned with fostering personal psychosynthesis.

In the first meeting a brief overview of course philosophy, objectives, and scope is presented. Discussion is encouraged but controlled so that most of the session is spent on experiential exercises. Between meetings the group members are asked to do homework. Assignments are given to the whole group and also to specific individuals to bolster certain personality aspects or to deal with feelings that could not be resolved during group sessions.

Every meeting is started with a "centering-down" exercise to induce relaxed alertness. Several variations are possible. The group members may be asked to get in tune with their breathing and to visualize that they inhale vitality and energy and exhale hang-ups and negative feelings. Or they may be guided through a head-to-toe body trip in which they are asked to be aware of and to relax various body parts. Or they may be asked to imagine a prism above their heads that collects cosmic energy; the imagined stream of energy is then directed through the body for cellular invigoration of the entire being of each person.

The following exercises are a sampling of the ones that we use. These must be presented within a cognitive context, not merely for the sake of experience alone. The teacher should participate in an exercise before trying it with his class. *Who Am I, Who Are You,* the body-exploration exercises, the Gestalt awareness exercises, *Now I Am Aware,* and the communication exercise are all mainly to increase self-awareness. The blackboard exercise and the strengths exercise are mainly to reinforce self-management.

With *Who Am I?* [Assagioli, 1965], each group member is asked to ask the question "Who am I?" and write the answer, ten consecutive times. The answers may emerge in the form of body states, images, feelings, symbols, colors, smells, life roles, persons, and so forth. After each exercise the group members are asked to share their experiences. (This exercise and the following one are useful both for self-awareness and disidentification.)

In *Who Are You?* [Lewis and Streifeld, 1970], group members are asked to form diads. One asks the question "Who are you?" repeatedly for ten minutes, while the other responds. At a signal the other asks the same question, and the first person responds. Group members are encouraged to ask the question as though they really want to know their partners thoroughly and to respond to their partners as though they really want to tell them who they are. In all diads the partners are asked to discuss their experiences. These are said aloud so that the rest of the group can hear them. This exercise is excellent for building inter-personal trust. Of sundry body-exploration exercises, we like the bioenergetics group in particular. [Lewis and Streifeld, 1970]

In the Gestalt awareness exercises [John Enright Seminar, Gestalt Therapy Institute, San Francisco], group members are asked to select something such as an object, symbol, feeling, color, or sound, and to completely identify with it. For example, in identifying with a rock an individual might say: "I appear cold and reserved but when someone makes contact with me I slowly warm up and respond to the attention. On the surface I seem monotonic, but on close examination some people see that I am enormously complex."

Now I Am Aware [Lewis and Streifeld, 1970] is an exercise in which each person is asked to become sharply aware of what he is feeling, doing, and thinking at the moment. Each takes his turn and makes explicit statements such as "Now I am anxious," "Now I see your face," "Now my hand is trembling."

In the communication exercise [Gordon, 1970], group members are asked to practice communication in imagination. Each is asked to think of a situation in which there is a block to his communication with another person. Then he is requested to make a list of his cognitive sets or biases evoked from the situation. Next he is asked to make a list of his emotional sets toward that other person. His imagination is elicited with full knowledge of his sets, to try active listening to the other person. He is asked to see whether he can really hear the other person and if this makes a difference in his set toward him. After active listening (feeding back to the other both the content and the emotions in the message), he is asked to try making "I" statements. He is then instructed to make note of how he is feeling and how different emotions are elicited toward the other.

In the blackboard exercise [Assagioli, 1965] the group is asked to visualize a blackboard on which first one number appears, then a second, then a third, and so on. The group goes on adding numbers but continuing to hold the previous ones. This exercise demonstrates how inept we normally are in controlling our mental functions but that we can be trained to strengthen our control.

The strengths exercise [Otto, 1970] has five parts. First, each person is asked to write "These are my strengths" at the top of a sheet of paper and to list strengths and resources that come to mind. Second, the groups break into diads, and each person is asked to become acquainted with his partner by giving a brief summary of the high points in his life. Third, each person prepares a sheet with the heading "These are what I see as your strengths." On this sheet he lists the strengths he observes in his partner. He then hands the sheet to his partner and states the reasons for his impressions. Fourth, he tries to help his partner identify a strength to develop further; fifth, he helps his partner formulate an action plan with a specific schedule for carrying it out. This exercise promotes positive, self-affirming attitudes. Similar statements for the group to explore are: "I like this about myself," "I like this about you," "I have this available to me," and "These are my negative attitudes (experiences, feelings, and so forth)." Each of these negative things has a positive aspect, and the person is then asked to make a parallel list of these positive aspects.

The course has been conducted for several groups of fifteen to fifty people—high-school teachers, community-college instructors, superintendents, high-school principals, other administrators of a high-school district, juvenile probation officers, and professional personnel of the Girl Scouts of America.

It is extremely difficult to measure the results of group training or to claim that certain changes in personal and group behavior can be explicitly attributed to the treatment. Several participants confirmed our conclusion that teachers who are trained only in the use of techniques need a theory to back it up. They said the techniques now began to make sense and that they liked the systematic approach of psychosynthesis. Many teachers were grateful that the course was not concerned with them as teachers but as persons. One said, however, that she knew that a self-realized person is also a better teacher. We found that most of the juvenile probation officers were eager to find new ways to cope with their wards. We encouraged them to start their own groups—which several of them did with children or with their parents, or both. The teachers also carried over the training in one of the high schools and thus continued to meet after they completed the course.

One of our more gratifying experiences resulted from group sessions with people from a continuation high school. The school has the difficult task of teaching students rejected as unteachable by the regular high schools. It is a relatively small school, staffed by about twenty persons. All joined in the course work, including maintenance and office personnel. The course was completed about three years ago; since then, the school has been humanistically oriented and has gained wide recognition for its exceptional success in reaching and motivating students who had been given up as losers. The principal and several of the teachers told us that the turning point in the teaching methodology of the school was largely due to the group experience.

We feel personally satisfied with the results and will continue to conduct the course principally for educators and other professionals who work with children. Although spiritual psychosynthesis is beyond the scope of the introductory course, we always include two or three exercises for exploring the higher domain, and the response to these has led to preparation of an intermediate course in which emphasis is given to spiritual psychosynthesis.

Most teachers attempt in some fashion to mold each student into the person the teacher would like to be. I try to state these desired attributes honestly and explicitly to my students. I also make clear that these are highly tentative views, subject to constant revision through interaction with my students and the rest of the world.

On the assumption that by modeling my own educational philosophy I may influence teachers-to-be to develop and model their own philosophy, I explicitly tell my students what my philosophy is and how I will attempt to develop it within the classroom. I expose them to the changing nature of my beliefs as well as to my commitment to continuing change. Modeling is so potent and influential on students that I try to be fully aware of the behavior I present and make my actions in the classroom a conscious and deliberate description of what I believe to be good education. While I may state that I hold a particular philosophy, it is my behavior that serves as the true delineation of my beliefs. If my behavior and my stated philosophy are not congruent, this will soon be evident to the students. When I say I wish my students to act in a humanistic way in their future teaching roles, I must act humanistically toward my students. When I say "I want my students to be . . . ," I must be saying "I try to be. . . ."

I want my students to be self-actualizing, lifelong learners who are capable of identifying and organizing their own educational and psychological needs, resources, and individual learning styles.

Toward this end I try to help students plan, organize, and be part of a rich environment for our classroom community (films, speeches, field trips, and participation in various schools). Elimination of busy work gives students some time to identify and prepare an environment that interests them. They can then work individually or in groups to organize these interests, thus living through the process of learning to learn and to grow.

When students have time during scheduled class meetings to work productively, on their own and in group projects, they have an opportunity to see a diversity of learning styles in operation. Questions are raised about the positive

---

Do As I Do

Modeling in Teacher Preparation

Raymond J. Roberts

need for different kinds of environments to facilitate different learning activities. Students learn the impossibility of one individual's assimilating more than a fraction of the available data. Seeing a film, for example, is a radically different experience for a visual learner than it is for an auditory learner. Each assimilates a different segment of the data although, superficially, the same information is available to both.

"Shadowing" is one activity I use to help teacher-trainees become aware of different learning styles. One student "shadows" or observes another as the "learner" identifies an area of interest and then organizes and pursues related tasks. Each student acts out the role of both "learner" and "observer," and then the "observer" describes to the class how he would provide for the observed learning style and psychological needs of the "learner" in a teaching–learning situation. Because of the basic similarities of the tasks chosen by academically oriented college students, the "observers" may see only gross differences and be unable at first to analyze the less obvious differences in learning styles. Subsequent questions and group discussion should point up the many subtle mechanisms involved in any learning process.

In addition to "shadowing," I use such activities as discussions, role playing, and simulation games to help students become aware of their own educational and psychological needs and the diversity of needs in others. As various types of growth are explored, we try to understand psychological health in a universe of rapid change and potential loneliness. One of my younger students described this as the problem of "growing gracefully."

I want my students to be open, divergent, critical thinkers who are able to select and analyze relevant data, recognize alternatives, develop personal values, and make decisions.

To encourage this, I try to maintain an atmosphere in which divergent points of view are accepted. I encourage disagreement and confrontation among the students and with me. I try to eliminate as many "badges" as possible so that students are not intimidated by symbols of authority. One simple device is to arrange the classroom chairs in a circle during discussion periods and to change my position from session to session so that no seat is designated as "the professor's." I also try to dress informally and comfortably and encourage students to call me by my first name. But most important, I try to be emotionally and intellectually honest. If, for example, I tell students I am trying to eliminate the traditional "truth-giving" role of the instructor and yet I act as final arbitrator in class discussions, students will quickly be aware of the incongruence of my actions and my words.

In group discussions alternative methods of attacking goals and identifying needed data are often listed and then discussed. During the group critique I resist making decisions for the class. The whole process falls apart if I do. After the ground rules have been set for the class (for attendance at class, participation in some of the exploratory type activities, or other such activities), the class makes its own decisions and I try to become a facilitator and consultant to the class. Students are sometimes reluctant to take over the decision-making process themselves. "That's the instructor's job," they say, or "You have more experience; tell us what to do." The temptation is often great to step in to resolve a dispute or to attempt to manipulate the class into going a certain direction.

I want my students to begin teaching as caring, supportive human beings who have such positive and accurate self-concepts that they can risk living examined, creative, and cooperative lives.

Accordingly I try to recognize and utilize the individual talents of students and encourage them also to prize diversity and support each other. Thus we can give and receive caring, acceptant behavior; we can show that it is good to be unique. The "difference" makes each person what he really is—a unique person with a special contribution to make.

A foundation of genuine support also makes constructive criticism possible. Criticism in a caring atmosphere can be used to bring about positive personal change. All members of the class can thus accurately assess their needs from a position of personal integrity and therefore risk living an introspective and experimental life, with all the mistakes inherent in creative growth. All members of the class, including the instructor, are then seen as creative, mistake-making learners and are supported as such.

The small group is the heart of this balance between support and positive challenge. A developmental and exploratory sequence of highly organized interactions moving from groups of two to fours and eights and so on can provide a base for developing critical, supportive, and cooperative interaction as a means of moving from individual to group goals. The sequence can also show the value of open examination in creative group process. Incorporation of values, clarification, and support may result in action groups that are established not only on the basis of skill-oriented goals but also on common values, such as studying ways of individualizing instruction based on a humanistic philosophy.

I want my students to become aware, active, responsible citizens, who value their personal freedom and prize diversity in others.

I try to provide opportunities for both group and individual responsibility in decision making about personal and group goals and processes. Experience in leadership positions in which students deal with the problems of helping groups define and implement decisions is important in developing responsible citizens. Each student should learn to deal with negative reactions to leadership activities that seem to reduce personal freedoms. Actual dissatisfactions need to surface and be dealt with. Role playing is often a helpful mechanism for dealing with negative reactions to authority.

To help students understand the role of the individual in group action, an opportunity is provided for evaluating the responsibility of individual class members. At least twice during a semester, small groups of students ask each other to write or state answers to questions like these: "Are you able to organize for a group-decided task and carry it to completion without supervision?"

"Can you let others pursue group-related activities in terms of their individual learning styles and needs?"

Perhaps most crucial is the students' evaluation of the decision-making process used in the class. They should consider the level of personal satisfaction gained in a student-directed class in comparison to an instructor-controlled class. Such an evaluation is not always favorable to the group decision process. Some students are uneasy assuming responsibility for their personal learning and for the direction in which the class goes. Others feel that the group method is inefficient, that they could cover more ground if the instructor provided more leadership. But if students are not to feel they are suffering because of some pedagogical whim of the instructor, these criticisms must be explored continually, particularly in terms of the psychological and educational needs they manifest.

The process of involving students in their own learning and in the decisions about the directions the class takes is laborious, time-consuming work. I have had much greater success with this teaching style when I have worked with students over the period of a year rather than one semester only. Such a process of growth needs ample time to deal with feedback and self-correction. But that ought not deter anyone from trying to implement some of these principles if only a short time period is available. Too often students are cut out of sharing responsibility for their own learning with the teacher's rationalization that there is not enough time to develop and refine positive, workable decision-making patterns. The greater the time limitation, the less dramatic are the results—but basic concepts can be explored and positive directions experienced. In a short period a bit more structure might be necessary than usual; we often do not have the luxury of waiting for students to make all the discoveries. Part of the challenge for the teacher lies in determining what kinds of activities need to bear his imprint and which lend themselves ideally to student responsibility.

The teacher-trainee needs, additionally, to investigate explicitly how a model can serve him in his future classroom. The student teacher needs to have field experiences demonstrating how various models can be used in specific academic fields and at different grade levels and how he can be faithful to his own beliefs while coping with the realities of an elementary or secondary classroom.

My students have had and will continue to have exposure to a wide variety of teaching styles from which they can choose their own; my classroom behavior provides them with only one alternative. Whatever their choices, they have at least an opportunity to observe and evaluate a conscious attempt to model a philosophy of education.

"Change affects everybody—those who view themselves as competent are afraid that with change they will no longer be seen as competent; those who view themselves as incompetent fear that they will more readily be found out." [Speech by Herbert Smith, Assistant Superintendent of Schools, Rockford, Illinois, 1972] Because of these and other fears and concerns, teachers, supervisors, and administrators find many rationalizations for opposing change. Pauline Levie, a curriculum specialist in a survey conducted for the San Francisco schools in 1972, has collected fifty statements made by various people who resist change. Some of these statements are given here:

"We're all too busy to do that."
"It's too radical a change."
"Let's make a research test of it first."
"The parents will never buy it."
"The union will scream."
"We've never done it before."
"It's against school policy."
"We don't have the authority."
"Let's get back to reality."
"That's not our problem."
"Why change it? It's still working OK."
"Can't teach an old dog new tricks."
"Let's give it more thought."
"The school board would never go for it."
"Not *that* again!"
"It's never been tried before."
"Let's form a committee."
"I don't see the connection."
"Maybe it will work in your department, but in mine . . ."
"We've always done it this way."

These rationalizations have considerable credibility for some personnel and militate against change. For many reasons, change is not rewarded by the system. Throughout many levels of the school system, significant aspects of the status quo tend to be reinforced positively, but possible and attempted reforms tend to be reinforced negatively. Hence innovations are frequently extinguished or stopped at initial stages. The beginning teacher soon hears the

Helping Teachers Change

Thomas Shaheen

rationalizations for the status quo and is subtly— and sometimes not so subtly—pressured to adopt and accept these rationalizations. Yet the beginning teacher, often eager for the challenge of improving the schools, has a strong desire to dream good things for children, to oppose ideas that lead the teacher to accept these rationalizations.

Faced with these enormous barriers and obstacles to change, there are schools and there are teachers who have sought and successfully implemented effective innovative practices. How is this possible?

Personal-Philosophical Directions

First, change occurs with considerable success when the teacher has a sense of mission, when he has a clear concept of the purposes, the goals, and the objectives of education. He sees that philosophy is more important than procedure, more effective than organizational patterns and techniques.

Effective change can and does occur when the teacher believes that the public schools must make a positive difference in the lives of children. Not only must the teacher have such a commitment, but both as an individual and as a member of the school system, the teacher must have such a philosophy, as well as objectives, well-defined, clearly understood, and accepted by the group.

The beginning teacher can be encouraged by examples of other teachers who dared to dream a little or a lot. The new teacher will gain heart by learning about the success of Beverly Carmody (see "Buena Vista Annex"), a young teacher who, with twelve other teachers, organized a school committed to the concept of continuous progress and an improved attitude toward young people. The beginning teacher will also enjoy the realized dreams of a small nucleus of teachers disturbed by the continued regression of Opportunity High School toward the repressiveness of other high schools in San Francisco. When the go-ahead light was flashed for them to form a new school and accept the concept that today's "kids are not steeped in original sin," they took up the challenge. These teachers believed in the kids and believed in their own abilities to create learning situations where growth, rather than problems, was emphasized.

Dreaming becomes action when the new teacher sees clearly the needs of kids, when there is recognition that dreaming and appropriate action will best serve the students.

The school system itself, which increasingly has moved toward perpetuation of the status quo, is more likely to reward the nondreamer, the person who poses little threat to the existing program. The new teacher—any teacher—who bucks this system must have courage, persistence, and determination not easily broken under pressure from colleagues. Dreaming brings threats to colleagues. The new, the untried program that is educationally sound and psychologically supported may not be professionally accepted. What supports within a system can increase the possibility for change?

In-Service Training

A system that has an active, innovative in-service training program dynamically related to the ongoing school program can encourage change. In-service training is essential, but in-service training as it exists must be changed; it can no longer stress the ritualistic, the procedural, the bureaucracy of hierarchial authority. The sense of mission must be emphasized, but it must be a sense of mission that will make in-service training a functional activity, translatable into the practices of the classrooms of today and tomorrow.

The content of in-service training must change. Teachers will dare to dream if they feel adequate to take up the challenges of change. Nor must the teachers be led to believe that change, individualization, and a new attitude toward children comes easily. But the excitement and joy that successful change and high expectations have for children are worth the effort. We must convince our teachers that through an effective in-service program they will find that Johnny *can* learn to read, that Johnny can learn to live fully and contribute much to society.

A new kind of in-service program will provide opportunities for teachers to work with their peers in small groups, to interchange experiences with fellow teachers, and to recognize that as teachers they uniquely have the know-how to offer much to each other about techniques and content. The teachers do not need "outsiders" (professors, administrators, specialists) to give them the background for techniques and contents. The outsiders contribute best in process, as generalists, not as specialists.

The in-service training for change must be based on the needs of teachers. It seeks to determine what each especially and uniquely needs. Effective in-service training for change will be individualized, not mass, instruction.

Encouraging Leaders

Positive training experiences, encouragement for change, and implementation of organizational facilitators can be mobilized by daring, sensitive leaders. These men and women may range from building principals to curriculum specialists and central-office personnel and superintendents.

Teachers soon get the message when they see an administrator who respects their desire for change and supports them, stumbling as they may be, in the early stages. Change occurs effectively when a teaching staff can agree with John Wise, principal of Rockford (Illinois) High School, who said that effective change came primarily when he decided to trust kids. Just as significantly, the support through those first difficult, often hectic, months is essential. In 1968, at a Rockford school board meeting, John Wise said, "When we decided to trust kids, we had a hell of a September, and October was not much better. By November we were beginning to see daylight, and we had a wonderful spring!"

The new teacher, often ready in troubled days to revert to the way he was taught, is buoyed up by a principal who stands behind his teachers until May and beyond. Long-term encouragement is especially needed to bring about effective educational change, and the new teacher needs encouragement always—but especially in those early days.

Fortunate indeed is the new teacher who has a principal who organizes the school day and the school program to eliminate the multiplicity of educational trivia that frustrate the teacher. Dreaming can exist and be productive for the beginning teacher if his principal is not concerned about the teachers' spending time and energy collecting money, running charity drives, doing statistical accounting, filling out time-consuming forms, attending to bureaucratic detail, doing textbook accounting, making checks of library books, and dealing with the endless details that demand attention. Industry long ago learned that it may be more profitable not to tie down its high-paid labor force with an accounting for insignificant details; education could take this cue.

Educational improvement will come for the new teacher when his principal can and does send out meaningful educational directives, when his principal respects the teacher as a person as well as a contributing member of the staff, when his principal involves him in decision making, when his principal structures staff meetings to indicate that he feels the time of teachers must be well spent, not wasted in dull, routine procedures. When the principal makes it clear to the teacher that effective change will be rewarded, that promotion goes to him who dares to innovate, his expectation can be great. When the principal values less the quiet, hear-a-pin-drop room than the bustling, learning-filled atmosphere of the open classroom, the beginning teacher has leadership that excites dreams.

Thus change is most effective when it begins with the teacher and is supported overtly by the structure and leadership within a system. Only when a teacher is ready to say confidently "The school, my program, is worth changing—and I can do it!" will change truly occur and our schools be better. The need is great, the task is hard, but the rewards are tremendous.

The issues of discipline, testing, freedom-structure, and values are far too broad for exhaustive coverage in a survey collection of readings. The following selections, however, raise major problems in each area, suggest specific approaches based on sound theoretical principles, stimulate critical discussion, and encourage further study. These articles deal with broad, basic questions, which every teacher, new or veteran, needs to come to terms with.

2 Recurrent Struggles

Values and Value Education
Jack R. Fraenkel

Jack R. Fraenkel, Professor of Interdisciplinary Studies at California State University, San Francisco, has specialized in social-studies curriculum development from kindergarten through high school.

Abuses and Misuses in Testing Black Children
Robert L. Williams

Robert L. Williams is Director of Black Studies and Professor of Psychology at Washington University in St. Louis. He has written many articles and made numerous public appearances in conjunction with his interest in problems of testing black children.

Aggression in the Classroom
Fritz Redl

Fritz Redl, Professor of Behavioral Sciences at Wayne State University, has served in the United States and abroad as director, teacher, consultant, and psychologist for many schools and organizations. He has received numerous awards and is perhaps best known for his books on childhood aggression.

Wrestling with Values

On all controversial educational issues we must come to terms with our own views and help our students do the same. Our attitudes and behavior, what we select to teach, how we choose to present subject matter, and how we interact with young people reflect our values. How values can be dealt with in the classroom and how values relate to two major issues—testing and aggression—have particular importance in our classrooms.

Jack Fraenkel, in "Values and Value Education," makes the case for value education and then proceeds to suggest concrete ways to pursue this goal. Helping students transform abstract notions into behavioral examples is worth considering and emulating in a variety of subject areas. Since we unwittingly transmit values all the time, a more refined understanding of how this process occurs may be helpful in moving us toward desired outcomes.

In "Abuses and Misuses in Testing Black Children," Robert Williams pulls together a good deal of the most recent information in this area. We must continue to search for ways of assessing strengths and specifying weaknesses, while not causing students untold damage.

Fritz Redl's article, "Aggression in the Classroom"—a concise, well-packed compendium of insights and specific suggestions—is a classic in the field and contains fruitful suggestions for productive classroom application.

One of the most important, yet neglected, areas in teaching is that of value analysis and development. It is probably no exaggeration to state that most teachers do not deal explicitly with the teaching of *valuing* in their day-to-day classroom activities. There are a number of reasons for this omission. Many teachers regard student values as essentially private concerns that should not be discussed publicly. Parents and other forces in the community often resist having controversial issues discussed, and values, of course, involve controversy. Some teachers believe that values must "be caught rather than taught" and question the probability of devising any program specifically designed for their development. Besides, they argue, the family, church, and other institutions are better equipped to deal with the matter. Some feel that any attempt on the part of teachers to influence or develop values in students smacks of totalitarianism. Some cannot decide what, or if, values should be taught and therefore decide to ignore the question entirely. A few simply say that they have more than enough to do "just trying to get the subject matter across" without worrying about values.

Objections like these suggest that teachers place most of their emphasis upon intellectual development and tend to ignore the affective area. Objectives, content, learning experiences, teaching strategies, and evaluative measures all tend to be selected, organized, and developed to promote learning in the cognitive domain more than in the attitudinal. Though the recent awakening to the ills of education in the United States produced a plethora of materials and suggestions toward reorganizing course content and improving students' thinking abilities, only a few writers have addressed themselves seriously to the question of value education. [Hunt and Metcalf, 1968; Oliver and Shaver, 1966; Raths, Harmin, and Simon, 1966] Several "methods books" make no mention of the topic whatsoever. Ballinger [1963], in reviewing a series of such methods texts, in fact found that "almost no attention *at all* is paid to controversial issues in any form."

Value education, however, is unavoidable. A teacher's actions, sayings, discussion topics, reading assignments, and class activities indicate that he believes certain ideas, events, objects, and people to be important for students to consider. Indications of value are suggested all the time in the classroom. . . .

This article is based on material that appeared in *Phi Delta Kappan*, April 1969, and has been adapted by permission of the author and the publisher.

Values and Value Education

Jack R. Fraenkel

Nonetheless, it must be admitted that in many instances what value education there is in a particular school or course is not developed through systematic design. What values are taught is determined implicitly through the selection and use of certain kinds of materials and assignments. It appears important to consider, therefore, whether we want values to develop in students accidentally or whether we intend to deliberately influence their value development in directions we consider desirable. It is my contention that the systematic design of appropriate teaching strategies to bring about desired values is crucially important and badly needed in education. We then have at least some control over the kinds of behavioral change we produce in students. If we allow student values to develop by chance, we lose this opportunity.

The question, then, is not "Should values be taught?" but rather "What values do we want to develop in our students?" and "How can they be developed?"

The teaching of some kinds of values appears logically and empirically justified if we are to maintain our effectiveness as teachers. As Fenton [1966] illustrates, certain behavioral values (e.g., specific rules of order in the classroom) must be established if we are to teach at all. Certain procedural values (e.g., encouraging logical analysis over illogical analysis) are also essential to our pedagogical effectiveness. Indeed, we could not do our jobs if we did not teach such values.

When we come to the question of values that promote a particular point of view (for example, monogamy is a good thing; divorce should not be permitted; money is the root of all evil), however, we are on much more difficult ground. . . .

The problem, of course, is that what acts or ideas are intrinsically good or bad will be defined differently by different men (or even by the same men) at different times. In a culture as pluralistic as ours, what is sacred to one individual may be anathema to another. Because our culture is so pluralistic, any attempts to develop one set of values as *the* set that all individuals should hold seems doomed to failure from the start.

There are, however, a large number of rather general statements (for example, "promoting the worth and dignity of all individuals") that the majority of Americans hold to be the goals of a democratic society and to which they at least verbally subscribe. . . . However, as is usually the case, they are far too general to be of much help in designing instructional strategies to bring about value analysis and development. Thus, we must be much more precise. . . .

Let us use a commonly accepted value to illustrate the point more clearly. Most Americans would agree that a "recognition of the dignity and worth of the individual" is a desired societal goal. But how can we tell when our students are recognizing the dignity and worth of others? As long as our goal remains so generally expressed, we cannot. Why not? Because it is not clear (and thus we do not know) what students *do* when they recognize individual worth and dignity.

Suppose, however, that we attempt to become more explicit as to what we expect. Can we identify certain behaviors in the classroom that we would accept as *some* evidence that students are recognizing "the dignity and worth of the individual"? For example, we might say that a student *waits* until others have finished speaking before speaking himself (does not interrupt others); *encourages* everyone involved in a discussion to offer their opinions (does not monopolize the conversation with his arguments); *revises* his own opinions when the opinions of others are more solidly grounded in, and supported by, factual evidence than his own (does not blindly insist on his own point of view); *makes statements* in support of others no matter what their social status (does not put others in embarrassing, humiliating, or subservient positions).

Notice that each of these statements indicates certain behaviors that we desire of students. To the extent that our students display these behaviors . . . , we have reason to believe that they are making at least some progress toward attaining the previously identified general goal of recognizing the dignity and worth of other individuals. This is not to imply, however, that such behavioral statements totally capture the essence of the more general goal. No concept as abstract as the worth and dignity of the individual can ever be fully and completely identified, let alone put into words. But we can try to describe as completely as we can what we believe such a statement to mean. . . .

We must also plan and develop appropriate teaching strategies to enable the teacher to reinforce these desired behaviors. Such teaching strategies need to indicate actual procedures for a teacher to use in order to encourage value analysis and the development of desired student values.

The most common means of teaching values employed by teachers in the past has been that of moralistic *telling*. Teachers have used a variety of exhortatory techniques, such as persuasion, emotional pleas, appeals to conscience, slogans, and "good examples" to help students learn to value the "right" objects, persons, or ideas.

A corollary of moralism is the argument for "exposure." According to this argument, the way to help students acquire certain desired values is to expose them continually to the kind of objects and ideas that possess such values (a painting by Rembrandt, a Mozart sonata, Caesar's *Commentaries*—in Latin, of course, and the like). In short, if we provide the "right" kind of atmosphere in our classrooms, our students will "catch" the values we desire them to possess. Our job as teachers, then, is to assure that we place our students in the kinds of situations and expose them to the kinds of materials that contain the kinds of values we want "caught." (Should any student not catch these values, why then, naturally something must be wrong with the student.)

The problem with these approaches is that they just haven't worked very well. "If admonition, lecture, sermon, or example were fully effective instruments in gaining compliance with codes of conduct, we would have reformed long ago the criminal, the delinquent, or the sinner." [Kimball, 1966] The sad fact is that exhortation rarely produces committed, actively involved individuals. Essentially, it involves one-way communication, yet several studies have indicated that one-directional, persuasive communications are relatively ineffective. [Festinger, 1964; Allport, 1954; McGinnies, 1966; Sykes, 1966]...

A study cited by Festinger [1964] introduced the use of fear and fear-arousing elements during training on oral hygiene. High-school students were divided into four groups, with three of the groups hearing appeals ... to use proper methods of oral hygiene. The appeals were characterized as strong, moderate, and minimal. The strong appeal contained fear-arousing elements, while the other two were more objective presentations of the facts. There were follow-up questionnaires to determine how many students had changed their practices to conform to the oral hygiene methods recommended. The relation between behavior and the degree to which students were made to feel concerned about oral hygiene was actually *in the reverse direction* from what one would expect from any simple relationship between attitude change and behavior. Festinger summed up his findings as follows: "All in all, we can detect no effect on behavior or even a clear and persistent change in opinion brought about by a persuasive communication." [Festinger, 1964]

A second approach to the teaching of values is that of the moral relativist. The findings of cultural anthropology in the last fifty to seventy-five years argue that there are no values seemingly that all people endorse. To quote W. T. Stace [1937] in *The Concept of Morals:*

The whole notion of progress is a sheer delusion. Progress means an advance from lower to higher, from worse to better. But on the basis of ethical relativity, it has no meaning to say that the standards of this age are better (or worse) than those of the previous age. For there is no common standard by which both can be measured....

This position seems to argue that there exists a plurality of value positions that one can take and that one value is as good as any other.

A corollary of this relativistic position is that of the logical positivist who argues that only judgments of fact can be verified. Judgments of value cannot. Judgments of fact refer to present or past realities; they are objective, describe relationships among things, and have assumed referents in nature. They can be tested publicly by anyone through observation or experiment. Judgments of value, on the other hand, cannot be publicly tested, for they deal with subject matter that is not subject to observation or experiment. Such subject matter deals with feelings and preferences and includes value terms that denote a quality of preference which an individual wants to express. Such statements also contain words like *should* or *ought*. [Hunt and Metcalf, 1968]

The logical positivist seems to overlook the fact, however, that such statements of value can be submitted to public test, if we can get some agreement on the value terms involved. For example, if I were to say that Nancy is a beautiful girl, this statement is testable enough if all of those concerned can agree on the meaning of beautiful. The key question seems to be, "Can the concepts in the proposition be defined in ways that (according to defining criteria) are clear?" Can we agree on the properties of a value concept and state, whenever possible, such properties in behavioral terms?

The central problem of relativism is that it ignores the fact that some values apparently are better than others and thus worth developing. Whereas moralism encourages an uncritical acceptance on the part of students of the values set forth by teachers (or other adults), relativism provides no guides whatsoever. Neither approach helps students to determine for themselves what it is that they consider to be important.

Thus, either deliberately or by default, students receive their values from a source outside themselves. They acquire what "society" deems to be important rather than determining this for themselves. In a society like ours, however, where many conflicting values exist, students acquire a number of values that are in opposition to each other. This polarity in turn furthers uncertainty on their part, yet neither moralism nor relativism provides them with any way by which to deal with the conflict that these opposing values produce. As Hunt and Metcalf [1968] suggest, to be told that one should always value both honesty and kindness doesn't help much when the two conflict.

Thus it would seem to make both logical and psychological sense to devise a number of instructional strategies that teachers can use to influence value development in directions they desire.

Let us consider first a teaching strategy designed to encourage students to identify and empathize with others faced with two or more undesirable and conflicting alternatives.

Festinger [1957] has suggested that when individuals are presented with a problem in which two "goods" are in conflict, they will expend effort to study the alternatives. With this in mind, the following strategy was designed.

1. An Affective Strategy That Develops Empathy for and Identification with Individuals Placed in Conflict Situations

Behavioral Objectives: Given the information in the following story, students should be able to:

a. *state* the alternatives open to Willie (the central character in the story)
b. *describe* at least two things that might happen to Willie depending on what course of action he decides to pursue; and how they think Willie would feel in each instance
c. *state* what they think they would do if they were Willie, and *explain* why they think they would do this
d. *describe* how they think they would feel if they did this
e. *state* what they believe is a warranted generalization about how people feel in situations similar to Willie's

In this strategy, students are asked to read a story (or have the story read to them, depending on age and grade level) in which an individual, as real-life as possible, is faced with a choice between two or more conflicting alternatives. Here is one such story that can be used with first-graders:

Willie Johnson was in trouble! He had been a bad boy in school this morning.

He had thrown his paint water at Sue Nelligan and the teacher had become angry with him. "Why did you do that, Willie?" she had asked. Willie couldn't tell her, because he really didn't know why himself. He knew that Sue had teased him a little, but that wasn't the real reason. He just didn't know! The whole thing put him in a bad mood. From then on, the entire day just went to heck.

In the afternoon he had pushed Tommy Grigsly in the recess line. He also had stamped his foot and yelled at the teacher. The teacher had become angry with him again. But this time she had pinned a note to his mother on his jacket.

Willie was really scared about the note! He knew it was about his behavior in class during the day. He was afraid that when he got home his mother would read the note and give him some kind of punishment. Then his father would find out, and he'd get it!

On his way home from school Willie was thinking about what his father would do to him. Oh brother, was he scared!

"Wow!" he thought. "I'll get killed if I bring this note home. I'd better take it off and throw it away."

He was just about to do that when he remembered what had happened to Billy Beatty when he was sent home with a note. Billy had thrown his note away and was sent to the Principal's office about it. Then Billy was in double trouble!

Wow! He *was* in trouble! He couldn't give it to his mother, he couldn't throw it away. What should he do? He had a problem, all right. He had to make a choice, but how should he choose? No matter what he did, the outcome didn't look too good! What should he do?*

Upon completion of the reading, the teacher can ask the class:
1. What things might Willie do? (What alternatives are open to him?)
2. What might happen to him if he does each of these things?
3. How do you think he'd feel, in each case, if this happened?
4. If you were faced with this situation, what would you do?
5. How do you think you'd feel?
6. Based on how you've said you think you would feel and how you think Willie felt, what can you say about how people feel in situations like this?
7. Why do you think people have different feelings about things?

This question sequence presents one example of a carefully thought-out teaching strategy. Students are asked to determine what alternatives are open to an individual placed in an uncomfortable situation (Question 1). No matter what Willie does, the consequences will be rather unpleasant. Thus the similarity to real life, for who among us has not been at one time or another in a somewhat similar predicament? Students are not only asked to analyze alternatives, however; they are also requested to predict consequences (Question 2). In Question 3, they are helped to identify the *feelings* of another, and then, in Questions 4 and 5, to empathize with those feelings and determine how they would feel themselves in such a situation. Questions 6 and 7 ask them to try to draw some conclusions about how people in general might feel in such situations. (It is to be emphasized at this point that there are no "right" answers to questions like the ones in this strategy, nor should there be. What we are interested in encouraging is a discussion about how people feel; such a discussion is impossible if there is one, and only one, answer that is "correct.") The assumption underlying this strategy is that, through empathizing with the feelings of

*The first draft of this story was prepared by Cornelius Mahoney, of Raphael Weill Elementary School, San Francisco.

another individual faced with unpleasant conflicting alternatives, students will be making affective responses so that affective learning may occur. The reactions of the teacher and other students to what a given student says will have some effect on what responses are reinforced. Students may be motivated to change their behavior and become more considerate of others facing conflicts.

Thus we see one example of a teaching strategy in the affective domain geared to the fulfillment of a specific objective—to encourage students to identify and empathize with individuals who are faced with a number of conflicting and undesirable alternatives and, through so doing, to become more considerate of others' feelings. But suppose that we had another objective in mind—to increase children's *sensitivity* to the worth and dignity of other individuals, especially those somewhat different from themselves. "To extend sensitivity, students need an opportunity to react with feelings and to identify with feelings of other people, whether in the reality of actual experience or as described in fiction." [Taba, 1962] It is also to be stressed that "feeling, values, and sensitivities are matters that need to be discovered rather than taught." [Taba, 1962]

Teaching strategies can be designed that will help students to discover such feelings of tolerance and sensitivity to others. One such strategy follows.

2. An Affective Strategy That Promotes Sensitivity to the Feelings and Needs of Others

Behavioral Objectives: Given the information contained in the following story, students should be able to:

a. *describe* how they think the central figure in the story feels
b. *explain* why they think he feels as he does
c. *describe* how they think they would feel in a situation similar to that of the central figure
d. *state* what they believe is a warranted generalization about people and how they behave

In this strategy, students are asked to read (or have read to them, depending on age and grade level) a story in which characters that are as real-life as possible express their feelings and show their emotions about other people, events, or ideas. Here is one such story that might be used with third-graders:

Anatouck was worried and scared. He had good reason to be! It was his first day at school in a strange land. Anatouck was an Eskimo and he had just come to California. He was eight years old, and he had never been to school in "the States" (as the main part of the United States is known to Alaskans). It was all like a dream—the sun and grass, the cities, the traffic. All were so strange.

Anatouck came from a land where it was cold and snow-covered all year round. He had spent the first five years of his life in an igloo. Then his mother and father had died in an accident. A short time later he was sent by missionaries to the mission school in a small village nearby. Here he met Mr. and Mrs. Barnaby, two teachers from California who were working as teachers in the mission school. He grew to love them and they loved him. They arranged to adopt him. Then when Anatouck finished the second grade, Mrs. Barnaby told him that the family (his new family) would be going home to California. Anatouck would start third grade in a California school!

Anatouck at first was very happy. He had heard many wonderful things about California. He even looked forward to going to school there. After he had been in California one week, however, he had begun to have doubts. The kids in the neighborhood his family moved to laughed at him. They called him names such as "flat nose" and "slanty eyes." He didn't like that much at all. Why did they call him such names?

And so today Anatouck was worried. It was his first day in the new California school. Would the children in the class laugh at him? Would they call him names? Would they giggle at the way he spoke? He hoped not, but he couldn't be sure.*

Upon completion of the reading, the teacher can ask the class the following questions:

1. What did you read? (What is this story about? What happened in this story?)
2. Why do you think Anatouck was worried?
3. How do you think he felt as he started out for school?
4. Has anything like this ever happened to anyone you know? In a story you've read? To you?
5. How did you feel? (Or why do you think people sometimes do things like this?)
6. After reading a story like this and talking about it, what can you say about people and how they behave? [Durkin, 1968]

The question sequence presents a second example of a specially designed teaching strategy. Students are asked in Questions 1 and 2 to describe and explain what they think actually happened to an individual in a specific situation. In Question 3, they describe how they think the individual *felt* about the situation. So far, the primary intellectual activity required is that of analysis. Questions 4 and 5 then enable the student to try to determine what his *own* feelings in such a situation might be, and then Question 6 asks them to try to draw some conclusions about human behavior in general in such situations.

These are but two examples of teaching strategies that can be used to further value education in public and private schools. It is important for us to develop such strategies. We must first identify and specify behaviorally what our objectives in the affective domain are to be, of course. We must also plan relevant learning activities (films that present value conflicts, open-ended filmstrips, panel and class discussions on controversial social issues, guest speakers, student field trips, essays on open-ended topics like "what makes me angry," role-playing, sociodramas, and the like) that will allow students to practice appropriate and varied behaviors. But we cannot leave the accomplishment of affective objectives to chance or to learning activities (no matter how varied or exciting) planned mainly for cognitive goals. Teaching strategies that identify specific procedures that teachers may use (such as the questioning sequences presented earlier) must be designed in order to help youngsters develop desired values.

---

*The first draft of this story was prepared by Cornelius Mahoney, of Raphael Weill Elementary School, San Francisco.

"If a tree is to be judged by its fruit, if the intelligence of a race bears any relation to its accomplishments, it seems difficult to draw any conclusion other than that the Black and Brown races are inferior to the white race." [Ellis, 1928]

Before considering the major issues in the dispute over testing black children, it is important to take a quick glance at the current status of the problem involving abuse and misuse in testing black children.

The dispute over the intellectual inferiority of black people and the corresponding problem of measuring black intelligence have created more controversy than perhaps any other single issue in the field of psychology. Some of the central disputants have compromised on occasion, but essentially there has been produced a sharp cleavage of opinion about the intelligence of black people and about intelligence testing in general. In a word, opinion is split over whether or not lower scores by blacks on the traditional ability tests are attributed primarily to genetic heritage or biased intelligence tests. It is seriously questioned today whether traditional ability tests may serve as valid measures of black intelligence.

In preparing this response, I carefully examined a vast array of publications dealing with one phase or another of the continuing controversy over abuses and misuses in testing black children. The single most salient conclusion is that traditional ability tests do systematically and consistently lead to assigning improper and false labels on black children and, consequently, dehumanization and black intellectual genocide. This conclusion is neither new nor surprising. The information has been known for many years. It was not until the Association of Black Psychologists generated some heat in this area by calling a moratorium on the testing of black people, however, that the real issues began to surface.

First of all, the meaning of intelligence is rather diverse; although considerable attention and effort have been given this concept, it is still ill-used and poorly understood. . . . Definitions of intelligence are so diverse that it would

Reprinted from *The Counseling Psychologist*, 1971, *2* (3), 62–73, by permission of the author and publisher.

Abuses and Misuses in Testing Black Children

Robert L. Williams

be impractical to list all of them here. A few examples are given as representative:

a. Intelligence is what the intelligence tests measure.
b. Intelligence is defined by a consensus among psychologists as the repertoire of intellectual skills and knowledge available to a person at any one period of time. [Humphreys, 1969]
c. Intelligence is the summation of the learning experiences of the individual. [Wesman, 1968]
d. Intelligence is the aggregate or global capacity of the individual to act purposely, to think rationally, and to deal effectively with his environment. [Wechsler, 1944]

It is clear from the preceding definitions that there is not only a lack of consensus among psychologists regarding the meaning of intelligence, but no absolute definition as well. Such confusion and ambiguity make for considerable difficulty in precise and accurate measurement.

Secondly, the most frequently accepted definition is that intelligence is based on the solution of brief problems of various kinds and on the quality of one's responses to a wide range of questions. The final, standardized test score, which is called the intelligence quotient, or IQ, is usually computed so that it is given a scale score for which the average of the reference population is about 100. Jensen [1969] and Humphreys [1969] claim that, in the general population, blacks are about 15 IQ points, or one standard deviation, below whites. Psychologists and educators incorrectly use IQ and intelligence interchangeably. The intelligence quotient is a symbol that refers to a set of scores earned on a test, nothing more. An IQ per se cannot be inherited. A review of the research on comparing intellectual differences between blacks and whites shows the results to be based almost exclusively on differences in test scores, or IQ. Since the tests are biased in favor of middle-class whites, all previous research comparing the intellectual abilities of blacks and whites should be rejected completely.

Bennett [1970], in responding to the Association of Black Psychologists' call for a moratorium on the repeated abuses and misuses of psychological tests and to Williams [1970a], dealt with such factors as test anxiety, amount of formal education, and uniform testing procedures. Clemans [1970] and Sommer [1970] give what appear to be the most frequent reactions to charges of abuse of ability tests, i.e., it is the user of the test who labels the child. In this regard, Newland joins in unison:

Ability tests do not label any children or adults. The adults who use them do that on the basis of scores earned on tests. Human beings do the labeling as well as selecting of the tests used to obtain scores in terms of which any such labeling is done. [Newland, 1970]

Similarly, Munday [1970] sees the criticism against tests as misdirected. Instead of criticizing the tests, Munday identifies counselors, teachers, advisors, and admissions officers as perpetrators of the improper uses of test results. From a black perspective, these critics are not dealing with the real issue.

Messick and Anderson [1970] perhaps came closer to the real issue than any of the critics when they made a clear distinction between the scientific and ethical considerations involved in testing black children. Many important issues, however, have been omitted from discussions in the literature. . . .

Scientific Considerations

Messick and Anderson [1970] point out that the same test may measure "different attributes or processes in minority/poverty groups than it measures in white, middle-class samples or for the same processes to be captured with a different degree of fidelity."

Translated, if this is true, then that test is invalid and should not be used in testing black children. In fact, not only is the validity of ability tests being called into question, but other such psychometric considerations of tests as reliability, objectivity, and standardization. . . .

Political Considerations

In addition to the scientific issues of testing, traditional psychologists have created a number of polemics that involve political issues. The literature is fraught with examples. For instance, take the case of Jensen [1969], who asked the question, "How much can we boost IQ and scholastic achievement?" For the next 123 pages, he proceeded to answer his own political question. The Jensen report, clearly a political document, was well known to the Nixon administration when the budgets for compensatory education programs were being sharply reduced. Boosting IQ is not a real issue; it clearly is a straw man.

Changes in test scores should not serve as the primary criteria by which educational programs are evaluated. If the goal and objective of Head Start, Project Follow-Through, and other compensatory educational programs are that of "boosting IQ," then the goal is misput, inappropriate, and irrelevant.

I submit to Jensen and to others several methods for boosting the IQ of black children:

a. Teach them the answers to the ability tests
b. Develop a black IQ test containing items drawn exclusively from the black world
c. Standardize black responses to white-oriented tests as follows: "What is the thing to do if you find a purse with ten dollars in it?" Correct answers: "Try to find the owner"; "Keep the money, and return the purse."

A concern with producing increases in test scores is similar to that of a physician, whose main concern is treating the casualties rather than the causes. We refer to this approach as "victim analysis." System-produced educational problems cannot effectively be changed by focusing exclusively on the victims. The system that produced the damage must be closely examined and modified.

Deficit vs. Difference Model Bennett [1970] makes the point that traditional ability tests merely reveal the "detrimental consequences of substandard opportunity." He believes that it would be better to remedy the "cultural deficit" than to discredit the test measures. Similarly, Wikoff [1970] argues that the culture of blacks needs to be improved and enriched. For too long psychologists and educators have believed in the mythology that low scores on a test indicate in fact a weakness or a deficit in the mental ability of the black individual. It has not been made clear that the individual may possess abilities not measured by a particular test. The deficiency may well be in the weakness of the test to measure black children—in the tester but not in the testee. Black Americans do not have an inferior culture; it is, indeed, different, but it remains a highly enriched culture.

A review of the literature on the major issues involved in testing black children clearly reveals two general conceptual models. The first group is classified under the general heading of a "deficit" model, whereas the second group is classified under the heading of a "difference" model.

The deficit model assumes that black people are deficient when compared to whites in some measurable trait called intelligence and that this deficiency is due to genetic or cultural factors, or both. To support this notion, such terms as "heritability of IQ," "cultural deprivation," and "the disadvantaged" have been invented to perpetuate the myth. Proponents of this school of thought assume that the intellectual and educational deficits experienced by the so-called culturally deprived are clearly revealed by such psychological tests as the Stanford-Binet, Graduate Record Examination, and Miller Analogies tests. These tests are devised to measure one's capacity to learn or, more specifically, what one has learned. The items are supposedly selected on the basis that individuals of the same age have had the same opportunity to become familiar with the content of the items. This assumption is not true. Two five-year-olds, one black and one white, from different cultural backgrounds will answer quite differently questions such as "What is the thing to do if another child hits you?" or "What is the thing to do if you find a purse with ten dollars in it?" The deficit model assumes a set of acceptable, standard responses. If the black child gives a response that is not validated as acceptable by the norm, he is declared as deficient in his ability to comprehend and to size up certain social situations, whereas the white child is considered adequate in his ability to make appropriate judgments.

If the black child scores lower on ability tests than the white child does, the difference does not mean that the black child is actually inferior in intelligence; all it means is that the black child performed differently on the test from the white. Test inferiority is not to be equated with actual inferiority. In this connection Jensen [1969] found that many disadvantaged children with IQs between 60 and 80 performed better on learning tasks than upper middle-class children having IQs in the same range. These findings suggest that the tests were a much better predictor of ability and capacity of middle-class children since these children performed at the expected level. The results suggest further that the tests underpredicted the performance of the disadvantaged children since these children performed at a higher-than-expected level. . . .

Briefly stated, the cultural-difference model asserts that the differences noted by psychologists in intelligence testing, family and social organizations, and the studies of the black community are not the result of pathology, faulty learning, or genetic inferiority. These differences are manifestations of a viable and well-delineated culture of the black American. The difference model also acknowledges that blacks and whites come from different cultural backgrounds that emphasize different learning experiences necessary for survival. To say that the black American is different from the white American is not to say that he is inferior, deficient, or deprived. One can be unique and different without being inferior. The model, therefore, makes a clear distinction between equality and sameness. . . . Instead of being confined by an egalitarian doctrine that confuses equality with sameness, the cultural-difference model recognizes that this society is pluralistic in nature, where cultural differences abound.

Language Difference vs. Language Deficit   Because of the vast cultural differences in black society and white society, significant language differences are present. Differences in language and dialect may produce differences in cognitive learning styles, but a difference is not a deficiency. Linguists do not limit themselves to defining dialect as the way words are pronounced: "Dialect refers to the linguistic structure of a people. The dialect is a fully developed linguistic system." [Baratz and Baratz, 1969] Instead of calling black language wrong, improper, or deficient in nature, one must realize that the black child is speaking a well-developed language commonly referred to as nonstandard English. Intelligence is frequently based quite heavily on language factors. It is a common observation that black children and white children do not speak in the same way. The differences in linguistic systems favor white children since standard English is the lingua franca of the tests and the public schools. . . .

Report of the Commission on Tests   A special Commission on Tests appointed by the College Entrance Examination Board indicated that the Board examinations taken by about two million high-school students a year failed to recognize and assess a wide variety of talents, skills, and mental attributes. [College Entrance Examination Board, 1970] Over the years many students, particularly black ones, have been grossly penalized. Basically, the Commission on Tests found the SAT, which measures fluency in English and ability to deal with mathematical and spatial concepts, to be discriminatory against certain minority groups. Although high verbal and numerical abilities are generally those required in traditional academic liberal-arts and scientific education, the Commission found these indicators to be too narrow for application to all who might benefit from college. The Commission recommended that the tests gradually be replaced by a flexible assortment of other tests measuring not only verbal and mathematical ability but many other dimensions of excellence. These dimensions included musical and artistic talents; sensitivity and commitment to social responsibility; political and social leadership; athletic, political, and mechanical skills; styles of analysis and synthesis; ability to express oneself through artistic, oral, nonverbal, or graphic means; ability to organize and manage information; ability to adapt to new situations; characteristics of temperament; and so on. . . .

The Jensen report [1969] led directly or indirectly to a number of changes in the President's program regarding Head-Start Programs, Project Follow-Through, and other compensatory educational programs. These and other reports must be considered political in nature. A few of the reports lead to positive change for black people, while others are quite detrimental.

In addition to the foregoing comments regarding education, it is clear from this discussion that ability and certain achievement tests play a major role in current educational procedures and consequently in determining what doors in life will be opened or closed to a black child. Tests are used to determine admission, grouping, selection, assignment to special classes, and educational tracks. If the tests are unfair (biased), then it is clear that they place (misplace) or label (mislabel) a certain portion of the populations in general and the black population in particular. Throughout the country disproportionately large numbers of black children are being misplaced in special education classes. Many states legally define the educable mentally retarded as those children obtaining an IQ below 80.

Statement of the Association of Black Psychologists on Testing Abuse At its annual meeting in 1969, the Association of Black Psychologists called for an immediate moratorium on the administration of ability tests to black children. The Association charged that these tests
a. label black children as uneducable
b. place black children in special classes
c. potentiate inferior education
d. assign black children to lower education tracks than whites
e. deny black children higher educational opportunities
f. destroy positive intellectual growth and development of black children
   In other words, black psychologists translated the whole abuse-of-testing issue into one of intellectual genocide of black children. Tests do not permit the masses of black children to develop their full intellectual potential. The tests are used to sort and consequently to misplace black children in special education classes.

Composition of Special Education Classes in St. Louis and San Francisco In St. Louis during the academic year 1968–1969, blacks made up approximately 63.6 percent of the school population, whereas whites constituted 36.4 percent. Of 4020 children in special education, 2975 (76 percent) were black and only 1045 (24 percent) were white. Thus, black children were being placed in classes for the educable mentally retarded about three times as frequently as their white counterparts. Again, children are placed in special education classes primarily on the basis of scores earned on biased intelligence tests.
   In San Francisco a group of black psychologists recently presented a document on testing abuses to the San Francisco Unified School District School Board. The document called for an immediate moratorium on ability testing of

black children until better and more appropriate assessment techniques are made available. The document pointed out that although black children constitute only 27.8 percent of the total student population in the San Francisco Unified Schools, they make up 47.4 percent of all students in educationally handicapped classes and 53.3 percent of all students in the educable mentally handicapped classes. The black psychologists pointed out that the consultants to the psychologists and psychometricians in the San Francisco Unified School District are not familiar enough with the black experience to serve as competent evaluators of black children. The document also pointed out that, of the psychologists and psychometrists who administered and interpreted the psychological tests, no black personnel were involved. The Association of Black Psychologists has recently reported that the San Francisco School District has honored the moratorium on testing and that no psychological tests are now being administered to black children for placement in special classes. . . .

Legal Considerations on Testing

It is clear that the continued administration of traditional ability tests to black children is a violation of the child's civil and constitutional rights under the provisions of the Fourteenth Amendment for equal protection under the law. . . .

The increasing number of criticisms in the literature and the possible large number of impending court cases regarding the abuse and misuse of testing black children strongly suggest that the cries of the black community be heard. [Halpern, 1970–1971]

Article XIV, Section 1 of the United States Constitution reads as follows:

All persons born or naturalized in the United States and subject to the jurisdiction thereof are citizens of the United States and of the state wherein they reside. No state shall make or enforce any law which shall abridge the privileges or immunities of citizens in the United States; nor shall any state deprive any person of life, liberty, or property without the due process of law; nor deny to any person within its jurisdiction the equal protection of the laws.

Diana et al. v. *California State Board of Education*   One case is reported by Leary [1970] of an eight-year-old Mexican-American girl who earned an IQ of 30 on the Stanford-Binet intelligence test, clearly placing her in the mentally defective range of functioning. Diana's mother had the test readministered by a school psychologist, also of Mexican-American descent, who translated the test into Spanish. Diana's IQ increased 49 points. In fact, of nine Mexican-American children retested in Spanish, all but one increased to above the cut-off score of 79 used by the California school district to place children in the category of the educable mentally retarded or the educationally handicapped.

Another case of misjudging is reported by Witty and Jenkins [1935] of a black child with superior intelligence who had an IQ of 200. She was rated by her teacher as lower in intelligence than a child whose IQ turned out to be 100. When a misjudgment does occur, the result will be to place the child into a curriculum paced to his measured abilities, where he is likely to progress only at the speed provided by the teacher. In fact, many black children probably have higher native intelligence than their teachers. These teachers frequently see the gifted black students as "problem children," "hyperactive," "disruptive"—when, in fact, the children are simply bored in the classroom. They are not being challenged by a teacher whose intelligence is average or slightly above average.

Hobson v. *Hansen* In a rather momentous decision in the United States District Court for the District of Columbia, United States Circuit Judge J. Skelly Wright issued a 182-page document in the case of *Hobson v. Hansen* in regard to abolishing the track system in District of Columbia schools. Judge Wright stated: "It is further ordered, adjudged, and decreed that the defendants be, and they are hereby, permanently enjoined from operating the track system in the District of Columbia schools." The District of Columbia educational track system was implemented in the high schools in 1956 and extended downward to the junior-high and elementary schools in 1959. The track system proved to be nothing more than another way of resegregating blacks and whites within the individual school system. As the evidence in the case became clear, grouping children on the basis of test scores was clearly a denial of equal educational opportunity to the poor and the majority of blacks attending school in the nation's capital. . . .

Children were placed in tracks based on such ability tests as the Binet and WISC. As the judge decided, when standard ability tests are given to low-income black children or disadvantaged children, they are less precise and less accurate; so also it is virtually impossible to tell whether the test score reflects lack of ability or lack of opportunity.

The judge, looking very closely into side issues of psychological testing and placement of track systems, pointed out the following damages inherent in the system:

By consigning students to specifically designed curricula, the track system makes highly visible the student's status within the school structure. To the unlearned, tracks can become pejorative labels, symptomatic of which is the recent abandonment of the suggestive "basic" for the more euphemistic "special academic" as the nomenclature of the lowest track. A system that presumes to tell a student what his ability is and what he can successfully learn incurs an obligation to take account of the psychological damage that can come from such an encounter between the student and the school and to be certain that it is in a position to decide whether the student's deficiencies are true or only apparent. The District of Columbia school system has not shown that it is in such a position. [*Hobson* v. *Hansen*]

The judge interpreted the testing and track system as a way of forcing the self-fulfilling prophecy—teachers acting under false assumptions because of low test scores will treat the black student in such a way as to make him conform to their low expectations. In concluding, the judge decided as follows:

As to the remedy with respect to the track system, the track system simply must be abolished. . . . Even in concept the track system is undemocratic and discriminatory. Its creator admits it is designed to prepare some children for white-collar jobs and other children for blue-collar jobs. . . . The danger that children completing their education will wear the wrong collar is far too great for this democracy. [*Hobson* v. *Hansen*]

Many cities have abolished the track system as a direct result of the decision rendered in the *Hobson* v. *Hansen* case. However, they have implemented other systems that are not called track systems but are just as lethal; for example, in one city the tracking system has been officially abolished, but three levels have been substituted in its place: academic curriculum, standard curriculum, general curriculum. It is clear from the inequality of education provided that educational tracking is one of the major aspects of the new system. In any event, psychological tests are used to determine who goes into the academic, standard, or general curriculum, each of which leads to different educational careers or futures. "A rose by any other name . . ."

Economic Considerations

Testing is a big industry. One of the major nonprofit testing organizations showed the following statement of income from tests for the year ending June 30, 1970:

	Actual 1968–1969	Actual 1969–1970	Projected 1970–1971
Admissions Testing Program	$17,424,015	$17,688,007	$18,520,800
College Level Exam Program	157,285	179,739	449,500
Puerto Rico Testing Program	211,697	259,850	233,000
Advanced Placement Program	973,823	1,236,065	1,363,000

Messick and Anderson [1970] point out that the social consequences of not testing are extreme. The economic consequences of not testing are also quite extreme for the testing corporations.

For many black children, the economic consequences of testing are quite extreme. As pointed out earlier, testing may determine which doors may or may not be opened to black children. Or, as Judge Wright in the *Hobson* v. *Hansen* case so aptly put it, the tests may determine that the child wear the "wrong collar" occupationally. As reported by Williams [1970b], a hundred minority-group postal employees were hired without administration of the usual screening tests. At the end of one year, by and large they received satisfactory ratings based on job performance. The employees were administered the usual screening tests at the end of a one-year period; they all failed. The tests certainly would have led to the unemployment of qualified persons. Lowering standards is not the issue; appropriate assessment is a vital issue, however.

Testing is a big business. The use of tests has become deeply imbedded in the American version of education. To some, testing represents an American dream; to others, it represents a horrible nightmare. Tests shape, in large measure, what is to be taught in schools. Teaching the test is not an uncommon phenomenon in American schools. Teachers prepare the student for the test to be taken. In many ways the tests may shape teacher expectations. If this assertion is at all true—and some evidence exists to suggest that it is [Goslin, 1967]—one strategy for improving or changing the educational system would be to change the content of the tests. . . . Items relevant to the black experience would bring about similar changes in classrooms. This effort might bring about a greater similarity between the predictor (tests) and the criterion (scholastic achievement).

While Bennett [1970] and others continue to declare the intellectual inferiority of black people, the courts are reaching decisions that negate their allegations. Thus it merely becomes an academic exercise to continue this "straw man" debate. Black professionals must be about the business of developing appropriate measuring instruments and black educational models for black children.

There's plenty of minor aggression in the classroom that nobody objects to. The real problem is the aggression that prevents good teaching and good classroom life. This aggression comes primarily from three areas.

First, it is an input from the home or from the community. A teen-ager gets hopping mad at his old man, but he doesn't dare let off steam until he gets to school. Now, the teacher didn't produce the aggression, but it's there and he's got to handle it.

Second is the discharge from within. Some youngster sits there daydreaming; all of a sudden, during a wild fantasy, he thinks of something that upsets him and he conks his neighbors on the head. None of them have done anything to him, and the teacher hasn't either. Something just burst out from within. (If youngsters are seriously disturbed, most of the aggression comes from way within, and neither they nor anyone else knows why.)

Third, the aggression is engendered right there in the classroom. It may be triggered either by what the teacher does that's right but that doesn't happen to fit the kid or by God knows what—the kid's reaction to the group or to other kids, or to something that maybe the teacher wouldn't have done if he had stopped to think. But anyway, it's reactive to something in the environment at the moment.

Now, if I were a classroom teacher, I would like to know how much of which of those three packages is exploding before me, because it makes a difference in terms of what to do at the moment. Most of the time we are not sure, but different sources of aggression smell different when we are confronted with them. Experienced teachers develop an uncanny skill at sensing "This is something the kid brought with him. I've got to help him recover from it before he acts it out." The outsider, though, wouldn't know.

Some aggression does not affect us directly because certain youngsters may be model pupils in the classroom, but then after school they may go out and

Reprinted from *Today's Education*, September 1969, by permission of the author and the publisher.

Aggression in the Classroom

Fritz Redl

rape or murder someone. So a youngster may be full of sick aggression without being a classroom problem.

On the other hand, there may be a great kid sitting over there who's bored stiff. He likes you a lot, but he gets mad at the fact that you bore him stiff. Finally, he's just had it, and he runs out and slams the door. A normal youngster like that whose aggression is classroom-produced is our problem. Too often, an article on aggression in the classroom concentrates on a few examples of youngsters who should have been in a mental hospital for the last ten years anyway and ignores all the other kids who bother us.

The term *aggression* is so overused now, you've got to watch out for it. Don't ever let anybody trap you into discussing aggression without first asking him: "Listen, brother, which aggression are you talking about? What actually happened?" Because aggression has a wide range—all the way from reacting to boredom to wrestling at the wrong time in the wrong place with another pupil.

Discharge of surplus energy or of displaced needs from the home or neighborhood; loss of control in the face of seductive equipment like a slingshot or a knife or whatnot; personal battles with adults, other kids, the group, or the teacher—all these fall under the heading of aggression.

The way Joe or Jane expresses aggression, while not the end of what we're looking for, certainly should be the starting point. Unless you know what lies behind their behavior, you will have trouble knowing how to handle it. Sometimes you may understand perfectly well how come. So the question then is what do you do to help him, which is a separate matter from knowing what was cooking to begin with.

I want to give special warning here not to make *aggression* synonymous with *violence*. The two are not the same, although they are obviously related. There is a theme in violence that we can legitimately call aggression. On the other hand, not all violence comes from aggressive drives. The behavior is aggressive, but the basis may be quite different. Let me give a few illustrations of violence that does not spring from aggression.

Panic coping   A kid may get scared stiff, so scared that he doesn't know what to do anymore. So he does something violent; he tears something apart. The fact that the behavior is violent is important. But this child is not hyper-aggressive; he is frightened and desperate.

The need to be heard   A frequent source of violence is the feeling that nobody listens. The child finally concludes that the only way to get someone to listen is to be violent enough. So when other avenues are blocked off, violence is a substitute for verbal and nonverbal communication.

The desire to display guts   If a kid is supposed to be tough, how can he show it? Who is going to believe it? "I'd better not let them know I'm scared. So I've got to find ways to show I'm brave." In order to do this in a peaceful life, he's got to create problems.

Demonstrating loyalty to the group code   This source of violence is not originally meant to be aggression for aggression's sake. ("If the rest of my gang thinks school is no good, I'd better show that I'm with them. So I put a thumbtack in the teacher's chair. I don't hate the teacher; too bad it's her rear that gets stung. But I'm a regular guy and I'm going to prove it.")

Risk taking—to study survival skills   For instance, how can a boy know if he can run fast enough to outrun the cop, unless he swipes something first? Or else picks a rat out of an ash can, whirls it by the tail, throws it in somebody's first-storey window, and then hops over the garage roof fast before they can catch him? A kid has to know how good he is in handling a dangerous assignment.

The stink and the dust produced in the decay of group psychology   If members of a group suddenly get anxious or panicky or wild or disorganized or elated or mad at each other, you get a lot of behavior that involves violence but that did not start as aggression. Although Joe and Jane may be doing something, they're not doing it as Joe and Jane but as members of a group.

Invasion of societal turmoil from the outside   Last on my list of violence that does not start with aggression but is secondary to it is, of course, an invasion of societal turmoil from the outside. Someone or something in the community ties a package of emotional TNT to the back of a kid and it blows up in the classroom. The kid responsible wasn't originally aggressive; he carries the whole load of community or neighborhood or subgroup aggression. As his teacher, you're just an innocent bystander. What he does has nothing to do with the way you taught him or whether you bawled him out or flunked him.

In short, there is some relationship between violence and aggression, but not a simple one. For teachers it's very important to begin to sense the difference between Joe's being loaded with personal anger at what you just did and the explosion that results when his TNT package goes off at a given time. They are different problems.

Now let me give a few abbreviated hints of what to do about various kinds of child behavior—hints that are not fancy enough to be written up much in books.

First, you sometimes need to get kids off the hook.   The aggressive behavior is beginning but without having really been planned, and if you get pupils off the hook now, they don't have to continue. Another way of putting it is that you sometimes need to cut a contagion chain without making a big deal out of it. And in most cases knowing how to do this is very important in dealing with a normally well-behaved child as well as with a wild one.

Take Joe, for example. He's sitting over there shaking imaginary dice, and at the moment, you're not too bothered. You catch his eye and he stops, but only momentarily. After a while everybody else gets interested. You want to cut that contagion chain now, because if you wait another five minutes, you'll have a mass problem on your hands.

If you interfere too early, everyone thinks you're a fusspot, a dope, or chicken, and you only aggravate things. If you don't interfere at the right time, you'll have trouble. Getting Joe off the hook at the right moment will stop his behavior without a big scene, and the rest of the group will not be too heavily afflicted. This skill of cutting contagion chains without making too much of a mess is, I think, one of the most important for anybody who deals with groups.

A second important technique for the practical handling of aggression in the classroom is signal interference. Signal interference in time saves nine. Very often teachers underestimate the possibility of stopping minor forms of misbehavior quite casually before the kid gets too carried away by it. They don't take the behavior seriously because it isn't bothersome enough, and by that time the situation is tense, the kid is already off his noodle, and anything they do now will have an explosive effect.

The big problem is that most teachers lack a good inventory of preaggression signals for their pupils. In some youngsters, the signals are easy to spot. Others apparently go aggressive all of a sudden from nowhere. That's because the teacher's radar doesn't pick up their signals. But if the teacher works at it, after a while he begins to get the messages from all around the room. One kid, for example, gets glassy-eyed and sits there quietly in a certain rigid position. If the teacher goes over and taps him on the shoulder, he'll go up like a rocket. Two minutes ago, if the teacher had gone around and said, "Come on, let's start working," that would have been fine.

A good many teachers—particularly those who are new to the classroom—do not know enough about the physiological and gestural signals that indicate the work-up to aggressive behavior. Everybody with experience understands them, but conveying this understanding to the other guy is hard. Apparently we don't think it's important because we don't have any fancy lingo for it, but if I were a beginning teacher, that's the kind of information I would like to have.

If you send me a kid with an unknown aggression work-up potential, I'd like to get to know that kid and figure out what he looks like before he goes off the handle. After that, I can tell at a glance that this is the moment to go over to him.

In observing classrooms and watching teachers with disturbed youngsters, I am constantly amazed at the terrific skill people with experience develop, and they can't ever explain it. What's more, they don't even mention it. They think it isn't worth discussing.

Let me describe one incident I observed: A kid is sitting stiffly at his desk, obviously determined that he "ain't gonna do nothing." The teacher walks over to him, pats him on the shoulder, and says, "Now, how about it? You don't feel so good, huh?" And he doesn't say anything. What does she do then? She says: "OK, I'll come back in a while. Maybe by then you'll be feeling better." That's all. She doesn't push him. ("Why don't you . . .? What's the matter with you? What kind of family do you come from, anyway?") She uses her judgment, and sooner or later he's over the hump. His face clears up; his posture is relaxed. Then she comes over and puts the pencil in his hand, and he starts working.

Now, number three: Watch out for the choreography of the dare. In our present society we all have an insatiable, unquenchable thirst for tribal rituals. We still perform tribal dances. Take this scene:

We have what looks like a relatively normal classroom at the moment. Here is Joe back there, who wishes I'd leave him alone. But he knows I'm a nice guy, that I've got to make a living, after all. And I'm pretty harmless, though a little crazy, maybe.

Still, somehow, the noise gets too loud, and I finally say: "Listen, you, you'd better stop that now." Then maybe things get worse, and maybe by this time I'm angry too. So I say: "All right now, if you can't be quiet here, why don't you go out and cool off?"

Let's assume I'm relatively lucky in my diagnosis, and the youngster gets up and moves to the door, but on the way he mumbles something under his breath. If I ask him what he said, he probably feels he has to lie—so I make a liar out of him. Or if he is decently honest, I have to send him to the principal.

The foregoing is one way the scene can be played. But it can also be played differently. If Joe is sensitive of his prestige in the group and I happen to have adults looking over my shoulder, then both of us become involved in a tribal dance. He has to say, "Make me," and I have to say, "All right, I'll make you." So either I try to bounce him or I call the principal or whatnot. Then for three weeks lots of procedures go on—all nonsensical and having nothing to do with the original issue. Joe's become a discipline case, almost.

What I've described here is a personal interaction, a limit-setting process of a very simple nature, really. Most of the time it works like a charm, but in the second instance it became a tribal dance. If I were a principal assigning teachers to study halls or other large groups, I would like to know how vulnerable they are to the tribal-dance routine, because in a dare situation the pressure is terrific. If you send me a kid who is tough, I don't mind. But I would like to know how involved this kid is in a tribal dance.

You see, some kids who are plenty tough don't fall for that kind of nonsense. In fact, some of my best delinquents would never be so stupid as that. If I really challenged them, they would think: "All right, so let the guy have his little victory for a change. So what! So I got out, I'm tough enough. Nobody will think I gave in." If, however, the youngster isn't really tough enough but has to pretend he is, then he has to do the tribal dance in order to impress the others with his plumage or whatever.

This is a big danger. And many a teacher could avoid many a large discipline problem if he were able to recognize the first drumbeats of a tribal dance. Very often we push relatively tough kids who mean well into tribal dances because we are unaware of the position they are in. At other times, we do not interfere when we should because we are too afraid we'll provoke a tribal dance when actually we wouldn't.

So the tribal dance is a whole phenomenon—separate from the usual problem of discipline—that is a rather deep psychological problem.

Number four: Watch out for the subsurface effect.   Whatever I do also has a side effect, and it is not always visible right now. If we are aware of what else happens besides the immediate effect of what we do, we won't simply say, "Because I blamed him for being noisy or because I praised him for being quiet, everything is hunky-dory right now."

So it's important to look with one eye to the possible nonvisible effect. I can do something about it afterward, but only if I'm on the lookout for it. Like that boy we've been talking about. Let's say he leaves the room and doesn't start the tribal dance. In that case, I'll want to make sure we have a brief get-together afterward to tell him that I appreciate his doing what I asked and that I'll defend his reputation with the rest of the kids. I'll say that there are no hard feelings; it was just that I couldn't let him get so loud in class. That's all; nothing more.

If you have to live with aggression, at least try not to breed it. We breed it, of course, by exposing even otherwise normal boys and girls to experiences, to space arrangements, to life situations that invariably produce inner frustration.

For instance, if I bore a youngster, I expose him to frustration. Or, if I have to delay giving help that is needed—say, a boy over there is stuck in the middle of a long-division problem and I can't get to him for a while because I have to be over here with the others—sooner or later he's had it, and he gets mad.

Or I may breed aggression if I intervene with too little sympathy. If a youngster is doing something interesting, something he likes, do I say "Get going this minute. Do you want to be late again?" when I could just as well say "Look, I'm sorry to have to break that up, but you know we've got to get out now"?

One final point: Don't forget that from time to time your own aggression will start showing. As you probably are aware, your hostile feelings and how you deal with them make a story no less complex and touchy than the ones just presented. That your anger may be righteous and justified is not the only issue. You must ask yourself some questions: "How does my anger make me behave in the classroom? Which (if any) of the behaviors it produces in me seem helpful in reducing youngsters' aggressive feelings, and which ones just make matters worse?" Figuring these out requires clear thinking and real objectivity, but it is worth the effort. Your professional obligation is to handle your own aggression in such a way that the individual pupil or the class can manage the spillover effect.

Critical Love from a Burned-Out Teacher
Joan Levinson

Joan Levinson is now working as a free-lance writer, researcher, and editor, following her experiences as cofounder and codirector of Bay High School, an experimental secondary school. She cofounded, with Herb Kohl and others, the New Schools Network to support experimentation in education.

Creative Structure
Marcia H. Perlstein

Helping Your Students Become Self-Directing
Clark Robinson

Clark Robinson has retired from an active career in education, having served as chairman of the Committee on Education at the University of California at Santa Cruz and director of the Graduate Internship Program in Teacher Education at University of California, Berkeley.

The Balance: Student Autonomy and Direction

Joan Levinson, in "Critical Love from a Burned-Out Teacher," tells her story with the artful "slice of life" finesse that makes the reader feel he's been there. Her philosophical statements are carefully intertwined with the illustrations that generated them. "Creative Structure" focuses on the increased freedom that balance ultimately brings.

Clark Robinson ends the section with "Helping Your Students Become Self-Directing." His points about practicing self-direction on increasingly complex levels can be replicated in any classroom.

Most of us who go into alternative teaching situations do so because of extreme frustration at the arbitrariness of public-school learning situations—specifically, the absurdity of fifty-minute periods, of syllabi, of semesters punctuated by periodic quizzes, tests, and final exams. We know that there must be better arrangements for learning, better ways to meet individual students' needs, more satisfying ways for us to relate as adults to younger people. We want to encourage young people to become autonomous rather than automatons.

So what happens when we find ourselves in a "free" school, free to be constructive and imaginative, free to do anything at all?

The teacher's initial mood is one of vague optimism about the possibilities of new approaches. The expectation is that students, long restrained from learning relevant subject matter, will really get into learning when the atmosphere is free and geared to their true interests.

Most of the young people who find their way to free schools are generally in bad shape. They tend to be supersensitive, aware of the absurdities of the public-school regimen, and in their souls they feel that in order to survive they must get out. Most of them are shaky and shy, unsure of themselves. Many move around in a daze—they inhabit a mental world of cotton wool spiked with needles of pain. Many are depressed a good deal of the time. For them there is no excitement in "real learning." They have a tendency to find the nearest couch and snuggle in until their nervous systems stop vibrating.

Teacher reaction to this reality situation is usually quite ambivalent. We are "on their side"; we do understand what they are feeling; we want to make it right for them. We too are supersensitive to pressure, often have deep feelings of unworthiness, are confused about values and about what kinds of activities are worth doing. We are not terribly different from the students.

But we are fairly sure that first we must do the opposite of what the public schools do—we must depressurize, deemphasize traditional subjects, orderliness, competition, and separation based on such labels as "student," "teacher," "bright," or "loser."

Critical Love
from a Burned-Out Teacher

Joan Levinson

A teacher starts out by teaching, usually subjects he knows, or subjects he has taught before in more traditional settings. He wants to make it better, more attractive to students. So he offers his course in physics, promising excitement in the study of electronics or optics or an exploration into astrophysics. At first, students come to class partly because it sounds interesting and partly because going to classes is what you're supposed to do in schools.

Pretty soon interest flags, the entertainment value of the course decreases, and the teacher finds himself with only one or two or sometimes no students at all. He is reluctant to lean on reluctant students and finds their lack of concern for physics a proof that it is, in fact, a meaningless pursuit. He begins to disdain his knowledge because of the repressive way he acquired it. He rejects the military use of physics and the commercialism of corporate use of scientific knowledge. He discovers that, for him, growth and mental health are in the woodshop, learning to use those forbidden instruments, his hands.

He doesn't want the hard work of tugging and pulling on the students. He isn't certain enough of what he stands for to be able to advocate any idea or course of action for anyone else.

In reassessing the role of teacher, many adults decide they don't want to teach at all. The act of teaching is seen as "laying your trip" on the students. And it's true, in a way. Because we "know" what there is to know and they don't, we control the situation. Controlling anyone is BAD. Everyone must be free to do his own trip.

Teachers don't want to teach partly because they need to take care of their own needs—learn how to fix cars or work a lathe or grow their own food.

But what about the students' needs? Most of them, quite clearly, still need from adults a sense of direction; some even want to learn subject matter. But because they are not really sure of the value of learning, given the laissez-faire (sometimes lazy fair) atmosphere of the free school, what usually happens is that the teachers use the school to continue their education in new areas, and the young students are left on their own—most often to do nothing but thicken the cloud of confusion.

Yes, we are sympathetic, but we are not always any more than that, and we do lay a trip on the students by compounding their lack of knowledge about what there is to do in the world. Book learning is limited in its usefulness, but it is one of the sources of growth. Though reading and writing seem anachronistic at times, we are still informed and persuaded, at least in part, by the written word, and we still need, more than ever, training and practice in thinking hard and clear and critically.

Knowledge has been misused or not used. Scientific technology is killing us, while at the same time it is prolonging our life span. Most institutions of learning are dysfunctional as places to learn. Accumulated wisdom has not prepared us for the world we find ourselves trying to change. Future shock is a reality, and there are no college courses dealing with it.

Hundreds of groups of people are saying a vigorous NO to the school establishment. We in alternative schools have said, "We can do it better ourselves."

And, on the whole, we have. Whatever happens or doesn't happen in free schools, there is at least the experience of an involvement in making something ourselves. But what we have made is not good enough. We say we want a new society. But we can't change things by not knowing about them. We can't influence people with ignorance. We can't grow personally powerful by refusing to learn.

We remain ambivalent about the act of teaching. How can we be sure that learning to spell correctly has significant value? Sometimes we feel it has nothing to do with survival; at other times it seems like a practical reality. Should adults interfere with the natural processes of children? What is natural? No one grows up without interference from some source, and it might as well be me as someone with less sensitivity. Maybe. Maybe not.

Still, it's possible that some of the stuff in books and in other people's heads might be useful in several ways. It will help some make it in the immediate future where skills and information help get jobs and places of influence. A knowledge of what has happened to the human race before our time can help put the situation in perspective. Maybe our problems aren't as new as we think. Maybe a little bit of knowledge is not a dangerous but a sustaining thing. Never has there been a more propitious time for creative thinking, for exercising the gray matter to come up with new ways to do things. Thinking hard is not only hard—it's fun too; far too many young people have never, thanks to their schooling, experienced the sheer joy of cerebration, of two nets of brain cells poking at each other, stirring up the circuits, producing maybe a new way of looking at the world. In our zeal for the rediscovery of skin and of the rest of the body and gut feelings and anger, let us not forget that the head is part of the body too.

Many free-school teachers, in their desire to be democratic and equal with young people, are doing them great harm. If the teachers in the public schools do not understand and do not want to understand the students and, therefore, leave them to grow themselves up in a vacuum, and if the free-school adults don't want to "lay trips" and therefore leave students with the same message: "Go and grow up by yourself without help from me," what is the difference for the students?

Society is doing the same thing. Amid the dying forms of a civilization choking on its excesses, it looks hopefully to those just sprouting up into the smoggy air, irrationally expecting young minds to have intuitions about how to go from here. But they don't, even though they are often possessed of a keener sense of the contradictions of the system than those who have been around longer. The young cannot save the old; they have even fewer ideas; if anything, they feel more impotent than their elders. By asking them to show the way now, we place on them a burden so heavy that we may be making it hard for them to grow into a strength that will enable them to lead in the future.

What we need are teachers who are knowledgeable, sensitive, stable, flexible, maturing people who are in better psychic health than their students. Young people need, as much as they ever did, adult guideposts—adults who know and say who they are, not because who they are is the only way to be but because it helps young people to define themselves in relation to such sureness. This does not mean that whoever they are today is necessarily who they are six months from now; if we are not constantly reexamining everything we ever learned and held of value, we are not as sensitive as we need to be to deal with young people. But it does the students no good for us to sit on the floor and cry along with them, "I'm just as confused as you are."

So far, we have not been very creative. We waver between rigidity of traditional schooling and the chaos of free schools. How many years of structureless chaos does it take to discover that, after a certain point, chaos is not growth-inducing? We have not yet found the middle ground, the place where balance and clarity of purpose give a natural structure to things.

Our problem is that we do not yet have a clear purpose. Schooling has traditionally been a preparation for participation in the life and affairs of adult society. But for young people who are rejecting mainstream values, who have no professional or job interest in their lives, no comfortable place to connect with the main society, the way to structure life and prepare for the future is not clear.

There are, at the moment, two choices for people who want to "do" in the cities: one is to try to work within sterile bureaucracies—government, education, medicine, law (where many are dropping out in frustration with the meaninglessness of their work lives). The other is to be involved in the chaotic, confused, always-falling-apart counterculture enterprises. Both are very difficult. There is too much stability in one, not nearly enough in the other. Money abounds and is prodigiously wasted in one and is almost nonexistent in the other. Real talents are always underused in institutions and always expanded in new enterprises.

What can schools prepare young people for? There are things to do in the world that might give us our forward momentum—everything needs to be changed, from the state of the air to the state of our minds. But there is no societal will to do what is needed—no organized channels and no money for the broad-scale changes that everyone agrees we need. The country stands still, looking nostalgically at the situation of twenty years ago. We wait. We are in a limbo time. It may last some time.

I am unable to give up the notion that structure supportive of learning is important and that abandonment of structure is a serious mistake. The impetus toward unfettered freedom came from conditions that were—and are—quite unbearable. The answer to overcontrol is not undercontrol; it is a delicate balance between freedom and structure, which must be constantly developed and nurtured.

Because concepts of control have been abused in many school systems, many young teachers feel that all structure is necessarily abusive, inhibiting, and patronizing. Many schools still maintain a pervasive kind of control that attempts to oversee every aspect of a student's functioning during the school day—his comings and goings, courses of study, use of time, expression of opinions, and so forth. The outcomes of these situations are comfortably predictable because the adult remains on top. Also, if the system is structured tightly enough, the adult experiences a protective isolation and distance from the students and a connectedness with other teachers who share his privileged position.

It is important to distinguish between structure and control. Control is arbitrary and excessive restriction. Structure, paradoxically, develops organically as a means of nurturing the autonomy of individuals within a context of social responsiveness toward others. Though some traditional programs across the nation have begun to break their control patterns and to involve students in decision making in their schools, the large majority have not started to question archaic assumptions about students. Alternative schools have, therefore, reactively brought with them a different set of misconceptions and fallacious assumptions about students and learning. Their excesses of freedom can be explained but can never be justified as responses to abusive control.

Those who adopt the reactive pose decide that countering the traditional forms of control requires turning around one hundred eighty degrees on every aspect of school functioning. Anything labeled oppressive must have its free counterpart in behavior of the opposite kind. If, under a system of control, the teacher was supposed to have all the answers, then under a system of freedom the teacher now has none of the answers. If, under a situation of control, the student is constantly in the position of underdog, then under a system of freedom the student is automatically right.

Creative Structure

Marcia H. Perlstein

A teacher in one of my human-relations classes once remarked, "Adults are more than grown children." In a chaotic understructured situation, this simple fact is not made clear. Proponents of unfettered freedom would say that there is no difference between an adult and a child and that one could learn as much from "jamming" in a friend's house as from spending time in a classroom. This may be true in many situations because adults in a reactively free situation haven't allowed themselves to work out the positive distinctions between adults and kids; they remain stuck in their own identity crises and are apologists for having "grown."

They're also apologists for many other things. They apologize for having learned or thought; they apologize for being proficient at reading, writing, and math; they underrate any experiences without the mark of childlike purity about them. While acting out their own conflicts against authority, they tend not to discriminate between authority and authoritarianism. Acting-out notions are not progress; they are reversal. The system they claim to disdain is still their reference point.

Many kids are confused by these kinds of adults. Inner-city kids often feel that the adults' position is being adopted out of fear rather than genuine preference that teachers are just not tough enough to take them on. Others openly scoff at them and do everything they can to check out the logical limits of the adults' stated philosophy. All this takes energy away from developing intimate and genuine relationships and working on basic skills and developing the important sense of self-worth and competence, which is the stuff of autonomy. Any genuine independence in people must be firmly rooted in security. In a curious way, children in excessively free situations remain as infantilized and unable to take responsibility as those in an excessively controlled one. If the norm is to do nothing and "play it cool," it takes tremendous courage to break that cycle to initiate some learning activity. It may eventually happen, but I'm not sure we have the luxury of time to wait it out. If some of this time and energy could be focused in a manner that respects the dignity and worth of every child, then that must happen.

It is all too easy for us who have skills to make a kind of choice that devalues academic activity; we can always turn back to it. Students ought to have the same option. We need to teach them to read, then give them the option of rejecting that particular skill. Before they've learned, we can never be certain whether the rejection is reflective of a real choice or "sour grapes"—they might need to appear to devalue what doesn't seem accessible to them in the first place. What are the alternatives? The chart on the next page suggests some.

Many public and independent school programs are grappling seriously with the issues of creative structure. Creative structure is based on the principle that adults are different from young people and that these differences can result in important mutual learning. Adults must set large outer parameters for young people and help them make choices within these parameters. It ought not to be a question of whether or not adults *should* intervene by setting limits, but rather what should be the *nature* and *extent* of adult intervention. Too little would be irresponsible; too much could be oppressive. Achievement of the appropriate balance is a conscious process that depends on the students' learning history, the students' social sophistication, the learning goals for the situation, the nature of the student–teacher relationship, and the structure of the school beyond the classroom.

	Abuse of Control (Teacher-dominated)	Abuse of Freedom (Student-dominated)	Creative Structure (Interdependence)
Teacher–Student Relationship	Teacher feared, hated by students, students patronized, not respected	Teacher laughed at by students who see lack of limits as weakness; students defied by teachers	Mutual respect
Rules	Rules handed down from on high by administration and teachers	Rules developed reactively after the fact	Some operating parameters set by adults, open to modification by students in terms of everybody's rights and needs
Relative Number of Rules	Many	None	Few
Curriculum	Finite body of knowledge must be covered—generally "factual" material supportive of status quo; specific content determined by curriculum guides and district fiat	Rhetoric; narrow range of materials reactive against status quo; subjective	Basic skills vehicle for further learning content; largely determined by interest, but represents broad range; specific content determined by teacher in concert with students
Evaluation	Teachers evaluate students on forms developed from above	Evaluation doesn't occur (often confused with judgment and not accepted)	Self-scrutiny encouraged for teachers and students—continuous feedback on both strengths and weaknesses; periodic written evaluation includes comments as well as credits; students evaluate themselves and teachers, teachers evaluate students and themselves
Preparation	All eventualities should be anticipated and prepared for	Nothing should be planned for—let it happen	Some things should be planned for but if something more meaningful starts happening, go with it; predict some outcomes, let others emerge; predict direction not speed or essence

Young people need to be helped to develop a sense of their own potency. [See "In Small Dreams," by Judy Bebelaar.] It is not enough for adults to set up a huge container within which kids have many options. The options must be seriously considered in terms of needs, interests, and aspirations. The real energy in any good learning system comes from options generated by the students.

An example from Opportunity II High School's requirements for graduation illustrates this point. The large container is provided by the San Francisco school district's regulations. Two hundred credits are required for graduation. The school provides the additional container—these credits can be earned through an academic morning program and a "school without walls" afternoon program. These courses fit broad categories in the social sciences, math, science, English, and electives. Students are given many options for earning these credits, and they soon develop many more of their own. They can take equivalency exams, organize their own classes under the guidance of a staff advisor, take independent studies, sign up for the on-location program, or select a number of courses organized by teachers and community resources.

In traditional schools the only route to a diploma is through a variety of very specific courses; at Opportunity II a student graduates when he decides it's time to go. The students make serious decisions regarding the speed and the nature of their own progress, with a little help from their adult friends. Many students are dissatisfied with the accumulation of two hundred credits as the sole goal. So quality is added as an important dimension of the large container; students work toward proficiency in reading, writing, and math. The beauty of the system is that it is almost entirely self-administrative for the students. A common denominator or standard is set for all, and each individual determines for himself how he wants to proceed with his own education.

Through a system of creative structure, students can also develop concepts of causality. If students feel manipulated (as in traditional programs) or ignored (as in excessively free programs), they have no opportunity to see their role in their present situation. They need to be helped to see clearly and easily the relationship between what they do and what happens to them. In many areas a student still has no opportunity to control what happens to him, but he does have control in some areas. We need to help him maximize his use of the control he does have. He must see that in many instances outcomes are determined not by supernatural or malicious forces but by his decisions. He must constantly be allowed to make decisions that show him the consequences are the results of his actions.

At Opportunity II one student spent an entire semester setting up rock concerts for women in prisons. This project was important to her, and she learned a great deal from it. She was encouraged to keep a log if she wanted to receive partial English credit and was told that she could also receive some elective credit in music. It was also pointed out to her that in choosing to concentrate exclusively in this area, she would not be meeting some of her other requirements. She had a valid choice; she could work on her requirements at a later date, or she could continue with the project. The important point was for her to know she was making that choice and that graduation was likely to be postponed. She was carefully helped with her decision; she considered her immediate needs and made her choice. The spontaneity and excitement of her involvement in her prison work was preserved. She took a one-month leave from school to concentrate exclusively on her prison work and then returned to several classes in literature, history, and civics. Her input is welcomed in all her classes. She is reading prison-related literature of protest in her literature and sociology classes and branching out beyond that area in her class on psychology of women. She has ample opportunity to share her experiences with other students and to consider her experiences from the vantage point of several different disciplines. The important thing is that this student has had a lot of space within some limits.

In a discussion of limits with students, the main emphasis ought to be on encouraging them to meet the challenge of responding to their own needs and simultaneously fitting this response into a framework that can be useful for them. Parameters are to help define, not to inhibit. Parameters can help students order their thoughts, clarify goals, and move forward constantly. Most importantly, if the structure is truly effective, it becomes almost invisible and the choices within the structure take precedence. Instead of concentration on what can't be done, the available choices must be so compelling and interesting that most energy and attention are focused on them.

This process ought to mirror the process that occurs in all situations, not just in schools. Never can we completely define our parameters, but we always have choices within them. We must constantly strive to increase our range of options and exercise our right of choice on every possible occasion.

"Freedom is the awareness of alternatives and of the ability to choose. It is contingent upon consciousness and so may be gained or lost, extended or diminished." [Wheelis, 1969] This central paradox of creative structure brings us full circle. A structure that is appropriately defined, justified in terms of the learning situation and goals, and carefully implemented can provide more freedom than is possible with no structure at all. Both superstructure and structurelessness inhibit the process of learning to make choices and therefore the opportunity to move toward freedom. In the overcontrolled situation, choices are eliminated; in the undercontrolled one we are often immobilized by spending too much energy in confusion and too little energy in exercising our options toward freedom. Within a structure students can be encouraged to avail themselves of opportunities that help them experience the progressive increase in potency and self-esteem. And once we, as teachers, disentangle ourselves from our rhetoric on both extremes of structure, we are free to seek our own personal balances and to make our own choices. Our students then can do no less.

A common dream of teachers is to imagine the many things they could do if they were free just to teach. Students have dreams of a freer classroom, too.

Imagine a room in which individual and group interests are pursued. Students work freely alone or in large and small groups. At times they move freely about the room, out of the room, or out of the building.

Imagine the classroom society ably assuming responsibility under your direction for the many nonteaching roles you have to do—taking roll, issuing hall permits, collecting money, making announcements, signing library referrals, responding to knocks at the door and telephone calls, and welcoming visitors.

Imagine being able to respect individual differences by letting students take differing assignments, follow "hot" interests, moving from a lockstep curriculum to one in which need and interest play the leading part.

Imagine being able to work intensely with an individual or a small group, free of concern for what the rest of the class is doing.

Imagine a classroom environment in which cooperation has largely replaced dog-eat-dog competition as a motivating factor.

Imagine a classroom where the reasons for "cheating" drop by the wayside, one by one; where students have come to value learning and reject mere symbols of learning; where students can study and learn together, at times correcting their own and each other's papers; where students don't feel that nothing is worth doing unless the teacher grades it.

Imagine your room as a social laboratory where students are learning to live now; where a student can be educated by the tremendous influence of his peer group under controlled conditions; where you can learn to relate to youth.

Helping Your Students Become Self-Directing

Clark Robinson

Imagine being free to leave your classroom at times; taking a group to the library, to the little theatre, or to another classroom; going to the office or attending a short meeting.

Imagine your room as a learning laboratory and you as its director, with twenty-five or thirty students working with you, exploring all the possibilities.

Some teachers see student conduct in the classroom as a direct cause of their teaching problems. Other teachers see this conduct not as the cause of teaching problems but as the symptom of teaching processes that somehow aren't working with today's youth. Freedom to teach comes only to those teachers who see behind the symptoms to the underlying causes and deal successfully with them.

Youth at every age seeks independence. Young people seek freedom even though they have not learned to exercise it in responsible ways. When their freedom needs are thwarted, there is trouble. As they grow and their personalities develop, they want to make more choices for themselves. If the school environment does not make this possible, they have two outs: (1) give up, cop out, accept a docile role, become a psychological or physical dropout; or (2) rebel, fight back, refuse to conform, attack the status quo, lash out against all authority. Either extreme is educationally disastrous. Young people need help to assume increasing responsibility for their learning as they grow up.

Growing up is extremely complicated. Too little adult control is bad, but so is too much control. Timing is important. Experience may come too early or too late or not at all. Young people can't be regimented on a standard timetable of education experience. Fair treatment does not come from treating young people as though they're all the same. They differ and must be treated differently. An experience may result in desirable learning for one person but harmful, traumatic learning for another. One person may have a limited background of experience, another a rich one. The characteristics of the parents, teacher, or other adult and the cultural setting radically change the learning possibilities inherent in each experience.

Although no single formula can be followed by teachers or parents to help a young person learn self-direction, there are some guiding principles that can be helpful. These principles are as applicable for parents as for teachers, and even for the community in its educative relationship with young people.

What do you believe to be the minimum essentials of a good learning environment for your classroom? What minimum standards of conduct do you believe are necessary to achieve this environment? Think very carefully about your answers, for you are determining a benchmark for conduct in your classroom. You are determined not to let the classroom environment fall below the standard, even though you have to impose some controls. You have called these standards minimum because you believe they can be surpassed as imposition gradually gives way to controlled freedom.

Now you are ready to begin.   Talk with the class about the minimum standards for classroom conduct. Explain why they are necessary. Explain your responsibility to the education and future of the students and to the principal, the school board, and the community. Moving from the old to the new is a gradual process; the solid ground of the old must be maintained until new solid ground is established on which to step forward.

After discussing and explaining the standards to be maintained, or even during this discussion, let the students know that you are not happy with your role of taskmaster and that you know they aren't, either. Talk about your ideas, and encourage the expression of theirs. Level with them about the kind of teacher you would like to be, and get them to level with the group regarding their hopes. Together, begin dreaming about how the class can extend its choice-making opportunities through self-control and how the resulting freedom can open up all kinds of new, enjoyable opportunities. This discussion has to continue over a period of time until all its facets are explored. Isn't that the way your ideas of controlled freedom came to you?

Some rules are needed along the way.   Drop back to reality and begin discussing the rules that will be necessary to maintain the standards of conduct that have been set. The object here is not merely to establish some rules—that's easy. The long-term purpose is to help students develop a new concept that is critical to the process of moving from imposed control to self-control. Students must come to understand that standards are ends, rules, the means. As ends, standards remain relatively constant; as means, rules can be changed at will. A rule can be adopted because it is necessary and then wiped out when it is no longer needed. In a classroom Utopia, possibly no rules would be needed, for each individual in his freedom would respect the freedom of others. This discussion you have with the students will stimulate a review of the whole philosophical basis for the envisioned educational changes. Stress the *order* outcome of controlled freedom at first, for students will comprehend and achieve it easier than the *learning* outcome to which it leads.

Level with your students.   The need to lay all the cards on the table to obliterate any semblance of your manipulating students cannot be stressed too strongly. You are honest in telling them that certain standards of conduct are going to be maintained—by you, if necessary—but that you don't like to do it. You are smart enough to know that your readiness to change is not enough, that the students must be ready too, and that this readiness can come only through a series of learning experiences extending over a period of time. How to provide them is your problem now.

No concept is too difficult if . . .   Many teachers wonder how to involve students, especially very young ones, in discussions of concepts that seem too mature and difficult for their understanding. Some years ago a conference considering the process of education gave an answer that has become a landmark in educational thought. [Bruner, 1960] Loosely paraphrased, the answer is that you can teach anything to anybody at any time and in an honest manner if it is presented at the appropriate level of maturity and understanding. The only limitation then is your ability to translate concepts from complex to simpler forms, from the abstract into the concrete.

Rules come and go as needed.   For the present you are the guardian of the standards of conduct needed for a good learning environment, so continue with the development of rules. This can go on for days. Rules can be added to as needed, done away with when not needed. Both processes provide fine learning experiences for students and for you when all are fully involved.

The signal to begin controlled freedom must come from students.   You provide experiences and try to build readiness, but the students must initiate the changes. One day students come to you with a proposal. "Why can't we?" they begin, as they suggest doing away with a rule that they feel is no longer necessary or as they exercise a freedom that so far they have not been able to exercise in an orderly manner. "A great idea, let's talk it over. It would be great if *we* can make it work," is the nature of your reply. Together, work out plans for a trial run. Don't abdicate your responsibilities as a teacher, but match their enthusiasm and join them in planning, feeling free to make any suggestions that you believe will help guarantee the success of the venture. As nearly as possible, make the only unknown their ability to assume the self-control that the plan entails.

Freedom is won, not granted.   Take little steps first; students must crawl before they can walk. Start with short-term projects that have definite beginnings and endings. Tip the scales toward success, but don't be afraid of failure; both are needed for maximum learning. There should be intrinsic rewards for ventures that succeed and only disappointment, never punishment, for those that fail. Stop any activity at once when the learning situation drops below acceptable standards. Evaluate the experience and help the class to see why it failed or succeeded. This evaluation is essential, since it helps internalize the experience and makes it educative. Be willing to try and try again with plans that are increasingly difficult and long-term.

When a class plans a "venture" activity, they must feel that they are responsible for its success. If you police the activity and discipline the stragglers, you are defeating its purpose, which is to move from teacher-imposed control to student self-control. If the activity degenerates and is operating below acceptable standards, you do not fly to the rescue to salvage it, but you reluctantly stop the activity and take charge. Wasn't that the agreement? Regretfully and openly you revert to the old authority role that you and the class are trying to leave behind. Students should see the contrast in the learning situation when they have permitted order to break down and when you have taken over and restored order. They should want to try again, always secure in the knowledge that you do want to give them every bit of the freedom that they can handle with responsibility.

Increasingly stress the end (learning), not the means (self-direction).   Your viewpoint at this point is that *your* responsibility is to learning, not to the enforcement of rules of conduct. There is little inherent virtue in order as an end, and it may be attained through means that are harmful; there is great virtue in the improved learning environment that an orderly classroom makes possible. So that the class will never be out of control, the teacher must be able to restore the classroom quickly to the standards of conduct established earlier. The primary teacher may ring a bell, a signal that all activity is to stop and the room is to become quiet; teachers of elementary and secondary students may use other means. This capability must be possessed but used sparingly, only as needed, if you are to maintain the confidence and respect of the class. You must not act in anger, frustration, or desperation, but as an agent of the class carrying out responsibilities already agreed upon.

Individual differences always complicate the process.   Students in any class differ in their desire and ability to exercise self-control and to become involved in learning. To move ahead only when consensus is attained would doom to failure the transition from imposed control to self-control. Throughout the long learning process there are countless opportunities to develop the concept that people differ and that differences must be respected. Experience is gained in the use of democratic processes. Be sure these experiences are internalized to strengthen the growth of democratic principles. Continue to stress the role you hope to fill as a teacher and relate this role to the democratic principles that are developed. No plan should be undertaken unless it has the enthusiastic support of the majority and the students have confidence in you. However, no plan can succeed unless it deals fairly with any minority. The learning experience needed by the minority may be a bit different, and different treatment may be necessary. Discuss this need with the class so that eventually they too believe that identical treatment for all may not mean fair treatment for each individual.

Students also differ according to their experiences in self-direction. Learnings not gained at each successive level of growth are missing at later levels. At a certain age students can no longer be controlled by the iron hand of the authoritarian teacher or the autocratic school system. The longer the transition from imposed self-control is delayed, the more difficult or even impossible is its achievement. You must evaluate your progress in terms of distance traveled, not in terms of where you are at any time.

The value of a process is measured by its product.   The values that come from self-direction—its products—are the real gains sought. While directing your attention toward a process, you also experience an increased capacity for learning. And with every gain made in student self-direction, you are freed to function more nearly in your new role as director of a learning laboratory. The environment for learning can then continually improve.

"Begin where they are" applies to teachers as well as to students.   You must do a lot of soul searching as you seek to determine where you are and where you must begin. The person you project in the classroom must be you—what you know, feel, and believe. You must have internalized—made yours—the philosophy that is to be the basis of your teaching. You too must learn from experience. Desired results will not be achieved unless you understand and are committed to the underlying philosophy of controlled freedom. The plan involves a slow, step-by-step learning process for you and the students. While each teacher must proceed in his own way, shortcuts cannot be taken; essential elements cannot be omitted. For the teacher who dreams of having the freedom to teach and the satisfactions of having really taught, a path is open.

The question of how learning occurs best is the major focus of educational psychology. Although we can't always make learning happen as pleasantly and effectively as we'd like it to, and there are no easy answers, we know a good deal about some of the major ingredients necessary for moving in a positive direction.

3 About Learning and How It Happens

Regarding Learning and Its Facilitation
Carl R. Rogers

Eleven Beliefs Basic to Decision Making
Eugene R. Howard

Eugene R. Howard is Superintendent of Urbana School District 116 and an Associate of CFK Ltd., an education-oriented foundation in Englewood, Colorado, for which he prepared *Improving Discipline in the Secondary School,* a catalog of alternatives to repression. He contributed a chapter, "Individualizing Education," to the *1971 Encyclopedia of Education.*

Gaming and Giving: Opposing Modes of Classroom Interaction
Marcia H. Perlstein

Assumptions about Learning

Any educational program, whether an effective one or a dismal failure, is based on some premises about children and how they learn. All too often these premises are unexamined, and the programs continue haphazardly. The relationship between assumptions about learning and the implications for teaching is delicate.

Carl Rogers, in "Regarding Learning and Its Facilitation," speaks from a humanistic vantage point. He specifies carefully the psychological conditions that must be met in order for a student to most happily and productively learn. Eugene Howard's "Eleven Beliefs Basic to Decision Making" follows. He discusses the assumptions about learning and ways for a school to act on these assumptions and give students responsibility for program operation "Gaming and Giving: Opposing Modes of Classroom Interaction" is based on the premise that learning happens best in an open, giving situation where teachers and students are unafraid to reveal appropriately their feelings about each other and the process they are mutually involved in.

How does a person learn? How can important learnings be facilitated? What basic theoretical assumptions are involved? . . .

Learning

Here are a number of the principles [of learning] which can, I believe, be abstracted from current experience and research. . . .

Human beings have a natural potentiality for learning.   They are curious about their world, until and unless this curiosity is blunted by their experience in our educational system. They are ambivalently eager to develop and learn. The reason for the ambivalence is that any significant learning involves a certain amount of pain, either pain connected with the learning itself or distress connected with giving up certain previous learnings. The first type of ambivalence is illustrated by the small child who is learning to walk. He stumbles, he falls, he hurts himself. It is a painful process. Yet, the satisfactions of developing his potential far outweigh the bumps and bruises. The second type of ambivalence is evident when a student who has been absolutely tops in every way in his small-town high school enrolls in a superior college or university where he finds that he is simply one of many bright students. This is a painful learning to assimilate, yet in most instances he does assimilate it and goes forward.

   This potentiality and desire for learning, for discovery, for enlargement of knowledge and experience, can be released under suitable conditions. It is a tendency which can be trusted, and the whole approach to education which we have been describing builds upon and around the student's natural desire to learn.

Significant learning takes place when the subject matter is perceived by the student as having relevance for his own purposes.   A somewhat more formal way of stating this is that a person learns significantly only those things which he perceives as being involved in the maintenance of or the enhancement of his

---

Regarding Learning and Its Facilitation

Carl R. Rogers

Reprinted from *Freedom to Learn* by permission of the author and the publisher, Charles E. Merrill Publishing Company.

own self. Think for a moment of two students taking a course in statistics. One is working on a research project for which he definitely needs the material of the course in order to complete his research and move forward in his professional career. The second student is taking the course because it is required. Its only relationship to his own purposes or the enhancement of himself is simply that it is necessary for him to complete the course in order to stay in the university. There can hardly be any question as to the differences in learning which ensue. The first student acquires a functional learning of the material; the second learns how to "get by."

Another element related to this principle has to do with the speed of learning. When an individual has a goal he wishes to achieve and he sees the material available to him as relevant to achieving that goal, learning takes place with great rapidity. We need only to recall what a brief length of time it takes for an adolescent to learn to drive a car. There is evidence that the time for learning various subjects would be cut to a fraction of the time currently allotted if the material were perceived by the learner as related to his own purposes. Probably one-third to one-fifth of the present time allotment would be sufficient.

Learning which involves a change in self-organization—in the perception of oneself—is threatening and tends to be resisted.   Why has there been so much furor, sometimes even lawsuits, concerning an adolescent boy who comes to school with long hair? Surely the length of his hair makes little objective difference. The reason seems to be that if I, as a teacher or administrator, accept the value which he places on nonconformity, then it threatens the value which I have placed on conforming to social demands. If I permit this contradiction to exist, I may find myself changing, because I will be forced to a reappraisal of some of my values. The same thing applies to the former interest in "beatniks" and the current interest in "hippies." If their rejection of almost all middle-class values is permitted to stand, then an individual's acceptance of middle-class values as a part of himself is deeply threatened, since to most people it seems that to the degree *others* are right, *they* are wrong.

Sometimes these painful and threatening learnings have to do with contradictions within oneself. An example might be the person who believes "every citizen in this country has equal right to any opportunity which exists." He also discovers that he has the conviction, "I am unwilling for a Negro to live in my neighborhood." Any learning which arises from this dilemma is painful and threatening since the two beliefs cannot openly coexist, and any learning which emerges from the contradiction involves a definite change in the structure of self.

Those learnings which are threatening to the self are more easily perceived and assimilated when external threats are at a minimum.   The boy who is retarded in reading already feels threatened and inadequate because of this deficiency. When he is forced to attempt to read aloud in front of the group, when he is ridiculed for his efforts, when his grades are a vivid reflection of his failure, it is no surprise that he may go through several years of school with no perceptible increase in his reading ability. On the other hand, a supportive, understanding environment and a lack of grades, or an encouragement of self-evaluation, remove the external threats and permit him to make progress because he is no longer paralyzed by fear. This is also one of the great advantages of the teaching machine, when properly used. Here the poor reader can begin at his own level of achievement and practically every minute step he makes is marked by reward and a feeling of success.

It is fascinating to me how completely we have tended to disregard the evidence which clearly supports this principle. Nearly forty years ago Herbert Williams, [1930] then a teacher, was put in charge of a classroom in which all of the most serious delinquents in a large school system were brought together. They were the "worst boys" in a city of 300,000. He could not hope to carry on much individualized instruction, and the boys were at all levels of school achievement. As might be expected, they were retarded intellectually (average IQ 82) as well as in their school achievement. He had very little special equipment. Besides the usual desks and blackboards, there was a large table in the room on which he placed picture books, readers, storybooks, and textbooks in various subjects, appropriate to all levels of reading achievement. There were also art materials available. There were but two rules. A boy must keep busy doing something, and no boy was permitted to annoy or disturb others. Each child was told, without criticism, of his results on an achievement test. Encouragement and suggestions were given only after an activity had been self-initiated. Thus, if a boy had worked along artistic lines he might be given assistance in getting into a special art class. If activities in mathematics or mechanics had engaged his interest, arrangements might be made for him to attend courses in these subjects. The group remained together for four months. During this period the measured educational achievement (on the Stanford Achievement Test) of those who had been in the group for the major part of this period increased fifteen months on the average, and this improvement was evident in reading, arithmetic, and other subjects. The increase was more than four times the normal expectation for a group with this degree of retardation, and this in spite of the fact that reading and other educational disabilities abounded. This incredible improvement came about through informal, self-directed, activity. It is my belief that studies such as this have been disregarded primarily because they provide a threat to the teacher. Here is evidence that the most unpromising students learn rapidly when they are simply given opportunities to learn and when no attempt is made to teach them. This must seem to many teachers that they might be deprived of their jobs and hence the information is simply not assimilated.

One reason for the success of this highly unorthodox and inexpensive venture must have been the attitude of Mr. Williams himself. He surmises that his interest in each child's home conditions, neighborhood, health, and in each boy individually may have stimulated the youngsters. He states that he wanted to get acquainted with each boy, and spent his time in this sort of activity rather than in teaching. That he had a strong and sympathetic interest in, and belief in, juvenile delinquents is shown by the fact that he went on to become superintendent of a highly progressive institution for delinquents.

When threat to the self is low, experience can be perceived in differentiated fashion and learning can proceed.   In a sense this is only an extension of, or an explanation of, the preceding principle. The poor reader is a good illustration of what is involved in this principle. When he is called upon to recite in class, the internal panic takes over and the words on the page become less intelligible symbols than they were when he was sitting at his seat before he was called upon. When he is in an environment in which he is assured of personal security and when he becomes convinced that there is no threat to his ego, he is once more free to perceive the symbols on the page in a differentiated fashion, to recognize the differing elements in similar words, to perceive partial meanings and try to put them together—in other words, to move forward in the process of learning. Any sort of learning involves an increasing differentiation of the field of experience and the assimilation of the meanings of these differentiations. Such differentiations, it seems to me, are most effectively made under two sharply differing kinds of conditions. They may occur when the threat to the *organism* is intense, but such threats are quite different than threats to the *self* as perceived. The combat soldier, for example, learns very quickly to distinguish the shriek of a shell going high overhead from the whine of one which is coming in his direction. He learns to discriminate very readily a normal footpath from one whose surface has been disturbed, since the latter may be a land mine. He is, in these instances, responding to threat of a very serious nature, but this is threat to his organism and not a threat to the self he perceives himself to be. In fact the more quickly he can learn these discriminations the more his self is enhanced. In the ordinary educational situation, however, such realistic life-and-death threats are rare, and when these exist, pupils respond well to them. Children learn traffic rules, for example, quite readily and comfortably. But humiliation, ridicule, devaluation, scorn, and contempt—these are threats to the person himself, to the perception he has of himself and as such interfere strongly with learning. On the other hand, as described above, when threat to the self is minimized, the individual makes use of opportunities to learn in order to enhance himself.

Much significant learning is acquired through doing.   Placing the student in direct experiential confrontation with practical problems, social problems, ethical and philosophical problems, personal issues, and research problems, is one of the most effective modes of promoting learning. Illustrations range from the class group which becomes involved in a dramatic production, selecting the play and the cast, designing and making the scenery and costumes, coaching the actors, and selling tickets, to much more sophisticated confrontations. I have always been impressed with the fact that brief intensive courses for individuals on the firing line facing immediate problems—teachers, doctors, farmers, counselors—are especially effective because the individuals are trying to cope with problems which they are currently experiencing.

Learning is facilitated when the student participates responsibly in the learning process. When he chooses his own directions, helps to discover his own learning resources, formulates his own problems, decides his own course of action, lives with the consequences of each of these choices, then significant learning is maximized. There is evidence from industry as well as from the field of education that such participative learning is far more effective than passive learning.

Self-initiated learning which involves the whole person of the learner—feelings as well as intellect—is the most lasting and pervasive. We have discovered this in psychotherapy, where it is the totally involved learning of oneself by oneself which is most effective. This is not learning which takes place "only from the neck up." It is a "gut level" type of learning which is profound and pervasive. It can also occur in the tentative discovery of a new self-generated idea or in the learning of a difficult skill, or in the act of artistic creation—a painting, a poem, a sculpture. It is the whole person who "lets himself go" in these creative learnings. An important element in these situations is that the learner *knows* it is his own learning and thus can hold to it or relinquish it in the face of a more profound learning, without having to turn to some authority for corroboration of his judgment.

Independence, creativity, and self-reliance are all facilitated when self-criticism and self-evaluation are basic, and evaluation by others is of secondary importance. The best research organizations, in industry as well as in the academic world, have learned that creativity blossoms in an atmosphere of freedom. External evaluation is largely fruitless if the goal is creative work. The wise parent has learned this same lesson. If a child is to grow up to be independent and self-reliant he must be given opportunities at an early age not only to make his own judgments and his own mistakes but to evaluate the consequences of these judgments and choices. The parent may provide information and models of behavior, but it is the growing child and adolescent who must evaluate his own behaviors, come to his own conclusions, and decide on the standards which are appropriate for him. The child or adolescent who is dependent both at school and at home upon the evaluations of others is likely to remain permanently dependent and immature or explosively rebellious against all external evaluations and judgments.

The most socially useful learning in the modern world is the learning of the process of learning, a continuing openness to experience and incorporation into oneself of the process of change. A static kind of learning of information may have been quite adequate in previous times. If our present culture survives it will be because we have been able to develop individuals for whom *change* is the central fact of life and who have been able to live comfortably with this central fact. It means that they will not be concerned, as so many are today, that their past learning is inadequate to enable them to cope with current situations. They will instead have the comfortable expectation that it will be continuously necessary to incorporate new and challenging learnings about ever-changing situations. . . .

Only the briefest summary of some of the guidelines [of facilitating learning] . . . will be presented here.

The facilitator has much to do with setting the initial mood or climate of the group or class experience.   If his own basic philosophy is one of trust in the group and in the individuals who compose the group, then this point of view will be communicated in many subtle ways.

The facilitator helps to elicit and clarify the purposes of the individuals in the class as well as the more general purposes of the group.   If he is not fearful of accepting contradictory purposes and conflicting aims, if he is able to permit the individuals a sense of freedom in stating what they would like to do, then he is helping to create a climate for learning. There is no need for him to try to manufacture one unified purpose in the group if such a unified purpose is not there. He can permit a diversity of purposes to exist, contradictory and complementary, in relationship to each other.

He relies upon the desire of each student to implement those purposes which have meaning for him, as the motivational force behind significant learning.   Even if the desire of the student is to be guided and led by someone else, the facilitator can accept such a need and motive and can either serve as a guide when this is desired or can provide some other means, such as a set course of study, for the student whose major desire is to be dependent. And for the majority of students, he can help to utilize the individual's own drives and purposes as the moving force behind his learning.

He endeavors to organize and make easily available the widest possible range of resources for learning.   He endeavors to make available writings, materials, psychological aids, persons, equipment, trips, audiovisual aids—every conceivable resource which his students may wish to use for their own enhancement and for the fulfillment of their own purposes.

He regards himself as a flexible resource to be utilized by the group.   He does not downgrade himself as a resource. He makes himself available as a counselor, lecturer, and advisor, a person with experience in the field. He wishes to be used by individual students, and by the group, in the ways which seem most meaningful to them, insofar as he can be comfortable in operating in the ways they wish.

In responding to expressions in the classroom group, he accepts both the intellectual content and the emotionalized attitudes, endeavoring to give each aspect the approximate degree of emphasis which it has for the individual or the group. Insofar as he can be genuine in doing so, he accepts rationalizations and intellectualizing, as well as deep and real personal feelings.

As the acceptant classroom climate becomes established, the facilitator is able increasingly to become a participant learner, a member of the group, expressing his views as those of one individual only.

He takes the initiative in sharing himself with the group—his feelings as well as his thoughts—in ways which do not demand nor impose but represent simply a personal sharing which students may take or leave. Thus, he is free to express his own feelings in giving feedback to students, in his reaction to them as individuals, and in sharing his own satisfactions or disappointments. In such expressions it is his "owned" attitudes which are shared, not judgments or evaluations of others.

Throughout the classroom experience, he remains alert to the expressions indicative of deep or strong feelings. These may be feelings of conflict, pain, and the like, which exist primarily within the individual. Here he endeavors to understand these from the person's point of view and to communicate his empathic understanding. On the other hand, the feelings may be those of anger, scorn, affection, rivalry, and the like—interpersonal attitudes among members of the group. Again he is as alert to these as to the ideas being expressed and by his acceptance of such tensions or bonds he helps to bring them into the open for constructive understanding and use by the group.

In his functioning as a facilitator of learning, the leader endeavors to recognize and accept his own limitations. He realizes that he can only grant freedom to his students to the extent that he is comfortable in giving such freedom. He can only be understanding to the extent that he actually desires to enter the inner world of his students. He can only share himself to the extent that he is reasonably comfortable in taking that risk. He can only participate as a member of the group when he actually feels that he and his students have an equality as learners. He can only exhibit trust of the student's desire to learn insofar as he feels that trust. There will be many times when his attitudes are not facilitative of learning. He will find himself being suspicious of his students. He will find it impossible to accept attitudes which differ strongly from his own. He will be unable to understand some of the student feelings which are markedly different from his own. He may find himself angry and resentful of student attitudes toward him and angry at student behaviors. He may find himself feeling strongly judgmental and evaluative. When he is experiencing attitudes which are nonfacilitative, he will endeavor to get close to them, to be clearly aware of them, and to state them just as they are within himself. Once he has expressed these angers, these judgments, these mistrusts, these doubts of others and doubts of himself, as something coming from within himself, not as objective facts in outward reality, he will find the air cleared for a significant interchange between himself and his students. Such an interchange can go a long way toward resolving the very attitudes which he has been experiencing, and thus make it possible for him to be more of a facilitator of learning.

Every decision about curriculum and the operation of a school is based upon a number of assumptions regarding young people and how they best learn. Most schools describe these assumptions in their philosophy. Typically, these statements are written in such general terms as to be of little help to individuals and groups engaged in positive change. In other instances school philosophies set forth principles that are contradicted in practice. Assumptions that can be translated into specific actions can provide guidelines for decision making by a faculty dedicated to building a warm, humane school environment that promotes self-directive learning.

In an institution devoted to systematic self-improvement, decisions regarding developmental projects should be based on two questions. The first, which should be asked when a project is in the initial planning stage is: "To what extent is the proposed path of action consistent with the school's published statement of its 'Beliefs Basic to Decision Making'?" The second should be asked as various stages of the project are completed: "To what extent did the proposed path of action result in the predicted outcomes?"

Answers to the first question are suggested in the eleven statements of belief about learning that follow. In each instance the premise as well as the implications for practice are presented. The second question, of course, can be answered only after a course of action has been undertaken.

1. Individual Differences   We believe that learners are different from one another. Each individual has his own learning style, his own set of interests, his own belief and value system, and his own set of goals and objectives. Individuals also differ in their level of maturity, the degree of responsibility they can assume for their own actions, and their level of motivation to exert effort for self-improvement.

Therefore at the school we provide well-defined options for learners. We organize the curriculum so that learners may proceed at varying rates, exercising content and process options as they go. We give learners choices from a variety of ways in which they can be successful and productive. We organize

Eleven Beliefs
Basic to Decision Making

Eugene R. Howard

the time schedule so that control of time is decentralized and planned by the individual interaction of teacher and student. We make available appropriate materials, facilities, and supporting talent to the learner at the time he needs them. The level and the kind of supervision given to staff and to learners are appropriate to the level of maturity of each individual.

2. Self-Directiveness   We believe that within each student the school should foster the maximum development of an inquiring, self-directive, and creative mind. We believe a major purpose of the school is to prepare students to continue to learn systematically when they no longer have a school to assist them. Self-educability is an essential ingredient of good citizenship.

Therefore, we seek and develop curriculum materials that stress teaching students to ask answerable questions, to differentiate between relevant and irrelevant information, to organize information, to support conclusions, and to withhold judgment pending the building of an informational basis to justify the judgment.

We organize each unit in the curriculum in such a way that the student may initiate learning activities to achieve his own objectives. Learning activities are preplanned by the staff so that learners can learn to plan and evaluate their own activities, thereby becoming progressively more independent of the school for their own self-improvement.

We evaluate school improvement projects on the basis of the extent that such projects are likely to foster self-directiveness and creativity as opposed to dependence on authority.

3. The Process-Centered Curriculum   We believe that learners are capable of self-initiated, lifelong self-improvement activities to the extent that they understand themselves, the learning process, and the evaluation process. We believe that the major objective of the school is to teach learners how to learn.

Therefore, the content of the curriculum includes the characteristics of the learner. (He is encouraged to ask, "How can I best achieve the agreed-upon objectives?") The content also includes characteristics of the learning and evaluation processes.

We teachers diagnose, prescribe, and evaluate in such a way that students learn self-diagnosis, self-prescription, and self-evaluation in their learning.

4. The Reality-Linked Curriculum   We believe that the ability to organize, interpret, and apply knowledge to real situations is more important than acquiring knowledge for its own sake.

Therefore, we provide units of instruction and projects that give students opportunities to organize, interpret, and apply knowledge. The staff seeks real situations in the local area and in other parts of the country, as well as in the school. We confront students with real situations, and ask them to draw conclusions and form opinions regarding the situations and to justify their conclusions and opinions by acquiring, organizing, and interpreting information.

5. Student Responsibility for Learning   We believe that the student, not his parents or the school, is responsible for his education. Parents and school should be pledged, however, to support and assist the learner as he utilizes the human and material learning resources available to him.

Therefore, the school does not utilize coercion, punishment, or artificial systems of awards as devices to motivate students to engage in learning activities. Rather, we encourage students to engage in learning activities that make sense to them and that provide them with a positive sense of accomplishment on completion. Positive reinforcement comes from the students' successful performance of tasks rather than from us or from the school.

6. The Interrelatedness of Knowledge   We believe that knowledge is by nature unified rather than fragmented, that subject matter fields are related, and the interrelatedness of knowledge should be demonstrated in the school. The concept-centered and problem-centered approach to knowledge is more realistic than narrow compartmentalized approach.

Therefore, we build interdisciplinary units into every course of study, when appropriate. The staffing plan of the school reflects the school's commitment to this concept.

7. The Positive Learning Environment   We believe that the success of the school depends upon every student's consistent, successful learning experiences. We consider a learning experience successful if it contributes to the intellectual development of the learner so that he seeks further similar learning experiences.

Therefore, we develop a side variety of learning activity packages, unipacs, project suggestion sheets, resource units, contracts, and depth units. We make every effort to suggest or assign to the learner the learning activities that are appropriate to his needs, interests, and ability.

We explore a variety of ways to make the learning environment positive. We initiate projects to improve each student's self-concept and his ability to provide other people with positive feedback when their activities merit it.

8. Utilization of Community Resources   We believe that students can learn in places other than classrooms, in groups that are not classes, and with people who are not teachers.

Therefore, we encourage and support student and staff learning experiences that take place in the most appropriate setting possible and that utilize the most appropriate talent and materials available. We try to locate and utilize a wide variety of personal and material resources both within and outside of the school.

The staff is organized so that a wide variety of talent—certificated and non-certificated, full-time and part-time—is available to help. We continue to explore the differentiated staffing concept and to adopt appropriate aspects of the concept.

9. Student and Staff Involvement in Decision Making   We believe that students and staff members should be involved in making decisions that directly concern them, that constructive dissent is highly valuable.

Therefore, we form student–staff task forces to engage in school improvement activities, and we make provision for the serious consideration of constructive dissent from decision-making groups and individuals. We also provide opportunities for students to learn how to organize dissent and focus it toward positive, constructive ends.

10. Open Communications   We believe that communications within the school should develop communication lines across age, clique, hierarchical, racial, social, and subject-matter barriers.

Therefore, we organize open, continuous discussion sessions ("rolling seminars"), discussion classes, forums, confrontation groups, and similar communications groups. The school's extracurricular activities are open to all students, regardless of academic achievement.

11. Motivation   We believe that coercion, punishment, and threat of punishment are generally ineffective to motivate staff and students to be productive, that people are more positively motivated if given choices of how to be productive than if offered only the choice of doing as they are told or refusing to do as they are told.

Therefore, the school's policies and procedures reflect trust in people rather than stressing distrust and fear. The school minimizes punishment and threat of punishment as devices for governing pupils' behavior. Written rules and regulations, when needed, are democratically developed and periodically reviewed.

Replacing the usual array of repressive and restraining devices is (1) a teacher–counselor system dedicated to fostering successful learning and open communications between school and home, student and staff member, student and student; (2) a reality-linked curriculum; (3) diagnostic and prescriptive teaching; and (4) opportunities for all students to participate constructively in shaping the institution in which they work. We organize the curriculum so that students can decide what they will learn, what materials they will use, and who will assist them.

Now we are ready to put our beliefs into practice and to answer the second question: "To what extent did the proposed path of action result in the predicted outcomes?" Answers to this question may lead us to reformulate some of our beliefs or the ways we propose to carry them out. Systematic self-improvement, like learning, is never-ending.

Students and teachers can feel either energized or enervated as a result of their contact with each other. Classroom interactions can be described as gaming situations when teachers and students see each other as the enemy. In the polar opposite—giving situations—genuine relationships can develop and replace the battleground tension.

While studying Berne's notion of games [1964], my psychology class discovered that games occur in a classroom when people say one thing but show through their actions that they mean something different, when responses become mechanical and general rather than specific and personal. Students and teachers stop trying to understand what they feel at the moment and instead respond to a recalled rather than present action. It is easy to slip into a general response; when many classrooms are similar, a situation repeats itself from one classroom to another and a student plugs in the response he learned from a parallel situation. Teachers tend to emulate unconsciously the styles of their teachers and classrooms. Both we and the students are so accustomed to gaming that we are unaware that gaming is replacing personal, open modes of responding. Stereotyped, role-bound behavior is expected and accepted.

Sometimes a game is so subtle that it is difficult to distinguish it from an honest statement of feeling. A student I once worked with often overreacted with wildly accusatory statements. He had a lot of insight into his own behavior; after an episode he would come to me apologetically to describe what had precipitated his outburst. He was entirely sincere at these times; from all appearances he was not gaming. But because of the repetitive nature of his behavior, because he infantilized himself in relation to me and seemed to feel

Gaming and Giving
Opposing Modes of Classroom Interaction

Marcia H. Perlstein

the need to "confess" (a patterned response), because most of his insights produced no change, he had inadvertently adopted gaming as a mode of interaction.

There are countless games that are not so difficult to identify. My students identified a number of games that they noted in teachers and in themselves. Here are some student descriptions of games played by teachers.

Rebecca was particularly struck by the following:

Ego-Antics

Teachers who are not very sure of themselves play this game. They try to prove to the students they know a lot, and the only way they can feel they know much is when they act like students don't know anything. If students don't feel sharp enough to start with, this kind of teacher can make them feel much worse. But if they do feel OK, it's good once in a while to stop a teacher who is doing ego-antics and ask him to explain himself.

Kim was interested in this one:

Those Darn Kids

Every time something goes wrong, instead of looking at what he's doing, the teacher lays a trip on and tells the kids it's their fault. When he talks to another person about his classroom and something that isn't going well, he always blames it on those darn kids.

Debby spoke of two games she felt had been played on her:

I'll Catch You

This type of game is played like this: The teacher will trip around the class and try to catch students doing anything wrong. She'll pick on every little thing, like papers without dates on them, gum chewing, or even whispering.

If You Want to Graduate

This is held over the students' heads from the time they enter high school. What teachers *don't* say is that no one little thing is going to stop a student from graduating, but they act like each one is. They use it as a way to get kids to do all kinds of things. They never think that maybe kids could do other things to graduate. After a while it makes kids want to say "I don't care if I don't graduate."

Joe noticed the "guilt trip," which he felt teachers often try to impose on kids:

We Teachers Have It So Hard

This game is all about teachers making students feel guilty if they don't catch on right away. They make kids feel that teachers have so many responsibilities and other more important things to do than maybe go over the work with the student.

Dave thought about teachers shoving down his throat material that had no meaning to him:

Eat It, It's Good for You

Teachers keep telling kids how worthwhile all of this is that they're learning and how lucky they are to be getting it. They say that if kids stay in school and study like eager little beavers, then they'll get some kind of fine job some day.

Most of us will recognize ourselves in some of these caricatures. Not everything a student perceives as a game is an intended one. But our intentions are essentially meaningless if they are received differently from what we meant. If we are being tuned out, scoffed at, categorized, labeled, and finally shelved, then even with the best of intentions we need to find another way to come across. We need not abandon all the attitudes we consider important, but we need to find a different way to express them.

My students also recognized that they played many classroom games. They were willing to name them, but, interestingly enough, they were unwilling to describe them in detail. Sample game names included *Nobody Loves Me, Follow the Leader, Laugh Guy, Cutie Pie, I Dare You to Knock the Chip Off My Shoulder, See How Bad I Am, The Teacher Doesn't Like Me, Getting By, I'm Slick,* and *Dig Me.*

> *I did not hear*
> *the words you said*
> *Instead,*
> *I heard the love*
> Mike

Whatever the variety of games in classrooms, consider them next to the opposite behavior, giving. Giving is far more involved than a literal interpretation of the term implies. As an alternative to gaming, giving is sharing oneself, being responsive to another, and making appropriate self-disclosures. What is perceived by students as genuine giving often elicits similar actions from them. The usual petty and divisive concerns then diminish and can be quickly worked through when they do occur. I have heard teachers discuss with a student some unpleasant aspects of the student's behavior, and the young person accepted these statements. The same words were used in other situations but were not accepted. A giving relationship makes painful information more likely to be heard.

My students identify a giving relationship as a central element for stimulating learning. Stephanie wrote a short description of Tina, her idea of a good teacher. She described the variety of ways in which Tina gave:

My idea of a good teacher can be illustrated by a woman who taught me during my last two years of high school. Her name is Tina.

Tina made sure that everyone participated equally in class; she had no favorites. Never do I remember her showing sarcasm towards a student or picking on a particular student. She was fair. If you were not doing well in class and seemed uninterested, Tina would talk to you and discuss with you how you could make class more interesting. She was more than willing to help you out with your work. She never let you slide into being stagnant or unproductive. She really made an effort to help you work to your potential.

School didn't begin at nine and end at three for Tina. She would get to school early and make coffee for students. Before school there would be a group of students in her room talking with each other and with her. After school, Tina was open for counseling and field trips. All of her counselees knew that she would have time to talk with them about a problem after school. If you had a problem and really wanted to talk to her, she would spend time with you and try to help you. She gave her counselees her phone number and told them to call her if they needed help out of school. Tina was very perceptive, too. She could tell if something was bothering you. At these times, she would ask you if you needed to talk to her or if there was anything she could do for you.

When it came to grading time, she would discuss with each student their work and give suggestions for improving their work. She took an interest in all of her students. She cared.

Probably the biggest reason why Tina was such a good teacher was that she never stopped growing. She was always willing to look at new ideas and try new things. She kept growing as a person. Twenty years from now, I feel that her classes will be even more wonderful than they are now.

Students characterize as *giving* all interactions that promote learning—situations where the teacher gives the student acceptance and warmth, gives the student a solid sense of being there. The teacher gives the student feelings of confidence and support and shares but does not impose personal information. With this basic attitude, a feeling of trust develops and the giving becomes reciprocal. Students feel free to express fears or inadequacies, to ask for help, to build upon areas of strength, and to diminish areas of uncertainty. For Mary this happened dramatically:

my ex-teacher
   what are you thinking?
that i have come a long way?
   a very long way indeed, from the loud-mouthed,
hot-tempered, little punk
to a more subtle, not-so-little punk,
   it is to you that i tip my hat,
for you taught me how to see beauty
   in this ugly world.
you were there when i needed assurances
   you gave me a chance to overcome my fears
and to hold confidence in myself
   you did not know, but if it wasn't for you,
i would not be here
   i'd be a whore
or a junkie
or dead—lying in some filthy gutter
you see, you taught me resistance,
to hold pride in myself
and for that i love you

Gayle felt her teacher gave of himself through revealing himself, presenting himself as a person (a concept emphasized by Jourard [1964]). She saw herself as lazy and unmotivated, but all that changed.

> Laziness and eventual motivation have, lately in my life, been related to my teachers. For example, when a teacher presents himself as another human being with certain specialized skills and insights to offer, yet at the same time exposes himself in his equally human weaknesses, needs, and feelings, I feel a certain respect and a certain freedom to learn. With this equal exchange, I usually feel the minimum of pressures and trust that this person—this friend—is a teacher by nature, and he's fulfilling himself by his giving. He has accomplished something if I have learned from his gifts, but if not, it is much more basically my loss than his failure.
>
> It is easily compared to the way one learns from a friend except that it is an acknowledged school situation and a bit more serious learning and concentrating should be done, yet the factor of equal human respect for what this *person* knows and has to give, without condescension, is what creates a conducive learning situation for me. Also the idea that the teacher feels you, too, might have something to offer makes things much more stimulating.
>
> And in cases where motivation is sort of lapsing, I find a bit of help in certain limitations, standards, and expectations. I guess I refer here to a sort of a "push" to get work done—so that it doesn't stifle others or myself in our learning pace.
>
> This school is truly incredible for me, it being a time of thriving on learning for me. I am truly being given a lot and, just as important, beginning to learn how to receive these gifts.

Gayle had participated in both highly structured traditional situations and in an extremely loose free-school situation. She wasn't happy at either place. At her new alternative school she saw as gifts the expectations her teachers had of her, the information they shared with her, and the small "pushes" they occasionally gave her. The trick with limits and pushes is that both have to be done artfully enough that the students can and want to succeed. The pitfall of gaming is particularly dangerous here. If the limits are too oppressive or the challenges too pressuring and competitive, then the motivation will diminish. The most exciting and effective kinds of requests we make of students are those that genuinely respond to both their academic levels and personal needs. The process includes mutual sharing, development of basic skills around meaningful issues, an open, constructively critical view of the world, logical ordering of concepts, and so on. Once teachers and students interact by giving to each other, the specifics fall into place.

But it is all too easy to romanticize the notion of giving without showing the potential difficulties. As teachers, we must try not to give in the sometimes ambivalent and unwittingly destructive ways we may have been given to when we were youngsters. We must prevent ourselves from giving in a patronizing manner; we have to look out for guilt-inflicting or anxiety-producing behavior where the reciprocation message is strong; we have to prevent our messages from carrying an aura of intimidation. We must neither infantilize nor create dependency. We need to avoid feeling that we are making a sacrifice, a feeling that often leads us to feel resentful or taken advantage of.

Pinpointing these problem behaviors in ourselves can be a conscious process and one that demands constant self-scrutiny. [See "The Difficult but Necessary Art of Introspection."]

Our aim ought to be toward mutual giving. The balance is delicate. Although we don't want to push students into reciprocation, we need to be available for and responsive to their attempts to give. We must be open to their sharing their experiences and their skills with us and with other students. As teachers, we can then model receiving behavior so that when we offer to share, the student knows how to be comfortably accepting.

The ideas about gaming and giving can be placed into sharp focus through a close look at the application of the giving process to a sample classroom situation.

Ideally the giving process can operate in five stages: (1) *Holding the moment in dynamic suspension*—stopping, standing still, and seeing what is occurring at a given moment in the classroom. It is being open and responsive to your own needs, the feelings of your students, and the interaction of the two. Something may happen that is unplanned but needs to be attended to immediately. All too often we feel inadequate to handle the unexpected so that we pass over it, pretending that it didn't happen. But if the cues are strong enough, they must be handled immediately. Whatever else is happening needs to stop temporarily, with attention turned to the undercurrents. (2) *Self-disclosing*—sharing your feelings with the students, in the present. Appropriate disclosure is different from placing blame, name-calling, confessing, and having tantrums. After the moment has been held, you can quickly try to get in touch with the feelings elicited (doing so takes quite a bit of practice) and communicate this response to the class. (3) *Eliciting a response from the students*—asking them immediately that they reveal something of their own responses to the situation. This keeps the process open and mutual. The assumption is that everyone is working together to improve classroom relations. (4) *Integrating feelings and cognitions*—assisting the students in understanding their feelings and integrating feelings with cognitions. (5) *Developing alternatives and planning a course of action*—reviewing the held moment in terms of other options, based upon the shared feelings and insights. The new information should help both you and students in making the next selection. The following example illustrates this method.

I was teaching a high-school psychology class; the students were getting very bored. I gave them several choices of activities for the following day, and they selected a lecture on Freud and sexuality. I got very excited, feeling it would be a real challenge to select aspects of Freud's theories that would be especially meaningful to the students and to organize this material at their level. (The average reading level in the class was about fifth grade.) I stayed up late working and returned to class the next morning quite enthusiastic. I began reporting my findings to them and soon found myself speaking more and more loudly (as the din from their part of the room continued rising), ducking spitballs, and feeling generally more and more anxious and uncomfortable. For the first time in many years, they were playing the student game with me. The invisible battle lines seemed to be drawn, and I'd become the enemy. I continued a while longer, pretending nothing was amiss. Then I realized that somehow the moment would have to be held in dynamic suspension and looked at.

holding the moment in dynamic suspension

I was feeling terrible; they were not learning, and pretending that all was well was merely compounding the problem. I stopped everything. The next step was to disclose my feelings to them.

self-disclosing

I almost turned to a game—"laying a guilt trip" on them. I wanted to tell them how late I'd stayed up the night before, how ungrateful they were, and how they weren't ever going to learn anything if they continued having those attitudes. Instead, I told them that I was feeling extremely uptight and a little bit bad; I was wondering why I had suddenly become the enemy. Things suddenly stopped, quieted down, and slowly but surely some of the kids began carefully considering my question.

eliciting responses

They had some major insights into the situation. They said I was talking over their heads and that they were feeling dumb. If I was going to play the teacher game, then they might as well play the student game. It reminded them of regular classrooms, so they returned to old patterns of dealing with the situation. They went on a while longer giving information of this kind and exploring a little more what it felt like to be dumb.

integrating feelings and cognitions

I immediately apologized for talking above their heads, said that even though I didn't like it I could understand how, when I was playing the teacher's game, they might slip into the student game. I had even mildly enjoyed throwing out a few fancy terms. I did remind them that they had asked for the material. I asked if it were presented differently, would they be interested. We then moved to the final phase of the discussion. We listed the alternatives on the board in a brainstorming fashion.

developing alternatives

Every possibility that we thought of went up on that board, whether or not it seemed worth anything. The choices ranged from continuing as we'd been, replete with a new arsenal of spitballs, to having the students research some material and bring it back to the group. There were many options in between. They ended up asking me to try the material again, with the option that they would stop me whenever they didn't understand something and ask me to include some more case studies as examples.

This illustration represents a positive approach to similar situations that I've handled differently—sometimes not so positively. We all fall into the trap of ignoring a game and proceeding with the lesson at all costs. The moment we cross the line from gaming to giving, students tend to follow suit. The time lost in "covering" the material is compensated for when problems are worked out and students return to the task psychologically prepared to cope with it. The mutual sharing develops an increasingly firm basis for whatever additional learning follows.

Most of us seldom reveal ourselves, especially across role lines (student to teacher, and vice versa). When we begin to do so, we often realize that we are revealing ourselves in a carefully controlled manner in order to obtain some planned response. We are trying to put across a particular image of ourselves. Once we stop playing that game, we can begin working, not on predicting outcomes, but on fundamentally changing the quality of the relationship. More often than not, if the tone is set, students respond in kind. With mutual openness established, receptivity to new learnings can be maximized. As my students and I continue sharing in this manner, my view of myself and my vision of my students grow fuller.

> *We do not need to reveal ourselves*
> *to others, but only to those we love.*
> *For then we are no longer revealing ourselves*
> *in order to seem but in order to give.*
>
> *Albert Camus*
> Notebooks: Volume I, 1935–1942.

Introduction to *Foxfire 2*
Eliot Wigginton

Eliot Wigginton has shared his experiences as a creative teacher at Rabun Gap-Nacoochee School through numerous public-speaking engagements and through editing the *Foxfire Book, Foxfire 2,* and *Foxfire 3.*

In Small Dreams
Judy Bebelaar

Judy Bebelaar helped develop the original proposal for Opportunity II High School in San Francisco and then taught there for seven years. Currently she gives courses in creative writing, American Indian history, and cooking. Works by her creative-writing students have been published in several magazines and anthologies.

Techniques for Achieving Potency and Pride

Students learn more when they believe they can. The achievements of Eliot Wigginton and Judy Bebelaar and their students are especially noteworthy because they led their students into activities which, prior to these projects, were activities students believed least that they could do.

In selections from his introduction to *Foxfire 2* (the second collection of articles on the local Appalachian culture produced by his students), Eliot Wigginton talks about beliefs about young people that helped them succeed. His awareness of their strengths and his ability to communicate his awareness to his students were central to their success. Wigginton stresses that even when local psychological and financial support is nonexistent, the ingredients necessary for positive outcomes can be found among any group of students and teachers anywhere.

"In Small Dreams," by Judy Bebelaar, follows. She speaks with feeling, knowledge, and conviction about ways in which she uses her subject matter as a vehicle for helping students make profound changes in self-concept. She helps them produce material that is recognized and genuinely valued by experts. Her students' magazine stands as a symbol of the kind of thing that can be accomplished when pride and potency develop in young people through their relationship with a significant adult.

One evening a couple of years ago, with some cicadas making a deceptively comfortable racket outdoors and the mountains easing from green to blue to purple, I sat down alone at a desk full of papers and photographs and note-books and articles torn out of magazines and loose paper clips and Bic pen tops and empty film cans and general trash like that; and I shoved it all around and got enough flat space to make an introduction to a book some high school kids and I had put together. That was the first *Foxfire Book*.

It was no piece of cake—that introduction. Mostly it was hard because I was trying to tell a lot of people who had never heard of us who we were and what we were doing. That's done now. This evening I sit down alone at the same desk, having just made another flat space and nodded to the mountains, pre-pared to do it all again; and I feel some sense of relief at not having to tell over again the story of *Foxfire*. Tonight I just feel like talking some on paper.

A lot has happened down here since that first introduction. But the cicadas outside are at it again tonight just like they were before. They haven't changed. The world goes on. There's something there to wonder at. . . .

You know and probably care deeply about some high-school kids. . . . You'd understand the day when I was in the office and Suzy was in the outside room and I heard her laughing—as usual—except she was really cracked up this time, and so naturally I had to go out and see what was happening, and she said just be quiet and listen. And Carlton, one of the tenth-grade kids, had been in the darkroom alone for an hour and I had forgotten—and God he was miss-ing his English class—and this string of muffled swear words suddenly drifted through the darkroom door. Yep. Carlton was still in there—oh, hell, that English class—trying to make a double-exposure print for Karen and Betse's burials article. And he was trying to figure out how to do it and burning up all this printing paper and coming closer and closer to getting it just right and talk-ing to himself explaining what was wrong like there were seventy-eight people watching. And Suzy had been listening to the struggle, laughing, when— BAM—out he came with a dripping wet print and a *There how does that grab you*—and it was beautiful, and we used it on the cover of the magazine that had that article in it (and in the book). And Suzy and I were both laughing, and

---

Introduction to Foxfire 2

Eliot Wigginton

then Carlton cracked up too. And we slapped him on the back and he punched us and we laughed some more. And then he went to English.

And when he got to English, he had to write five hundred times, "I will not be late to class any more."

And the teacher read some poems aloud that nobody listened to, so she spent the whole hour reading to herself while the kids hacked off—or slept. Sort of like us in church five minutes into the sermon. You know. . . .

Sometimes, on cicada nights like this, I do a lot of thinking. Mostly it's thinking about stuff that's happened since the first *Foxfire Book* came out—about letters we've gotten, schools we've seen, groups we've visited and talked with. We made some good friends through that book—friends who intuitively understood what we were saying, knew they were saying it too (though in different ways), and got in touch. And sometimes I am overwhelmed by optimism when I watch them at work with those fragile, humane experiments like the Opportunity II school in San Francisco, the Young Film Makers and the *Fourth Street i* and the Teachers' and Writers' Collaborative in New York City and Interlocken's Crossroads America Program. I *know* it's making a difference.

But inevitably the optimism I feel when I dig in with those people and share their adventures—inevitably that is tempered by the sounds of human cicadas that endure and drone on and on endlessly into the night.

"I will not be late to class any more."

And they never understand.

Sometimes I lie awake at night and think about all that. Strange stuff to think about, I know; and I probably wouldn't except that it constantly colors my life and the lives of kids I care about.

What do I say, for example, in answer to the stacks of letters I get from teachers asking questions like, "My pupils are so listless, so uninterested. How can I motivate them?" Or, "I would like to start a project like yours. Would you please tell me exactly how to go about doing so from beginning to end?" How can I answer questions like that, knowing that the only way it can work is for the teacher to push back the desks and sit down on the floor with the kids and really listen to them for the first time, and see what they can all come up with *together* that *might* work in the context of their own particular school and community—and then try to find ways to make it work for as long as it seems worth doing—and then find another. Knowing all the while most teachers won't bother to do that. Knowing they want texts and learning kits and packets that tell them how. Knowing they're missing the greatest adventure of all. And so are their kids.

How do you get to these teachers?

And what do I say to kids who ask me for one good reason why they should stay in school and stay straight when they've just been humiliated in front of their classmates for answering a question wrong or just been punished for doing something that deserved no punishment (or something they didn't do), or just flunked a course by one point—a course they'll now have to repeat. Or a kid who's on the verge of running away?

What do I say to those faces?

And what do I say to a state's education organization that's trying to prevent the teaching of journalism by any teacher not properly credentialed in that area, knowing I never had a course in journalism or folklore in my life? What do I say to them, knowing our magazine has been written about in virtually every publication of any note in this country—but has yet to be mentioned, after seven years of operation, in our own state's education publications (and there are several). I should think that at least half the time of such organizations would be devoted to ferreting out projects of some potential worth, helping them when they need it most (as we did often during those first three years), and putting them in touch with others who can act both as support, as valid critics, and as invaluable resources. We operate in vacuums.

What do I say to them?

I lie awake and think about that stuff. I can't help it. And I am filled with dread at the thought that that mentality will prevail, driving out the next Pat Conroys, Herb Kohls, Jim Herndons, and Jonathan Kozols in the process—along with the fragile, humane experiments. Because I know that if it's a lost struggle everyone loses: the kids, the society that gets them next, and the teachers who scurry back to the safety of their texts and shelve their imaginations and their enthusiasms and their dreams for better times.

Then I remember Myles Horton—constantly engaged in causes bigger than himself—and what he says to people who lie awake at night: "You must not worry about things you have no control over. Make peace with yourself, choose your battle carefully, fight there and there alone to make things right, and leave the rest." And that makes a certain amount of sense. If our battle is to go roaring into a school, try to change it, and get fired in the process, then that's one thing. But I am rapidly reaching the point where I believe my battle is with a tiny group of kids who happen to be working on a magazine called *Foxfire,* and with what happens to them in the process of that involvement. And that is all I can afford to worry about. They are my challenge now. Period. . . .

That is what I find myself doing. For the record, then, and for those who are still reading and curious, and for those who have written and asked, these are the principles I operate by today. They will change in time, but for now, these are my touchstones.

First, I've found that the world of most of my kids is filled with so much negative energy imposed from outside sources that they have no choice but to withdraw into themselves and their circle of friends for sanity, safety, and some sense of belonging. Examples come to mind immediately: the shopkeeper who automatically suspects the kids are going to steal; the waitress who automatically assumes the kids are going to make a mess and be a pain in the neck; the dormitory, home, or classroom where, whenever the kid hears an adult call his name, he recoils, wondering, "What am I going to have to do now?" or "What have I done this time?" Or where a kid is met at the door with that special gaze designed and perfected through years of practice that says, "I'm here, see? Any trouble and you're going to wish there hadn't been, and I'm not kidding." The air is charged with it.

How many times have I seen the effects of a great day evaporate like mist before the door of a classroom or home? A fourteen-year-old gives a talk before a group of 450, is mobbed afterwards by people wanting to ask questions, thank him, or get his autograph on the article he wrote in the last *Foxfire*; and that night, giddy with happiness and accomplishment, he is met at home by a mother who chews him out for forgetting to make his bed that morning. He says, "But, Mom, let me tell you what just happened to me." And she says, "I know already. Don't tell me. You got caught smoking, right?"

And then those adults wonder why there's no communication; wonder why the kids don't want to come home at night. What choice have we given them? . . .

The obvious corollary is that not only do we too rarely share a kid's ideas and joys and triumphs, and not only do we put them in situations where they *can* triumph, but we also do not trust them. They cannot be in such and such a place unsupervised. They cannot be left with this decision. They cannot be expected to carry out that task. And so we retreat behind rules that bind them.

To say kids *cannot* be trusted is the most personally damning statement any adult can make, for it simply reveals either that he can neither create nor endure the kind of atmosphere in which a kid can try and perhaps fail (read *learn*) and yet not be damned; or that he is not an inspiring enough individual to make them want to participate *with* him as responsible partners in a common goal.

I'm not just spouting idealistic jargon. I've seen it work the other way. The Hill School, for example, where kids can work alone on independent study projects in most of the campus buildings far into the night; or another school I know of where the kids even have the responsibility of deciding at the end of the year which teachers get rehired; or our school where an inspired work supervisor has turned over the supervision of the campus work crews to the kids.

Too many of us fall short of that love and patience and self-confidence it takes to work with kids as equal partners. We must do better. There is so little joy in the world of most kids. The recognition of worth and accomplishment is so strained and so stingily parcelled—and our condemnation so freely given that it completely overwhelms the elation of any positive, shared experiences. I find it no mystery at all that kids tune us out.

And if you think I'm exaggerating, you're probably part of the problem.

Second, I believe that in most cases, the most rewarding and significant things that happen to a kid happen outside the classroom: falling in love, climbing a mountain, rapping for hours with an adult who is loved or respected, building a house, seeing a part of the world never seen before, coming to some deep personal empathy with a kid from another background and culture, or genuinely understanding some serious community or national problem.

These are all things that may *later* give him the motivation necessary to *want* to be able to write correctly and forcefully, or *want* to know history, or *want* to understand the complexities of nature and man through biology, botany, psychology, anthropology, or physics. But we too often ignore these events, seeing them as "irrelevant" or "froth." Until they are acknowledged as important and relevant to the student's existence, all he does inside those walls is doomed to seem meaningless and without reason. What we must realize is that the walls of those buildings we imprison kids in now must come crashing down, and the world must be their classroom, the classroom a reflection of their world. The two must work as one.

The purpose of our schools, then, must be to help our kids discover who they are, their loves and hates, and the stance they are going to take in the face of the world. It becomes our responsibility as teachers to put them in situations where this testing can go on; to create for them memorable experiences that they will carry with them like talismen and come back to touch a thousand times during the course of their lives. I'm convinced, for example, that a student learns more about himself and life generally in three days spent with an Aunt Arie (who went no further than the fourth grade) than in four years of high school English.

We've gotten everything mixed up. We saw a man in a factory say, "I can guarantee that if you put piece A and piece B and piece C together according to this blueprint, you will get the following result, and I can guarantee it will happen every time." We saw that, and it seemed good.

And so we took it to our schools. "Put text A and kit B and qualified teacher C before the students of this land, and we can guarantee they will all read at level D at the end of one year." We tried that, and it was not good.

But now we cannot stop. We have substituted understanding *Silas Marner* for understanding the communications (no matter what form they may take) of others. We have substituted the dates of the Spanish Armada's great battles for an understanding of history and how it works and how the past affects the present. We have substituted the use of clay molds of little figures and the copying of pretty pictures for creativity in art. All in the style of technology. "These tools and these ingredients and these instructions will yield these results. Follow them. At the end, you will have a well-educated student, ready to think for himself and take his place in society. This we can predict." And it does not work. And we are reaping the harvest now.

We have ruled out the possibility of anything worthwhile, new, or creative coming out of random behavior, play, or the testing out of a kid's own ideas in any area from art through zoology. And so we have eliminated those activities. And we expect our kids to learn from their mistakes.

We have ruled out the possibility of his being able to make competent decisions regarding his life, his environment, his conduct—even his bedtime—so we make those decisions for him. And we expect him to be able to walk out of our schools self-confident, ready to make competent decisions regarding his life, his environment, his conduct. . . .

We have separated him from his world—have made it irrelevant to our tidy curricula—and yet we count on him to know what to do with that same world and have creative solutions for its problems, when our time with him is done. Amazing.

And third, I'm afraid we've become a nation of nomads with no sense of that security or serenity that comes from being able to say, "Here is where I belong. Here is my place, my time, my home, my birthright, my community. Here I am loved and known, and here I love in turn."

And it happens to my students. Over half of them move away permanently. They are giving this county away. Our tax assessors are all land developers from outside the area. Parents have no family left to sell the farms to, so they sell them off and watch "second home" extravaganzas take their places. . . .

The only way I can see to get our kids committed to our neighborhoods and our communities is to get them so involved in their surroundings that they become determined that the community's destiny will be in *their* hands, not in the hands of commercial rapists. They must feel that they are essential to the future of their homes. The alternative is to watch them leave, creating a vacuum filled, in our county's case, by ten thousand summer lots all priced so high that even if they *wanted* to come back someday they couldn't afford to.

Too often we fail to see any common bonds between ourselves. Maybe if we set about with our kids creating some fertile ground for those bonds, we'll find how close our interests and our instincts and our needs as human beings really are. And maybe we'll find again the rich wisdom in that sense of shared responsibility and love that once existed.

Until that time, we may have to resign ourselves to a world where our kids flee home leaving their parents behind: lonely, embittered, bewildered islands on a whole wide street full of people.

As I said, I'm far from having all the answers for myself or anyone else. But those things I believe. They are the platforms from which I work in Rabun Gap. I am convinced that we, as adults, must constantly cling to, affirm, and celebrate with our kids those things we love: sunsets, laughter, the taste of a good meal, the warmth of a hickory fire shared by real friends, the joy of discovery and accomplishment, empathy with the Aunt Aries and their triumphs and sorrows, the constant surprises of life; and we must hope that, as teachers, in the process of that celebration and that empathy, we will build in our students' souls such a reservoir of warmth and hope and generosity and energy and self-assurance that it would carry them through hell. That is surely what those who do not have that reservoir will face.

Foxfire is one means I have stumbled upon to help with that building. It is not enough by itself. There are hundreds of other ways. But with Myles Horton in mind, it is that way I have chosen, for me, for now. It isn't going to work for all my kids, but I believe it's worked for some; and I'm constantly revising to make it work for more.

And I have to believe that if a man is doing that, then, though cicadas ring forever in his ears, he may not be praised, but he at least will not be damned, for he is doing everything he can in his small part of the globe to help, in his small way, to set things right.

in small dreams
    your hands
        are warm towels
            soothing my face

Jose Flores

Long ago, there was a belief that words had magical powers, that poetry and
incantation could transform the world around us and our lives. I believe it's
true still. What's more important, I've watched my students come to believe in
the mystical power of poems—their own and others. Many of my students,
during my six and a half years of teaching, have written good poems; there
have been many fine lines, striking, beautiful, or deep. But I've often been frustrated trying to convince a student that something he or she had written was
good. My attic and my file cabinet at school are full of folders of work I
thought too good to throw away, while the students thought them too worth-
less to bother taking home. And (a kind of mirror image of the same problem) I
often found it difficult to make a criticism without destroying a lot of the self-
confidence I'd carefully nurtured. Even a preface like "You know, I wouldn't
bother to tell you this if I didn't think enough of your work to try to help you
improve it" didn't seem to help.

My students lack self-respect and confidence in their academic abilities. I
have taught in a continuation school and two experimental schools designed
for students who rejected or were rejected by traditional, large high schools.
Usually the rejection was mutual. But I think most of what I've found true
about students and poetry would apply well anywhere. Even "average" and
"good" students experience some damage to their self-esteem and their views of
themselves as writers in our competitive, label-hungry, and track-conscious
systems.

Students have been exposed a lot to the negative power of words and of
writing, the "bad magic" of words. I'm thinking of the clever labels dreamed up

---

In Small Dreams

Judy Bebelaar

by "educational psychologists" to explain why young people are failing in schools. I have a paper in my take-home folder now in which a bright (and academically talented) student refers to herself and a friend as having "retarded ideas," being "misfits" who sought their only possible refuge in drugs and drinking. This student came to our school after becoming convinced she would "flunk out" of the city's college prep school. The pressure and competition there effectively paralyzed her, and she hated it.

In addition to the kind of damage this kind of word power has done to students, making them feel that someone else has determined forever the exact limit of their talents and potentials, much of the positive magic of words has been destroyed. Poetry especially has been deadened and entombed by unimaginative educators. My own pet example is the teacher who, instead of teaching us Shakespeare's magic, had us memorize footnotes for a daily quiz.

I've invented, discovered, or stumbled across some techniques to help re-awaken in young people a belief in themselves through the magic of words—of poetry. But all the techniques in the world won't help if you aren't genuinely excited by words, poetry, and young people. I've found some ideas through working with Steven Vincent (of Poetry in the Schools through the Poets and Teachers Collaborative). Usually the success of an idea depends upon an individual class and the person working with the class.

Sometimes a student's writing problem is a kind of paralyzing block. That blank piece of paper before him scares away all thoughts, words, or ideas. If this is the case, I suggest a box of words cut out from magazines—*Life* was great for this purpose. I try to choose words that look good (large letters, interesting type) and are vivid and descriptive—*limestone* instead of *green, stripling* instead of *tree, leap* instead of *walk,* and so on. Scissors, paste, construction paper, scrap wood (for mounting words—usually free at lumber companies), or a pile of extra magazines (to find a word someone wants) are all that's needed. Here are some of my favorite examples of the results:

Pyramid wheels make fear a cross: Perspective
Bird readers, moon matters.
Sugar portraits,
    Smothering monuments.
        Rise . . .
            dreams
               die.

                Rebecca Castro

The quiet passing
   of dreams
How do you say it?
   Help.

Geanetta Ross

"Street poetry" helps students who are paralyzed by a blank sheet, too. I initiate a silent walk, providing students with notebooks and paper and asking them to write down interesting words or phrases they overhear or see on walls, signs, sidewalks, or newspapers. I ask them to describe vividly a few details they notice. Sometimes providing an appropriate incentive for whoever makes the longest list, if they don't seem wild about the idea at first, helps. Then I duplicate a long list of everyone's contributions and ask the students to re-arrange, add, and subtract words to make a street poem of their own. My class walked down "skid row" one day and went to the park the next. The contrasting results said a lot about our city.

Another technique involves the sense of listening. I've found that writing to music works much better when I help individual students establish the imaginative landscape. I ask, "Where are you?" or "Is it night or day?" or "Are you alone or with people?" and so on, until their own imaginations take over. Sometimes it helps to be a secretary for a reluctant writer, like Frank, who invariably sits in the corner of the room nearest the door, escapes as soon as someone notices him, and speaks very seldom—although he does smile more often now. As he said the words, I wrote them down.

> Tall trees, leafy and green
> I stand alone, looking at the blue sky
> It's sunny and warm
> But it's a waste of time.
> And it's only my imagination.
>
> I've been in the country once
> When I was about five
> My parents took me on the train
> It was hot
> Big fields, trees
> A lot of people
> I liked it there
> I visited my cousin.

> *Frank White*

Communal poetry works well too. I sneak in a grammar lesson by assigning a part of speech to each person. They invariably ask, "What's an adverb, again?" I ask people to try for unusual words, words that are vivid and particular. One of my favorites is this one:

> Concepcion's Dream
>
> Fickle peacocks manipulate
> Jealous cockatoos
> Their red banners flying,
> Radiating tailfeathers.
> Smiling crookedly,
> Drunken cranes stumbling amid lush green meadows
> In her dream.

It's a good feeling to cooperate on a work.

From Andre Codrescu, a local poet, I learned "lists": a list of places you'd love or hate to be, a list of things you'd like to buy—real or imaginary, or this list of what poetry is:

a poem is
    a bee
            or a frog
                or a pot of honey
                                a wish
                        steaks
                    ice cream
            that melts in your mind
                    not in your hand
        barbequed chicken

                            space
                                or a grain of sand
twilight
        the air we breathe
    a soul-drenched dead child

                pomegranates, mangoes, and avocados
lunacy
        and clarity

            it's the north, the south, the east, and the west
    a spotted turquoise ladybug

            a fire
            a festering wound
            a blister
            a scream, a wail

flashlights, nightsticks, guns, badges
                a kick
                a jab

illumination, the light, ecstasy

            a sensual assault
            peeling off the layers of the mind

            a blood-filled flea
                a mushroom
                    syphilis of the soul

                        it is a separate reality

Writing in response to student-made picture collages also produces good results. Lawrence McGaugh, a Berkeley poet, used this technique in the classroom.

                wizard of oz
rocket ships to the moon
westclock, lady scott
locked behind windows, reaching out
            summer fat man
wilted daisies, oranges, listening
            nixon promises, peace, Indians
the blue meanies, green and yellow
            stripes, football uglies
screaming yellow ladies flying
            through downtown at night

                anne murphy

Partly, this works well because the combination of images and the phrases call to mind a response from a deep part of the self and tap the subconscious, the well of poetry.

Writing about dreams does the same kind of thing:

Ayuda

You wake up in the morning
            diciendo "ayuda!"
me quieren matar
            they want to kill me
and then I can hear
            someone's footsteps
es mi madre diciendome

"que es lo que te pasa?"
            she walks in my room
ai silencio
            por un minuto
then I answer
            "fue un sueno
                mui pesado
                    only a nightmare"
but I am awake now

                Piedad Morales

A technique I call "association boxes" also taps the subconscious. To introduce the idea, I explain the idea of free association and talk about the relatedness of poetry. I draw a box in the middle of a blackboard and ask students for words with a lot of depth and meaning. I choose one word I think will work well and draw three or four boxes connected to it. Then I ask for associations and draw more boxes connected to these words.

Here's one student's poem in reaction to *hate*:

> red horse hate
> funky evil raggedy ghetto project rats
> crazy evil sadistic lies
> hate unfaithful people cruel
> lies!
> funky unnatural bats and dogs
> son of a bitch!

I also use lots of examples of good poetry. Contrary to popular belief, students enjoy figuring out poems that at first appear alien and indecipherable. My students' favorite is a sixteenth-century poem, "To His Coy Mistress." (A discussion of the poem invariably ends in speculation as to whether or not Andrew Marvel would have made a good pimp and whether—even though it's a fine poem artistically speaking—its male chauvinist tenor doesn't destroy its effectiveness.) I think number two among the favorites is Ezra Pound's translation of "The River Merchant's Wife," which also leads to discussion about love and family-arranged marriages and medieval Japan.

Students almost always know what a poet is talking about. The idea and feelings are not alien, only the words on paper are. I think too many teachers dismiss a lot of good poetry because it seems too sophisticated or difficult for students who can't read or who have difficulty expressing themselves without lots of spelling and grammar errors. Usually my high-school students are immensely and justifiably pleased when they've figured out and learned to appreciate a poem that I've told them most people don't get introduced to until they're in college. We share the belief that good poetry, knowledge of the deepest kind, should not be the sacred possession of the fortunate few who go to college.

It seems that many poets feel that way now too—poetry has too long been coffined and confined. Lately teachers, students, and poets, through the Poetry in the Schools Program, have been working successfully to restore the magic. This program was brought to life by Steve Vincent, a young poet. I have watched my students encountering poets (mostly young also), absolutely absorbed in the magic of hearing a poet read from his own work and respond to theirs. I have always published my students' work—the best of it—as attractively as I can with school supplies and my minimal typing ability. But always only a few really valued the publication—some other teachers, a discouragingly small number of students, and my friends. After a few visits by poets, however, I noticed people hoarding the publication and taking extra sheets of the pages with their own poems. And now they like to read aloud what they've written. This seems to show that they realize they've produced something excellent, recognized not only by the teacher, who would like it anyway, but by poets, whom they see as people producing fine work. An authority on their side really matters—there have been so many against.

Many of my students state, often and emphatically, that money is one of their primary goals in life, and they know, from questions they've asked the poets, that even if you have a few books and honors to your name, earning a living as a poet is difficult if not impossible. Still, they sincerely respect and admire the poets who visit us. When the school district threatened to cut off funds for the program, students responded with many letters about the value of the program—forceful, indignant, and impassioned letters. (These convinced the district.) Even though the students' stated goals are sometimes materialistic, they really identify with the artistic and humane goals of the poets. Poets aren't alien, bookish creatures. Most of the visiting poets have been young; all have been black, brown, Asian, long-haired, or women.

Due to their reinforcing contact with young poets and positive results with these techniques, poetry has become a comfortable communication tool. Mary's definition of poetry pleases me immensely and says a lot of what I've tried to say:

> poetry is the essence of life
>   digging, searching deep within the soul
>
> the conscious, subconscious
>   writing from the heart
>   meditating, complicating
>   searching for the word
>
> the word to create your image
>   which briefly passes through your head
>
> the ecstasy of
>   finding what you mean
>   to feel what you feel
>   to read what you wrote
>
> *Mary Dacumos*

Poetry has been used as a psychotherapeutic tool. It can help people grow. It can help them escape the confines of mediocrity or hopeless inability our systems have unfairly imposed upon many because of narrow definitions of what is subnormal, normal, bright, or gifted. It can give them an outlet for the part of themselves that hides behind what is often a cynical, practical exterior. They see very well the way the world goes, and they'd like to push it another direction.

Parents often ask why all the poetry in our publications has to be so sad or bitter. It's because the kids care a great deal about what's happening. I think they feel something very akin to what Ishmael Reed expresses in his introduction to *19 Necro-Mancers From Now:* "Manipulation of the word has always been related in the mind to manipulation of nature. One utters a few words and stones roll aside, the dead are raised, and the river beds emptied of their contents. . . . The Afro-American artist . . . is a conjuror who works JuJu upon his oppressors; a witch doctor who frees his fellow victims from the psychic attack launched by demons of the outer and inner world." [1970]

I think my students feel that they too are "detectives of the metaphysical, about to make an arrest." [Reed, 1970] So they attack what they find unjust or offensive or evil. And I think they're beginning to believe that what they express is not just a comforting relief but that it may really affect the world. That may not sound earth-shaking to many people, but considering that many of these students have had little faith in the written word—that words have done a great deal to confuse, humiliate, bore, or deaden them—it *is* earth-shaking. Some of the poetry samples that follow are fragments; some are poems. They express bitter, angry, and sad feelings. I think all of them represent powerful magic, good "JuJu."

hey, black people
are we really proud?
of the four and five letter words
written on our walls?
of the scars
on our faces
left by razors
held in black hands

same black hands
from the same black ghetto
with the same rats that
bite the same
black babies
while your lanlord
calls the roseman
to bring mo roaches

and what
about black junkie pushers
programming black minds
with white psychedelic drugs

and i caught you
smiling again

and hey black people
are we proud of the
many black youth
victims of involuntary niggerslaughter
being buried
while we stand tall?
fists held high
and mechanically
echo hollow
black powers

wake up
black people

bullets have already
been sent to malcolm
and martin
all our heroes
are dead
or dying

the bus ain't coming
        and we know
the train to glory ain't coming to
carry us
home

       Michael Montgomery

Prismed by trampled drops
    Elasticized by dreams far too large for anyone
      Shrunk with sorrow
        Accelerated by fear
        Halted by love

       Larry Stoiser

life is but one heavyset dream
    failing and rejecting death
life a paper doll,
      burning in a paper bag

      Maya Mosely

Fear has a way of exposing itself
One cannot leash that which has no solidity
Madness oozes from every pore
Its smothering power takes over
We creep in the bathroom and flush the toilet

      Rebecca Castro

and the burning temperature of pain rises faster
and faster, locking your bones
with locks of torture
ringing out your black soul
tighter and tighter
until it spits out
the cry of
emptiness
    and
      nothing

     Ken Buchanan

But some poems state the magic of the beautiful. They express love. And as imprisoned as they are in the city, most of my students seem to identify the positive with nature and wildness.

young apple trees standing
like bumble bees
sweet apple trees
fruit, flower, bigger seeds
shouting excited spraying leaves
big, little, tall and soft
you'll call

Ursula Smith

Although there has been a proliferation of new programs during the last decade, very few offer the productive learning opportunities that are necessary for today's youth. Too many projects are organized by people who offer innovation for the sake of innovation alone. Many initiators articulate high ideals but don't carry them through in practice; others isolate themselves to the extent that survival becomes nearly impossible. Many fight valiantly against insurmountable odds. Few genuinely integrate theory and practice, examine themselves openly, and continually struggle to improve. The articles in this final section discuss some efforts worth viewing. Most of the programs arising from these efforts have been developed within traditional public schools with no additional budgetary expenditures. The secret involves extensive reordering of priorities and application of sound educational-psychology principles in regard to young people and how they learn.

4 New Options

Youth into Adult
Mildred G. McClosky

Mildred McClosky is Education Director for Catalyst. She was formerly Curriculum Coordinator for the innovative Graduate Internship Program in Teacher Education at the University of California, Berkeley. She authored *Teaching Strategies and Classroom Realities* as well as *Youth into Adult.*

Participatory Youth Programs
Mary Conway Kohler

Currently Executive Director of the National Commission on Resources for Youth, Mary Kohler previously served as Referee of the Juvenile Court in San Francisco and Special Consultant to the commission that created the Family Court of New York State.

Antioch College-West
Pattilou Schultz and Lance Dublin

Pattilou Schultz, Resource Coordinator for Athenian Urban Center, has been a consultant for the Far West Laboratory for Research and Development in Career Education.
 Lance Dublin, Assistant Dean of Antioch College-West, is also consultant to a number of postsecondary institutions, including Texas A and M, Lone Mountain College, and the University of the Pacific.

Skeleton of a Growing Child
Cynthia Embree

Cynthia Embree is now working as Assistant Coordinator of Student Volunteer Programs at Drake University, Des Moines, Iowa.

Experiential Learning

The idea of extending the boundaries of the classroom beyond the traditional walls has gained special credence in the last ten years. From elementary schools through colleges, students are venturing forth into field experiences of particular interest and concern to them. The effective programs include seminars to enable students to understand and organize their experience.

Mildred McClosky, in "Youth into Adult," sets forth a multidimensional model of worthwhile programs for youth with both a philosophical rationale and criteria for observing experiential learning. Her model sets the stage for Mary Kohler's article, "Participatory Youth Programs," which gives concrete examples of exemplary programs that provide the challenges, satisfaction, and learning alluded to in the McClosky model. In addition, Kohler carefully describes the characteristics of the teacher or other helping adult who sets these programs in motion. Pattilou Schultz and Lance Dublin follow with "Antioch College-West," a description of a total college program that utilizes the principles of experiential learning. The first part of this section closes with Cynthia Embree's "Skeleton of a Growing Child." As a participant in a school-without-walls program, she served as a teacher's aide while obtaining college credit. She communicates some of the combined frustration and exhilaration that a program of this kind offers. Her experience illuminates the theory and vivid description in the preceding articles.

It is important to ask, along with specific questions about how schools function, more general questions about the development from childhood through youth to adulthood. Only by continuing to ask these more general questions can we avoid waking up someday to find that educational institutions are finely tuned and efficiently designed to cope with the problems of an earlier day. Among the more general questions, we need to ask how it is that the young become adults.   [Coleman, 1972]

One of the greatest agonies for youth today is the postponing of maturity, the dangerous, wasteful prolongation of adolescence. As young people reach biological fullness, characteristically they desire to explore new paths, try out adult roles. As they stretch toward adulthood, they must learn both to exercise and control their awakening powers. For this they require the opportunity to engage in significant social activities, and the recognition from older people that they are indeed progressing toward the adult status for which they yearn. In our present society we have failed to provide such needed transitions from childhood to adulthood.

In most primitive cultures there are "rites-de-passage" celebrating adolescence as a period that begins with puberty and leads to adult obligations and privileges. Biological maturation is honored. Marriages are often prearranged; social and occupational roles are assigned. Thus adult status is quickly reached through routes that are clearly prescribed.

In freer and more complex societies like ours, where choices exist in religion, mating, education, and occupations, adolescence has become a tortuous stage of delayed development. Wrestling with numerous decisions, each young individual must now create his or her own identity. A plethora of difficult choices, however, is not the most serious problem facing adolescents today. Vast and rapid social changes have occurred that have created a host of new obstacles for youth en route to adulthood. Even a brief examination of these forces demonstrates how arduous the journey has become.

Youth into Adult

Mildred G. McClosky

Abridged from materials prepared for the National Commission on Resources for Youth (1971–1972). Copyright © 1974 by Mildred G. McClosky.

Until fairly recently, adolescence was of limited duration. Unless youth went to college upon graduation from high school or earlier, young people were expected to support themselves. Once they obtained jobs, their adolescence was virtually ended. Now partly because of the greater affluence of parents, adolescence no longer has a definite cutoff period. Since postgraduate education has become essential in many fields, for many college youth a state of dependency continues even into their thirties.

For the majority of youth, ordinary jobs are becoming difficult to obtain. With increased automation and the need for advanced skills, employment possibilities have declined for the average teen-ager. As a consequence of longer periods of required schooling and fewer opportunities for unskilled jobs, more and more of our young people are now indefinitely stuck in an adolescent limbo—despite their biological maturity and their psychological need for involvement in the adult world.

With the demise of the extended large families of the past, youth have become virtually locked into their own age group. Having little access to the working world of adults, adolescents have become heavily reliant on their peers. With their parents off at work, removed from their children, adolescents can no longer mix with them as freely as youth did in the past—for example, when they helped in the small family store or worked on the farm. With few adults around to model themselves after and without many younger relatives to care for, adolescents have become a subspecies of their own, with teen-age language, customs, and values. Although age segregation may have some desirable effects, most of the results are troublesome. On the positive side, today's adolescents have developed marked capabilities for sympathy and leadership within their own groups. Unfortunately, however, this interest in their peers is often accompanied with a suspicion of authority from outside the group and an inability to relate easily to older or younger people.

There is little that today's youth can depend on with certainty. Knowledge becomes outdated quickly. Fads and fashions wither fast. World politics shift and twist. Every day brings something startlingly new to absorb. The span of each generation has become shorter. Five years, sometimes even two, make a significant difference in outlook, style of dress, "hip" language, and goals. Many adolescents can no longer fully understand their older brothers and sisters, while the gap separating them from their parents increasingly widens. Planning for adulthood becomes harder, for how can one plan anything for sure?

This is a generation in which the average teen-ager has spent approximately 18,000 hours sitting passively in front of the television set. Add the hours watching movies, listening to radios, reading newspapers and magazines, and they far exceed the amount of time most young people give to formal schooling. Although we cannot yet fully gauge the effect of television and other forms of mass media on the sensibilities and values of the young, we do know that

Prolonged Adolescence

Pervasive Peer-Group Culture

Rapid Change

Mass Media

there must be considerable impact. Youth have been exposed to racial issues, to poverty, to all forms of violence and injustice. As the mass media have helped to make this nation smaller, countries abroad familiar, and even the moon accessible, youth have inevitably become sensitive to the vast national and international problems begging for solution. Some become increasingly restive with their lack of effective participation in the world around them.

Growing Numbers of Youth in Crisis

Each year more youngsters leave home. Many troubled youth remain at home, but for them it has come to mean daily arguments about conflicting values, a battlefield where they cannot communicate their personal problems. Some are in crises of one kind or another—a bad trip, an unexpected pregnancy, an onslaught of suicidal depression, serious problems at school, or profound loneliness. Alarming numbers of youth are attracted to drugs or to strange religious cults either as a way out of life's complexities or as a desperate means for excitement, challenge, and camaraderie.

Youth's Increased Social Commitment

In the past decade large numbers of adolescents have expressed feelings of explosive impatience. Both overstimulated and underused, many of them were no longer willing to sit back and wait for adults to cure the ills of society. Some insisted on social action immediately. They wanted to join with adults, or lead them, in community action for better housing and health conditions, more effective schooling, job training, civil rights. Both privileged and underprivileged youth became dramatic about their dissatisfactions. Witness the "long hot summers," the number of student riots, the violent protests, and general malaise of the late sixties. In the past couple of years, the wilder outbursts of youth have abated. While many young people are seeking private solutions, others are still throwing themselves eagerly into volunteer activities of social import. Many more would become involved if they had the opportunity.

In a nationwide survey of 2000 high-schoolers in 1970, *91 percent* of the students said that they would be willing to delay their own personal interests for a year to work on such problems as pollution, poverty, race, and education. [*Today's Education,* 1970]

New Laws on Voting

During the Vietnam War, when many eighteen- to twenty-one-year-old males were drafted for military duty, an appalling irony became apparent. If these young men could be called upon to die for their country in an unpopular war, should they not have the right to vote for or against such decisions? Partly in response to this overwhelming question and partly in response to the growing impatience of the young with their prolonged adolescence, the right to vote at eighteen was granted to American youth. Thus we have finally ritualized adolescent entrance into society by officially declaring eighteen a time of civic adulthood.

Maturity, however, cannot be legislated. To transform youth into adults, a multitude of experiences are needed. Youth must participate in the adult world and find adults to emulate. Young people have to see what happens or fails to happen when adults work together on significant tasks. They need to learn first-hand the various options that await them. Trying out different roles for themselves, they can then learn what more there is for them to learn, and they can begin to make informed choices about the kinds of adults they might wish to become.

Fortunately in the past decade we have had some vivid examples of what responsible youth can do. A number of new services and informal institutions have mushroomed across the country—hot lines, free health clinics, halfway houses for parolees or the mentally ill, "rap centers," drug-prevention and rehabilitation centers, community action programs, creative civic-arts projects, experimental school programs, and youth tutorials of all kinds. Many of these programs were initiated and designed by the young people themselves. In others, youth and adults worked together in effective collaboration.

In 1967 the National Commission on Resources for Youth was established by Mary Conway Kohler to discover, develop, and disseminate ideas for worthwhile programs involving youth in significant activities. The Commission was particularly concerned with demonstrating the power of youth to help themselves and others—if the adult world would only encourage their participation. Through the National Commission, in the past six years several hundred programs have been uncovered and others developed.

Working as a consultant for the Commission, I had the opportunity to investigate firsthand many of the participatory youth projects throughout the nation. I discovered that despite their vast diversity, the most compelling projects had several characteristics in common. Although the model is far from crystallized, I believe it would contain the key features of the successful participatory youth projects I had the privilege to observe.

They [model programs] would involve youth in significant tasks that both young people and adults recognize as important. More than do-good or make-work activities designed to keep teen-agers busy or to make them feel virtuous, they should be addressed to some crucial problem—such as community health, pollution, drug addiction, unique concerns of minority groups, crisis intervention, communication across age groups, or special services needed for older citizens. [See "Participatory Youth Programs," by Mary Kohler.]

They would provide challenge, offering youth a chance to do something difficult. The tasks would require a full expenditure of both mind and spirit. They would offer participants the opportunity to perform at higher levels than they had previously believed possible. (Like all of us, youth probably operate only on one one-hundredth of their actual potential.)

They would offer active learning in an age of increasing spectatorship. Learning through experience, through direct observation and involvement, is not only a natural way to learn, but it is especially suited to the restless energies of youth.

Characteristics of Model Programs

They would relate theory to practice, demanding more learning to guide further practice. Youth participating in such projects would be stimulated to learn intensively about the issues involved, to reflect seriously on their experiences, to test ongoing theories and assumptions, and to consider what more they need to learn in order to solve the problems involved.

They would give adolescents some genuine knowledge of the many occupational options in the adult world. Through their own eyes youth could find out about the world of work, professional careers, and social services. They could test out their own interests and potentials and thus become better able to make informed choices about their future careers and possibilities.

They would provide a community experience. They would offer to youth a sense of community—the feeling of belonging to an extended family—and the exhilaration that results from being associated with others in significant activities. With the reduction in size of the nuclear family and the decline of the extended family, youth need both a center for their changing selves and the warmth and protection of friends.

They would demonstrate new types of youth–adult alliances. They would strive for an effective balance, a delicate partnership between young people and adults in which each age group would offer what it uniquely could.

They would promote genuine maturity. Most important, within each program, the youth would be encouraged to exercise adult responsibilities and to discover their capacities for adult roles. The adolescents involved in these model programs would participate actively in decision making, governance, and leadership activities.

These characteristics might constitute some of the essential features for the eventual model of programs that could, indeed, change immature youth into responsible adults. The widespread practice of such programs might then transform future periods of adolescence into genuine transitions to mature adulthood.

In Atlanta, Georgia, high-school students rescue the remains of a 7000-year-old Indian culture from bulldozers. In Coos Bay, Oregon, they locate ruptures in the city sewage mains and prevent pollution of their waterfront. Between Oregon and Georgia hundreds of teen-agers and their communities are harvesting the rewards of an important educational idea. The brand name varies. Some educators call it participatory education; others term it experiential or action learning. Whatever the label, the principle is the same: young people learn by doing, particularly when the doing demands decision making. The teen-agers in Atlanta and Coos Bay are living evidence of that premise in action.

At its best, experiential learning complements traditional teaching methods instead of competing with them. It assumes that different students are susceptible to different learning techniques and that the best education matches its methods to individual needs. Additionally, important academic skills are best developed when these skills are seen as vehicles for the solution of problems of genuine concern. Thus, students who begin to care for their younger charges want to learn to read better so that they can pass this skill on; others working in day-care centers feel the need to understand some basic theories of child development so that they can examine questions they have raised about their young charges; those who have learned a good deal about their own local culture may want to improve their writing skills in order to communicate to others outside their locale. Countless examples abound where young people feel the need to know everything, ranging from historical methodology to anthropological and archaeological concepts to linguistics, sociology, and psychology. They learn a good deal through their experiences; a strong problem-centered seminar can help them organize these findings cognitively and gain competence in a variety of disciplines. And, most importantly, experiential learning responds to several

Participatory Youth Programs

Mary Conway Kohler

Based on address given to the National Association of Secondary School Principals in Dallas, Texas, May 1973. Developed into an article with the assistance of Lynn Jabs.

basic adolescent needs that are neglected in many American classrooms. [See the preceding article, "Youth into Adult," by Mildred G. McClosky.] A good experiential learning program deeply involves young people in all phases of its operation. Some of their basic needs are met through meaningful input regarding major decisions.

Three premises about decision making are basic to the operation of a good experiential learning program:

1. Teen-agers are capable of making good decisions.
2. Decisions are never right or wrong, only better or worse.
3. People draw self-respect from their successful decisions; they draw insight from decisions that don't work.

Ordinary school programs sometimes expose students indirectly to the processes and responsibilities of decision making, but such an important skill requires more conscious cultivation. In most classrooms, responsibility does not extend beyond mere obedience. In too many schools, students are considered responsible only when they complete assignments promptly. They make a decision about whether or not to complete the assignment, but seldom do they have any say in how best to achieve results.

Too often education consists of cataloging the accomplishments of other people without ever convincing the young person that he too is capable. The decision making that underlies experiential learning reinforces the adolescent's dubious sense of identity. The fact that "I have decided" generates confidence in "me as an important person."

The sense of self-worth is further enhanced by a feeling of social worth. When people are valued by others, they tend to value themselves more. [Coopersmith, 1967] Young people can know they have made effective decisions when they see their projects operating well; it is also important, however, that their efforts are taken seriously and recognized by the community. Currently, youth are much in demand as consumers, but they are rarely accepted as contributors. Career training often promises future recognition and appreciation but ignores the fact that young people need to feel valuable now. What is more, they *are* valuable, but neither they nor adults can appreciate their value without adults helping them utilize their energy and imagination. [See "Youth into Adult."]

The decisions students make must ultimately shape the programs they are involved in. They must be helped to see the constraints under which both they and the adults operate, but within these parameters they can be helped to exercise increasing responsibility. They can learn that good decision making involves self-assignment; this skill also includes choosing among objectives and selecting means for achieving selected goals.

Young people need challenge and intensity. Even if they are hostile at first, they drop their defenses when their decisions are taken seriously. Apathetic young people shed their indifference when offered the chance to carry out a program that they have planned. In general, youth are eager to find worthy outlets for their abundant energies, which are otherwise dissipated in restlessness or misdirected into mischief.

School officials who choose experiential leraning as part of their response to these adolescent needs face unlimited possibilities. The challenge is to identify and develop the possibilities that grant the teen-agers maximum responsibility. Administrators often equate experiential learning with temporary placement in a community agency or industry. Although it is by no means the only kind of experiential learning, involvement with a preexisting community organization can provide tremendous learning opportunities for teen-agers.

In a San Francisco project called Mission Possible, students with an interest in health services work at the local hospital. The San Francisco program meets three of the essential conditions for a good community-based experiential program. First, the young people are doing or observing work that is important to the operation of the hospital. Some agencies relegate teen-agers to made-up jobs, because the young people lack skills necessary for more interesting work. They forget that the point of experiential learning is to develop the skills of teen-agers, or at least to expose them to the kinds of skills that they may want to acquire. By moving students from one part of the hospital to another and giving them meaningful assignments, Mission Possible opens for them a wide range of learning experiences. The San Francisco students rotate from department to department: in the laboratory they perform simple tests; in geriatrics they feed elderly patients; in administrative offices they answer inquiries and maintain files.

Second, Mission Possible has the support of the hospital staff. Community organizations often accept teen-agers without understanding that the adults who work with them must take some interest in their progress. In Mission Possible, doctors are concerned enough to devote their time to lectures, and other staff members willingly explain hospital procedures to the young people. This concern underlies the importance of the work that the teen-agers do and provides many of them with their first adult models apart from parents and teachers.

Finally, the program receives adequate supervision from the school itself. School counselors monitor the students through notebooks and a questionnaire that students complete. The students have personal access to counselors with whom they can discuss the problems and progress of their work. Seminars enable them to raise relevant questions and to study certain areas in depth.

The need for continuous school supervision cannot be overemphasized. Shoving a student into a work opportunity is not enough; he must have guidance in interpreting his experiences and relating them to his career goals. He must also have the opportunity to integrate experiential and academic skills.

Finding and supervising community opportunities that provide these three components requires selectivity and a resolution not to squeeze young people wherever they fit. Some schools assign the entire task to special nonprofit agencies, which handle all community-placement projects. In Philadelphia, an organization called Kaleidoscope researches placement opportunities, matches them with students, and supervises the students as long as they are on the jobs.

Schools that "go it alone" should pump parent–teacher organizations, service clubs, chambers of commerce, and professional and trade associations for placement ideas and contacts. Student-operated research bureaus can also investigate community needs and opportunities. In Minneapolis, 200 high-school students earn credit for their work in day-care centers, nursing homes, city agencies, and elementary schools. Many of the opportunities were unearthed by the Department of Student Involvement, which is run by students and teachers from two Minneapolis high schools. In other programs the schools appeal directly to community leaders. In New York City's Executive Internship Program, for example, school officials arrange one-to-one matches between students and executives in banks, libraries, media stations, hospitals, and universities. The students spend a semester watching, working with an executive, and recording their observations. Weekly sessions with a school counselor encourage students to evaluate their progress.

Some schools develop their own work environments where students are trained before they are sent to outside work assignments. In Flushing, New York, city students from John Bowne High School run a farm where they grow vegetables, raise poultry, and operate farm equipment. After learning basic agricultural techniques, the students are offered summer work on farms in up-state New York. Students in Manual High School of Denver, Colorado, manage their own construction corporation, which bids on urban-renewal contracts for sidewalk repair and building renovation. The teen-agers do their own bookkeeping, draw up plans, work as foremen, and constitute the labor force. Teachers serve as advisors, a local craftsman instructs the students in construction techniques, and the project has union support so that students can readily be placed in regular jobs.

Placement in community work situations often leads to specific job opportunities for teen-agers. The primary object of experiential learning, however, is to acquaint young people with the process of decision making, which is valuable to them for whatever they do. Administrators who limit themselves to arrangements with preexisting community institutions often overlook an entire battery of experiential learning situations that can originate in the school itself. Many of the best programs begin when students or teachers spot a gap in the services available within the school or from the school to the community. Students in Philadelphia have organized Operation Venus in response to widespread ignorance about venereal disease. The teen-agers run a telephone service for their peers and schedule speaking engagements with church groups and parent associations as well as radio and television appearances. In Mamaroneck, New York, teens have set up a comparable program to help their peers cope with drug abuse. Other peer counseling programs do not specialize in any particular problem. The Unwinding Room at Ste. Marie Goretti High School in Philadelphia is simply a place where troubled students can talk to student counselors about problems with sex, family, courses, or friends. The student staff members receive training from professional psychologists, but the room is off-limits to adults. In New York's Upper Manhattan Outreach Program, students are paired with a community health worker. The teams visit residents in East Harlem to talk with them about prenatal and postnatal care, medicare benefits, pest control, poisoning from lead-base paint, and health care for the elderly. In San Diego, California, the students from an economics class have set up an information booth in a local shopping center. The students ask customers about their complaints and do research to locate the source of consumer problems.

Besides counseling services staffed by young people, many schools operate programs in which students act as educators, either for their peers or for younger children. In the Open Campus program in Swampscott, Massachusetts, students teach minicourses in organic cooking, bike repair, and Hinduism. In Petaluma, California, students work in two-member teams to teach courses on such topics as "Computer Applications" and "Current Problems in the United States." The Petaluma students are paid for their efforts, and their class members receive full academic credit.

Teaching younger children is a natural situation for experiential learning. Underachievers often master reading or arithmetic concepts for the first time when they teach them to younger students. The daily decision making on tools and techniques receives positive reinforcement through the progress of the younger child. The Youth Tutoring Youth program of the National Commission on Resources for Youth has met nationwide success by offering teenagers wages or academic credit for teaching language, reading, and other skills to elementary-school children. Students have also taught successful nutrition courses in Cairo, New York, and creative writing in Philadelphia.

In Enfield, New Jersey, high-school students run a Living History Center where they prepare portable resource libraries that contain multimedia materials on a variety of topics to be used by teachers of young pupils. In preparing the slide–tape presentations, the students gain a thorough knowledge of their subject as well as important technical skills and experience in communicating ideas through visual and audio media. The Enfield project began as an attempt to preserve local history. Because the discovery of a local heritage inspires a special kind of community spirit and because it requires the coordination of otherwise isolated disciplines, it is a valuable field for experiential learning projects. When students in Georgia excavate the remains of an ancient Indian civilization, they learn something about the geology, history, and archaeology of their region, not to mention the communication skills that they develop in reporting their discoveries. In Blanding, Utah, Navajo teen-agers collect the oral traditions of their Indian community by interviewing to gather the stories and writing to record them. A similar project in Appalachia resulted in a quarterly magazine and in the famous *Foxfire* book, a rich collection of the folklore and tradition from Rabun Gap, Georgia.

Other successful experiential projects involve environmental studies. Students in one high school brought a successful antipollution suit against a national railroad, while in Beverly Hills, California, students run a recycling center and edit an environmental newsletter. Other schools, such as Grossmont High School of San Diego, arrange construction projects in which teen-agers design, finance, and build an entire house. The work requires a broad range of decisions from students who plan, construct, and furnish everything from the foundations to the window curtains. They even auction the house at the end of the year to cover the cost of the project.

In each instance an important community function remains unfulfilled until students are mobilized to perform it. Because their work responds to an authentic local need, the decisions the young people make become genuinely important and the project is able to satisfy many basic needs of adolescents.

The feeling that should animate experiential learning was captured for me in a comment from a boy I met in a New York prison. Among the sad-faced young people in that institution, this boy was distinguished by his cheerful energy. A question or two revealed that he worked with the institution's printing press. When I asked why that brought him so much satisfaction, he promptly replied, "Without me it wouldn't work." In the same way, experiential learning offers many teen-agers their first opportunity to be indispensable.

The Helping Adult

It takes a very confident adult to handle with equanimity a teen-ager's feeling of strength. Teachers who work with experiential learning programs possess a cluster of traits that uniquely qualify them to direct these projects. They can precipitate youthful decision making without controlling it. Nearly all adults are reluctant to share their authority with teen-agers, and the way in which this sharing operates is delicate and difficult. Adults cannot pretend they have no say, and let teens take over entirely; sharing is not the same as forfeiting or dominating. The effective adult knows when to intervene and when to step back.

A prevalent misconception about adults who work with young people is that they themselves must act like teen-agers. This is particularly false in experiential learning, which assumes that adolescents need to interact with adults. Large classrooms and depersonalized neighborhoods mean that many young people do not know any adults aside from their parents. During adolescence when they must disengage themselves from their families, young people need other adult models. In addition, they need to glimpse the options available in the adult world. The parameters of adolescence are delineated well enough by the teen-ager's own experience and that of his friends. Adulthood, however, remains strange territory. The only people who can be trusted as scouts are those who have been there—adults themselves.

In experiential learning, effective teachers use their adult status as a compass for mutual exploration, not as a weapon for defense of their egos. Teen-agers are accustomed to strong-arm methods from their elders and may be disbelieving or bewildered by adults who do not claim authoritarian privilege. The adults must stand enough beyond their own adolescent authority crisis to understand this response and to reaffirm their confidence in teen-agers as people who are ready to assume authority of their own. This attitude is impossible for adults who have not conquered their own insecurities. The absolutist temptation is almost insurmountable for a sagging ego faced with thirty potential subjects. Experiential learning requires adults who have resolved their own hang-ups about identity and prerogatives to a point where they do not have to work them out at the expense of the teen-agers.

Interestingly, a teacher's idiosyncrasies matter less to students than does the integrity that makes the teacher trustworthy. The adult's confidence in his own worth, matched with an intensive interest in the young people and in the quality of their experience, is more important than a pleasant personality. One very successful experiential program is led by a short-tempered man who shouts at the teen-agers and interrupts them in midsentence. Another project in a Puerto Rican community is run by a soft-spoken woman, hardly older than her students. The manners of these two adults could not be less alike, yet underlying the quiet smile and the gruff orders are the same confidence in and expectation for the students. And the students respond to these adults, who come on without apology for who they are. Students want to be able to take seriously the adults who lead them, just as much as they want to be taken seriously themselves. This is impossible without adult integrity, a certain frankness about who we are, what we can do, and what we believe young people can do.

The same frankness precludes the "right answers," which are stock in trade for many teachers. Knowing that no answer is final is perhaps the single realization that unifies adult experience; yet educators often use arbitrary facts to camouflage the relativity of "answers." Such dissemblance, well-intentioned as it may be, is a disservice to the young people who are later confounded by ambiguity. In experiential learning, teen-agers learn that being an adult means learning to use mistakes, not being infallible. They discover that decisions are negotiable and absolute answers are rarely available.

Clearly these principles must be experienced before they can be understood. The adults in experiential learning restrain their own tendencies to dominate and intervene so students can experience these principles. The adult role is like that of an advocate who draws out of the students alternative plans of action. When problems surface, adults and students examine potential solutions. While the adults may contribute their own ideas, they remember that their first function is to generate ideas in the young people.

The advocate role calls for great subtlety. The adult serves more as a supportive presence than an active influence. Yet he retains responsibility for the quality of the experience that engages his student. It is unreasonable to suppose that young people who have little prior experience with responsibility can shoulder it without discomfort. The adults in experiential learning understand that some frustration and discouragement are inherent in all social decision making. Extraneous confusion, however, can be minimized by an adult who has mastered the art of offhand suggestion. Adults who are able to activate latent qualities of leadership and commitment in young people give precedence to the teen-ager's individual development over other project results.

This schedule of priorities doesn't exempt the adult from an emotional commitment to the project itself. Students and adults who are partners in pursuit of a single goal become increasingly able to share their feelings about their work, themselves, each other. Often the adult can liberate the human component of their interaction by expressing his own enthusiasm or by listening responsively to the eagerness of the students. Many adults become so preoccupied with what they can give to young people that they never notice what the young people want to give in return. In experiential learning, young people find themselves in circumstances that press them to discover and use their own stores of resourcefulness and reliability. Such opportunities grow naturally out of mutual projects where the adults have an enduring faith in the capability of the young people, an unfailing sensitivity to their needs, and an honest acceptance of the interdependence between themselves and young people.

None of these characteristics is possible unless the adults involved are willing to risk themselves emotionally, psychologically, and perhaps even professionally in their work. They are asked to have faith in untested capabilities, to respond to limitless needs, to admit vulnerability. In addition, they must maintain a delicate balance between ambiguity and chaos. Ambiguity tempts the teacher to take over. When the young people seem especially inept, the adult can issue a few quick orders and get the program on its way. The accomplishments may be impressive, but the students have been squelched again, denied even an apprenticeship in decision making. Chaos, on the other hand, leaves teen-agers without direction. Their discussions circle endlessly around decisions without ever grasping one and translating it into action. Intentions disintegrate, self-confidence collapses, and frustration sets in. Adults in experiential learning must chart a course between these two equally disastrous extremes. Young people must sense that their decisions are respected and that great things are expected of them. If they suspect that their planning can be annulled by adult fiat, they will never feel committed to their work. Nor will they feel responsible if the adult does not set inescapable standards that indicate his own sense of responsibility to the program and belief in the teen-agers' abilities to meet these challenges.

By now, administrators may wonder where they can find such a special breed of humans. This description of adults suited to experiential learning undoubtedly errs on behalf of the ideal. At a more basic level, an adult is qualified to participate in experiential projects when he believes in young people and practices the principles that experiential learning tries to instill in them. Nearly all schools employ some adults who accept and act on these ideas. Most schools also exist within communities with problems that can be translated into experiential learning projects, and the teen-agers in every high school have needs that remain unmet by traditional teaching methods. Adolescent needs, community needs, and adults who understand decision making—the components for experiential learning—are waiting to be coordinated in every American high school.

Schools are filled with students who have been oversupplied with information but are impoverished when it comes to self-confidence, responsibility, and the skills necessary for successful adulthood. In experiential learning, educators have the tool to redress this imbalance. The task may seem monumental. Indeed, the challenge is equalled only by the dangers of leaving adolescents unequipped to make decisions in a world whose alternatives multiply so rapidly. Yet if the hazards of neglecting this type of education are obvious to all of us, the rewards of accomplishing it supersede the hazards in schools that have tried it.

This sampling of successful school-initiated projects should prove that the possibilities are limited only by the imaginations of students and school officials. Every community has services that go unperformed for lack of interest and funds. Every town has a heritage that goes unrecorded. Every neighborhood needs new buildings. Every environment has streams to clean up and scrap to recycle. School administrators should see in each of these "problems" an opportunity for their students.

The needs and rewards are unmistakable; the potential for successful experiential learning lies latent in every school. It remains only for teachers and administrators to marshal the imagination and determination that led to clean water in Coos Bay and salvaged history in Atlanta and to discover more capable young people involved in projects all across the country.

Antioch College-West does not have a science department, a psychology department, a tree-covered campus, nor a hundred-member faculty of PhDs. Instead, the college draws upon the unique resources of the community— human, institutional, and physical—to make possible highly individualized undergraduate degree programs. The University Without Walls design is utilized, and the college has a basic commitment to experiential learning. The program attempts to educate people for an uncertain future that requires continual invention and the use of new ways to organize information. Through individualized educational processes, both faculty members and students attempt to define new roles for themselves; outside resources are called upon to offer expertise and assistance. Students are prepared for the time when new institutions will be recognized for their educational value and new forms of representation will be created to replace the degree.

Ideally, the staff of Antioch-West would like to make it a place where students come to find persons who can help them define their needs and goals, organize the necessary resources to reach those goals, and then provide a mechanism to translate and describe the skills developed and information mastered so that others understand it. But for now, the college provides socially acceptable certification and therefore establishes documentation and evaluation procedures and awards a degree.

The degree requirements of Antioch-West are individualized, although each student follows a common process. Students do not merely accumulate a predetermined number of credits to graduate; they engage in a set of learning experiences that allow them to meet their own goals and needs.

Since Antioch-West relies heavily on the use of resources in the community, it does not duplicate these same resources "in-house." Instead, faculty members are sought according to who can best contribute to the *process* of education. These people spend most of their time advising students and managing the associated responsibilities, which include locating internship sites, working with field resources, and helping plan and document a student's learning. Faculty members engage in only minimal classroom activity and more often are working with students on projects and independent study.

Not only faculty members but also students accept a redefinition of their roles. Each student takes on major responsibility for defining, developing, implementing, and evaluating his own program.

Antioch College-West

Pattilou Schultz and Lance Dublin

Students are from sixteen to fifty-five years old. They come from a diversity of cultural and socioeconomic backgrounds and represent a range of traditional and nontraditional college histories and learning styles. What they have in common is a search for a model of undergraduate education that can be adapted to their particular situation, a dissatisfaction with curricula in other institutions as a means to help them prepare for *their* futures, and a desire for an education while unable to afford the luxury of removing themselves from the world where they must support and raise a family.

Antioch-West attracts many older-than-average students, who are often already in work situations that require additional learning strategies. The student and advisor first examine the setting to ensure that the student's job is appropriate to his degree interests. Then they address the following questions: How does the student function in that setting? Which functions does the student perform from memory and habit, and which can be further developed with additional knowledge and skill? What kind of mobility does the student desire in the job setting? What components of the job are changeable?

These students must also establish learning goals and objectives early in their programs. In view of these goals, they consider their needs and determine what changes in the job setting are necessary. Sometimes these changes include getting a better overview of the job, increasing the job responsibilities, assigning new tasks, or identifying a project incorporating outside resources as well as the job. The student and advisor may also consider what outside activities the student should be doing to complement and supplement the learning taking place in the job setting.

A landscape architect, for example, wanted a broad liberal-arts education; some preschool workers needed to continue working full-time and to follow a program with heavy emphasis on child development and related subjects; a mental-health aide wanted training and background in another field, since his hospital was being phased out. These people felt that the traditional academic programs would not utilize sufficiently the knowledge and skills that they'd gained through their work experiences. A simple work program would not provide the cognitive exploration they sought either. They needed an experience-based situation closely related to a classroom component. Antioch-West had such a program.

Each student works closely with a core faculty advisor and advising and degree committee throughout his program. Together, the student and advisor review and summarize the student's past learning experiences, identify the student's needs, establish educational objectives, and develop a plan to meet those objectives. The advisor also helps a student locate resources and works with him to document the ongoing learning. The advisor and student strive to maintain a relationship of delicate balance between dependence and autonomy. The advisor must play a strong role in the learning experience, but the student must develop a sense of autonomy and refine his independent learning capabilities.

The advising and degree committee aids in the evaluation and planning process. This committee is made up of the student, advisor, and professionals

Antioch-West Programs

as well as others from the community who have expertise in the student's area of interest. Ultimately, this committee decides the student's specific degree requirements and certifies when he has met those requirements and is ready to graduate.

Students are encouraged to utilize a wide range of learning settings in their educational programs. These may include internships, apprenticeships, projects, seminars, workshops, tutorials, or independent study. Many students transform their current jobs into learning situations. The classroom and study situations are means to aid the student in clarifying, understanding, and building upon his field experience.

One student worked as an apprentice to a museum administrator, another did videotape interviews of the Ellsberg trial, and a third helped care for birds injured in an oil slick. All these students took classes that helped them understand and increase their effectiveness in their fieldwork. The classroom experiences ranged from art to television and film to zoology and biology. Some students developed projects to pursue major problems; they chose activities and classes to help them discover solutions to these problems.

As the student sets his degree objectives and designs a program, his past learning experiences—college work, jobs, readings, personal experience—are reviewed and evaluated. In order to receive credit for them, a student must be able to demonstrate the learning that occurred in each of these past experiences and show how they contributed to his present degree objectives. This gives the student recognition for learning done in a diversity of settings, not just in a traditional college, and aids him in gaining a perspective on his learning and making plans for the future.

In the documentation process, all of the student's experiences and learnings are synthesized and recorded. The student pulls together his learning experiences and examines them, which gives him increased understanding of the specific skills developed and the information acquired through an experience. Documentation also makes it possible for the student to demonstrate clearly the skills and knowledge he has developed and the ways in which he can use them. In this way, his learnings can be transcribed and represented to the outside world. If documentation is not taken seriously—given time and thought—it serves only as a recording device and not as a learning process.

These components support a philosophy of experiential education. Experiential learning focuses on information-seeking, on the process of learning, and on preparation for continual learning. It is a student-centered process rather than one involving passive responsibility in learning. The student is encouraged to explore his feelings and reactions in the kind of challenging, frustrating, ambiguous, and perplexing situations he is likely to encounter. He is involved in making decisions and taking risks.

Since the student is the consumer of his education, the first task of the program is to ensure that he accepts experiential education as a valuable learning process. He must become aware of his responsibility and role as an active participant. The student must be motivated, not necessarily toward a goal but at least toward exploration. Without this motivation a student may allow his experience to suffice for the core of his learning; he may merely perform job responsibilities or internship duties. This is not enough in experiential learning. The student must actively pursue the skills and knowledge he seeks. He must be exploring ways to integrate these experiences into his whole program.

Students choose an experiential activity with different goals and needs in mind. Some seek practical experience in an area of career preference or possible graduate study. Many want to put theoretical knowledge into practical use. Other students seek to develop and expand certain skills or learning styles. Another group simply desires to explore an area or setting that appeals to them. And a final segment, of mostly the older-than-average students, wants to change their present job into a valid learning experience.

When a person enters Antioch-West, he develops both long-range and short-range goals and objectives. These goals might reflect roles the student hopes to play, keeping in mind the philosophy of the college that a student should experience a variety of roles. Or the goals might reflect knowledge he wants to acquire, often in conjunction with academic learning, or skills he wants to develop or expand.

The student's experience is examined with these goals in mind. The student and advisor ascertain whether the setting meets the student's stated and secondary needs, how it relates to the rest of his program, and how it ties in with his long-range goals. These goals and objectives are continually revised, added to, and commented upon throughout the experience. As a student participates in an activity, the new information he acquires can shed light on other possibilities in that setting or somewhere else. Or the new knowledge may prove an assumption false and require a change of goals.

This constant analysis and examination form an important learning strategy. It prevents the experiential learning setting from turning into "just a job." It keeps the student from falling into rote or unplanned activities and patterns. This process also helps determine when it is time for the student to leave that setting.

Many institutions are expanding their definitions of legitimate learning to include experience-based activities. While this is encouraging, these activities must really be experiential in order to be valuable.

Experiential learning is a process. It is not synonymous with cooperative education, in which a distinction is made between work and study. It is not comparable to a career-training program, which has a goal the training of individuals for certain roles in agencies and institutions. It is not the same as a quarter of fieldwork, in which the student works independently in the community, reports periodically to the professor, and writes a final paper on the experience to gain credit. Experiential education is the organized use of experience, analysis, and documentation, together with cognitive exploration.

Experiential education can be a means to move our society toward a redefinition of work and learning so that the artificial distinctions between them can be broken down. There is no reason why people should ever stop learning. If a job can become a learning experience and the necessary support systems are made available, then learning can take place continually.

(Forgive me for writing thus, unanalytical. I am not a scientist at heart, social or otherwise. I trust these ambling words still give a glimpse of my experiences this semester.)

I. Opportunity

Opportunity for all those beat down, squelched, repressed, regressed, bored, and otherwise messed over by the public high school system.

Opportunity for me.

II. What I learned this semester.

What I learned from my supervisor. (What can I do.)
What I am. (A child, a woman.)
What I learned at a public high school. (Many old children,
many young–old, laughing, grumbling, singing with gutsy soul baritone,
freaked out, strung out, hippies, soul brothers; high on pot, coke, reds,
Schlitz, Hell's Angels; poets, lovers, haters, actors, dealers, and
painters, and a seventeen-year-old father who has lost his first child
already.)

III. Carolyn. (Or: Keep the Faith, baby)

My first job—my first student to tutor.
I gave Carolyn big things to do—inspiring things.
Asked her what she wanted to study ("I don't know")
Wanted her to start a vocation study project (wants to be
a probation officer) with research, interviews, relevance.
Asked her to write about her ambitions, why go to college
("I don't know. I don't know")

Skeleton of a Growing Child

Cynthia Embree

Nothing.

Only dark head bent
Ebony eyes to the floor.

I will be firm, realistic, serious.
    Tell her like it is.
I begin with certainty
    (green-brown eyes to the floor, wall, books, hands, meeting anything
    but the long, young, arms, legs, body stretched out in the chair, not
    knowing where to reach or how far—the dark child-woman I'm terrified
    of losing)

"Carolyn," I say,
    "You said you wanted to go to college.
    That is your choice, not mine,
    But if you want to do that you are going to have to
    start finishing your assignments.
    I've given you two or three things to do, and so far
    you haven't done any of them."

Ebony eyes to the floor.
Long legs shift slightly under the table.
Reaching the limits of the tiny counseling room.

Feeling out of place, out of time,
Out of right, out of knowledge,
My shoulders sink.
    Green-brown eyes to the floor.

"How come, Carolyn?
Am I pushing too hard?
Am I bugging you?"

"You not buggin' me."

"Are you gonna do it, Carolyn?"

"Yeah, I'm gonna do it."

She leaves.
I know she's gone
I never could fight, talk to people either.

Now I've tried both at once and lost.

Try meeting in the middle.
Start again, with simple stuff.
No big ambitions, plans, projects,
vocational-occupational-scholastical-confusional
excesses.

A play—*The Miracle Worker.*
   How Annie brought an angry child out of the darkness
   with a word.

"I want to teach you—oh, everything the earth is full of ...
everything on it that's ours for a wink and it's gone, and what we are
on it, the—light we bring to it and leave behind in—words, why, you
can see five thousand years back in a light of words, everything we feel, think,
know.

And share, in words, so not a soul is in darkness, or done with, even in
the grave. And I know, I *know*, one word and I can—put the world in
your hand." (Can I?)

"I wanted to teach her what language is.
I wanted to teach her yes." [Gibson, 1957]

(I wanted to know that yes myself.)

      Carolyn digs it.
      Reads, writes questions, answers,
      Talks to me
      (Still, "I don't know,"
      But less often.)

Wednesday morning drama class.
      Teacher has a meeting and
      leaves me with the magic wand touch
   to change a table, chairs into a
   counter, bus, living room, museum.

The actors play and live their parts,
      laughing, arguing, wise-cracking,
      ribbing each other and me.
And in the middle comes
   the teacher, with open arms and a
   sassy greeting for her loves:

"Did ya miss me class?"

Carolyn (with a smile, knowing it won't hurt):

"Aw, we don't need you.
Cynthia's our teacher."

IV. Raymond.

Raymond is my friend.
Comes in with his special lady-killing wink,
just to bug me when I'm working
("Hey, white girl, Whatcha doin' ")
and I love it.

Talks to me in his journal.
Told me once, not me, really, but the wall;
   (did he know I was listening?)
he's so lonely—then quick changed the subject,
smooth as black velvet, not missing a step.

What can I do? Anything?

Talk to him. Tutor him. Let him hug me.
Give him homework to do. Take him to lunch.
Be myself and a friend.

(Can myself and a friend and teacher ever meet in one? Stop changing,
running from each other, playing hide-and-seek?)
                     Raymond, I love you.

V. My Supervisor, Head Counselor and Teacher

My friend, backboard, catalyst, and
passport into the world again.

Sick, sick, beaten and weary of wandering, running in and
   out of the unending, intricate passages of my mind.
Spent six months of horrible idleness,
running against, from, and into my Self and wanting out.

I made a phone call.
   "Hello, is there something (anything left in this whole world) that I
can do (am I capable, have I any worth left)?"

   "Oh! I *want* you!"
She took me in:

"There's lots to do.
Here I am, here we are, look around and
see what you want."

She put me in places I thought I would die in
(and I didn't).
Then watching her, playing at teaching,
talking to kids, chasing them down,
calling their games, guiding them through
    ("You guys are *great*—this is college-level
    stuff and you're reading it. Digging it."
    Anxiety. Schizophrenia. Suicide. Hallucinations.
    Big words—they fight—and fight through—
        and love.)

Watching her, I knew I could never do it,
but wanted to.
(*Talk* to those kids?
Know them?
Is it possible, for anyone but a miracle?)

I did try.
A few successes. Many tears.
    (Mostly for my old sorry self—still looking for something worthy to
fill up my empty hours—telling myself I wanted to save these children—
meaning me.)

I kept saying:
    "It's not enough. I want to do more.
    (*Make* me do something, make me come out of this gutter—*pull*
    me out.)
    I don't have enough to do."

She brought me back, repeating my own
    repetitions and adding:
    "Take what you asked for;
    Do with what you have before
    asking more."

    Like a slap, awakening me from a
        self-induced nightmare.
        (Though one of many slaps—one of
        many dreams—like a bad TV serial
        that must run its weekly course until
        actors, audience, producers weary of it
        and it fades,
        dies.)

She showed me herself:
    her strength and energy,
    her own unhappiness, frustrations.
    Showed me the paths (many, rocky, wandering)
        to the worlds of those kids
        (excuse me, those Students—
        they call themselves that, and are.)

She gave me a promise—the same she gives to all:
    "All I can, to help you on your way,
            that I will do.
    The path is yours alone to find."

Pray God,
May that promise someday
be mine to give.

VI. (Not) The End.

What I learned.

What I learned was a bunch of platitudes:
    Know thyself.
    Kids are people, people are kids.
    Learn by doing.
    To err is human; to forgive (especially thyself) is divine.
    Don't cry over spilt milk.
    Keep the faith, baby.

What all I learned was platitudes, but
I learned them gutsy and I learned them crying.
I learned them good.

Learning Our Differences
Rodney A. Clark

Rodney A. Clark is Professor of Education at California State University, San Francisco, California.

Reach, Touch, and Teach
Terry Borton

Director of the Dual Audio Television Project for the Philadelphia Board of Education, Terry Borton is also a lecturer at the University of Pennsylvania. He has authored two books, *Reach, Touch, and Teach* and *Find Your Own Way.*

School Climate Improvement
Eugene R. Howard

Buena Vista Annex
Beverly Carmody and Cora Meek

Beverly Carmody teaches a class of fourth- to sixth-graders at Buena Vista Annex, San Francisco Unified School District.
    Cora Meek is an elementary-school teacher in the San Francisco Unified Schools.

Community High School
Jay Manley

Jay Manley is currently serving as Associate Director, Experimental Schools Project of the Berkeley Public Schools, in charge of teacher training.

Beliefs into Action

Included here are the programs, large and small, which represent humanistic thrusts and integrated efforts in a variety of areas.

Rodney Clark's "Learning Our Differences" discusses ways of helping students to assess themselves. Terry Borton, in "Reach, Touch, and Teach," offers an interdisciplinary curriculum sampling based on important principles of affective education. Next, Eugene Howard, in "School Climate Improvement," gives another example of beliefs about young people that are important in operating schools.

The two final articles describe full school programs where serious learning occurs in settings that have been designed and modified by the originators of the schools. In "Buena Vista Annex," Beverly Carmody and Cora Meek talk about an urban elementary school designed and operated by teachers in concert with parents and paraprofessionals. They help their students develop important basic skills while experimenting with methods that allow individual students and teachers maximum freedom in meeting these goals. Jay Manley closes with "Community High School," a high school within a school, which actively sought to integrate the notions of community and autonomy and developed a curriculum and structure that support these concepts.

These are merely a sampling; once the concepts are understood, the variations are infinite. New programs can be initiated on any scale. Any classroom can become an open one, any teacher can legitimize outside experiences and integrate the learnings with classroom materials.

If you, the reader, are a teacher considering a move toward innovation, you might find the broad outlines of this book helpful in your beginnings: first, look inward and understand as much as possible about your own strengths and defenses in functioning with students, then view your stance on major issues in the field, next research recent findings on how learning occurs, and finally, find out how others have attempted to put some of their beliefs into action. Your program may then still be your own, but it will also reflect the thoughts and struggles of some of your predecessors.

For teachers, much of what is said about individual differences seems to have more to do with the sameness of learners than with differences. Means, norms, standard scores, all seem to lump learners together rather than treat them as unique. This is only partly because teachers do not understand the science of measurement.

In their communications, measurers themselves often have not carefully separated their measurements from the variables being measured. They have allowed teachers to develop rigid interpretations of measurements as though they were "real"—for instance, teachers have been allowed to think children "have" IQs. And teachers have even been urged to use statistics about groups as though they were data about individuals.

Learning Assumptions about Human Behavior

In order to escape this paradox, it is important that teachers reexamine what human difference really is. It is essential that teachers do this task for themselves.

In our living experiences there is pervasive feedback for each of us, which tells us that all human beings are different. We know vaguely that we are all a part of each other, but we know indeed that each of us is unique. The same living experiences that teach each of us the universality of differences also teach us to deal with unique others by making assumptions about them. These assumptions are part of each self's concept about what the world is like and the people in it. Such assumptions are part of the private "reality" each of us has devised.

Having developed a basic set of assumptions, the educated human being can expand his assumptions through continuing evaluation of experience. The continuing evaluation will involve collecting data—some of which is quantified— and testing new feedback against previous learnings. Under some circumstances, such as therapy or trauma, changes can push into the basic set of assumptions, but for each of us there is a core of "knowledge" about human behavior almost not available to evaluation but which affects evaluation because it influences all criteria, values, and motivation.

Reprinted from *Educational Leadership*, March 1967, *24* (6), 485–489, by permission of the author and the publisher.

Learning Our Differences

Rodney A. Clark

Since all learning involves evaluation and since evaluation springs from an individual's assumptions about humanness, all learning involves significant elements, unique and unmeasurable. School procedures have traditionally left to chance the development of these basic assumptions about humanness. Learners were not helped to evaluate anything so personal, so intrinsic to the self. At best, students were told what assumptions to have.

Now educators are recognizing that if we facilitate the development of each learner's full potential, we must not ignore the core from which we start with him. And slowly we are admitting that we cannot tell a learner what to value, by what to be motivated, by what criteria to judge what is love, what is satisfying, what he needs. These he knows. They are part of his self.

Educators who particularly value the democratic processes and those who have investigated "mentally healthful" interpersonal relations have discovered that they tend to share assumptions about humanness. It is not surprising then to find that democratic processes are most effectively carried on through mentally healthful interactions. Nor is it surprising that mentally healthful, democratic interactions between teachers and learners enable each learner to develop assumptions about humanness which, while unique, accept the potential of all men to move toward openness, autonomy, love, and complete self-actualization.

Some assumptions about humanness that learners develop from mentally healthful, democratic interactions with teachers and peers are predictable. . . .The learner will recognize that all humans are different. From this he will realize that, whatever the differences of individuals, for each self the differences add up to infinite worth. The learner comes to know that behavior is explainable. He sees that each human chooses his own becoming and therefore each human is uniquely purposeful. As he finds that all humans are striving to be fully effective, he accepts all behavior as the behaver's attempt to be effective.

Teachers who have learned these same kinds of assumptions will put them together to understand that learning is a changed relationship among elements of the complicated process of the individual's becoming effective. From this definition of learning, teachers will move into the teacher–learner relation so as to help learners evaluate the consequences of their efforts to be effective. They will assume the validity of the learner's assumptions about effectiveness as humans, but they will help the learner evaluate even these assumptions if they become available to introspection.

Again it can be predicted that, if the mentally healthful, democratic interactions in a school are rich, varied, and deeply evaluated, each learner will develop along four facets of effectiveness. These have to do with loving–lovable, coping–capable, expressing–meaningful, and integrating–autonomous.

Four Facets of Effectiveness

Each of these facets moves from experiencing the world to a concept of what the world is like, to a concept of how the self is related to the world, to a concept of what the self "should" be like, to a concept of what the self needs.

Loving–Lovable   A human's first interaction with the world is through being cared for. Without care, he would perish. From the quality of this care the infant learns about love—its plenty, its warmth, its sensibility, its limits, its demands. As he learns about being loved, he acts out what he is learning—by loving. Through loving and reactions to loving, he learns a concept of being lovable. The experiences of being loved, loving, and becoming lovable move through interactions with mother, father, siblings, peers, other adults.

The loving–lovable syndrome is well developed by the time a child comes to school but is certainly not finished. School activities and teachers contribute much to the concepts. Peers gradually become more influential than teachers, but helpful teachers contribute importantly to the evaluation of peer experiences.

In adolescence, each learner must review his concept of loving–lovable and make decisions about how he will form his maturity around it. Fortunately, he can choose to learn to be different in loving and be lovable in ways other than he has ever known directly if teachers will help him. His loving will be observable to a large degree, but being lovable will be entirely private to his self-system.

Coping–Capable   The second facet of effectiveness arises as each human tries to use the world. He learns what things can do to him and what he can do to them. Gradually he learns what he can make things do to each other and how he is affected by this interaction. He learns to cope with the world as it is or to change it, to use the world and to be used by it, only if and how he chooses. Then, through experiencing and evaluating his efforts to cope, he learns a concept of being capable.

Teachers know a great deal about helping learners develop coping skills. They are likely, however, to help improve the observable efforts at coping and leave to chance the private learning about being capable.

There are four general areas in which coping–capable learnings develop. The first of these areas (perhaps each of the others to some extent depends on it) is *communication*. The learner experiences naming, defining, describing, discussing, listening, reading, writing, "appreciating." In addition he communicates through music, art, drama, and dance. And as he evaluates how these activities satisfy his needs, he learns a concept of being a communicator. It is this private concept that will determine what he does with his communication skills.

A second set of coping skills enables a learner to live with people. It must be remembered that for every skill about interacting with people the learner also develops a concept about his self as interactor. He alone knows how he defines being satisfied and capable and this determines what interactions he will attempt.

It is convenient to group a third set of coping skills under a category dealing, not with people, but with the physical, chemical, biological, empirical world. We can predict that coping with the world will bring some realization that phenomena are explainable; that explanations are discoverable; that there are "laws;" that these laws are relatively "true;" that through these laws things become more useful. What the teacher cannot know about directly is the learner's private definition of being a capable user.

The fourth set of coping experiences in our classification are those dealing with quantifying and calculating. The learner must conceive of himself as a quantifier, a calculator, a problem solver, one who uses numbers efficiently, one who can expedite relating to things and people by calculations, or else he will not engage in mathematical activities.

Expressing–Meaningful   The third facet of effectiveness is the process through which a self's efforts to be expressed provide a concept of being meaningful. Of course, being meaningful comes out of being lovable and capable. These tell us *what* we are to start with, but each of us needs to go on to discover *who* we are. As we express—that is, make external in the world—what we are, we learn about a scheme of things. We come to "know" that there is a purpose for our purposefulness, there seems to be a reasoning about it all.

Our efforts to express ourselves are observable. They are the things we make, create, build, own, our style of living—any procedure by which we put outside our self what we value, believe in, hope for, in order to show it to others or to make it better known to our self. It would be foolish to assume that children or adolescents, because their definition of being meaningful is still meager, are any less involved than adults are in building this concept. We assume that learners must express themselves. While they cannot be "assigned" to do so, they can be helped to recognize needs and to match needs with appropriate expressions.

Integrating–Autonomous   By autonomy we mean a concept that the self is satisfyingly choosing its own becoming. It is a concept that is mentally healthy but unfortunately is not commonly developed. The basis of its development, however, comes from the need of each self to integrate all the self's needs. In other words, the self needs to resolve conflicts between needs—it is important not to need to go and to stay at the same time.

For children, experiences with choice making, standing alone, and going one's own way develop a concept more of independence than of autonomy. For adolescents, however, choice making per se, independence per se, rebellion, reevaluation, redecision, new directions are almost the essence of becoming. Integrating all his newly aroused needs and reevaluated self-concepts consumes the motivational power of the adolescent. From this cauldron he must deal directly with the concept of autonomy. All his definition of maturity goes into this concept.

Since the concept of autonomy is the most sophisticated facet of effectiveness, it—more than others—continues to be developed throughout adulthood. Perhaps it is not surprising that few selves become autonomous. It is obvious, however, that the more teachers can be helpful in the evaluation of integrating experiences the more they will contribute to the mentally healthy, democratic potential of the new generation of adults.

The foregoing description of human effectiveness provides a base from which to reconsider the place of "measurement" in helping learners. Admitting that no measurement is "real"—only an approximation, a probability—we are adding the complication here that intrinsic learning, being unique, privy to a self, cannot be measured. Besides, it becomes obvious that intrinsic learning is not quantifiable.

In the sense that each self is lovable with no strings attached, no matter how each self privately defines *lovable,* then being lovable is infinite. There can be no more or less, only difference.

Much the same can be said for being capable. Each human is so able to do things, each puts together his abilities in such a complicated way. We can compare only isolated skills, never a total pattern of skills. That is, we can judge coping skill in a specific instance—typing speed, for example—but the capabilities of various typists to live effectively is another kind of guess entirely. And no matter what we guess, each typist has an entirely unique basis for guessing otherwise.

Who is meaningful? We all are. What is our meaning? It cannot be measured. Our meaning is not a matter of quantity—since I mean nothing without you, I cannot mean more than you.

It seems that we can talk about being almost autonomous or about not being very autonomous. But, privately, the self conceives its actions as choosing its own becoming or it does not. (This is complicated in discussion because we assume each human does choose his own becoming whether or not he has this self-concept.) Therefore, even if each person's autonomy were not privately defined, we still could not compare autonomies.

Then what can we measure? Obviously not any intrinsic learning. But we can use measurement very effectively for helping a student with the other side of the process of becoming effective. For instance, while "lovable" cannot be measured, we can observe acts of loving. By collecting and quantifying data about loving acts, we can increase the feedback to the learner about the consequences of loving acts. We can observe the learner's use of skills (coping), certainly see, hear, feel, his modes and products of expressing and how some kinds of integration of needs are externalized. We can collect data about the experience side of becoming effective. We can count events, measure change in skills, determine criteria for skill performance, objectify data about attitudes through scaling procedures, inventory interests, test hypotheses, compute probabilities, and so forth. Yet our purpose in this is for feedback to the learner. If we increase the feedback to the learner about the consequences of his efforts to be effective, then he will evaluate what the feedback means to him.

We may cease to measure some things and collect data about other qualities, but we will nevertheless need to know the probability that our data are reliable or valid. This kind of quantification will build the effectiveness of teachers and learners the more it clearly increases the flow of feedback to learners.

In summary, the deep, pervasive, intrinsic learnings that are the very self-concept of the learner, are unique and private to the learner. They cannot be compared or quantified externally. Teachers can facilitate this learning by increasing the significance of the learner's experiences and the quality of his evaluations of experience.

Teachers will truly facilitate learning only when they accept that the learner chooses his own becoming. Each child, adolescent, adult, culturally disadvantaged, delinquent, neurotic, nonreading or otherwise handicapped learner knows more about what he is doing than does the teacher. We cannot measure the learner. We can measure things external to him in order to increase the usefulness of data for his evaluations.

There are two sections to almost every school's statement of educational objectives—one for real and one for show. The first, the real one, talks about academic excellence, subject mastery, and getting into college or a job. The other discusses the human purpose of a school—values, feelings, personal growth, the full and happy life. It is included because everyone knows that it is important and that it ought to be central to the life of every school. But it is only for show. Everyone knows how little schools have done about it.

In spite of this, the human objectives describe the things all of us cite when we try to remember what "made a difference" in our school careers: the teacher who touched us as persons, or the one who ground out our lives to polish our intellects; the class that moved with the strength and grace of an Olympic team, or the dozens of lessons when each of us slogged separately toward the freedom of three o'clock. What we learned and what we became depended to a significant degree on how we felt about ourselves, our classmates, and our teachers. The schools were right—the human purposes were important. But with the exception of those teachers who were so rare we never forgot them, the schools did little to put their philosophy into practice.

Recently, however, a variety of programs have begun to build curricula and teaching methodology that speak directly to the human objectives. These programs, stemming both from within the schools and from various branches of psychology, point the way to a school practice that not only recognizes the power of feelings but also combines academic training with an education directly aimed at the student's most important concerns. Schools may soon explicitly teach students such things as how to sort out and guide their own psychological growth or increase their desire to achieve or handle their aggressive instincts in nonviolent forms.

The new impetus has a variety of names: "psychological education," "affective," "humanistic," "personological," "eupsychian," "synoetic." Some of these names are a bit bizarre, and none has yet gained wide acceptance. Taken together, their presence indicates a growing recognition that in the world's

Reach, Touch, and Teach

Terry Borton

present state of social and moral turmoil the schools' traditional second objective can no longer be for show. Riots, poverty, war, student rebellion, swollen mental hospitals, and soaring crime rates have involved an enormous number of people. They have generated a broadening conviction that society is as responsible for the psychological well-being of each of its members as is each individual. And that conviction has created a receptive audience for new kinds of educational critics.

The new critics do not simply attack the schools for their academic imcompetence, as did the Rickovers of a decade ago. They are equally concerned with the schools' basic lack of understanding that students are human beings with feelings as well as intellects. Jonathan Kozol has given a gripping sense of the "destruction of the hearts and minds of Negro children" in his *Death at an Early Age*. [1967] In *How Children Fail* John Holt [1966] has shown that even in the best "progressive" schools children live in constant fear, which inhibits their learning. Paul Goodman's *Compulsory Mis-Education* [1962] has made a powerful case for his contention that "the present school system is leading straight to 1984." The intuitive warnings of these "romantic critics" have been backed up by statistical evidence from the largest survey of education ever conducted, James Coleman's *Equality of Educational Opportunity*. [1966] This survey correlates academic achievement with attitudes such as a student's self-concept, sense of control over his fate, and interest in school. The study concludes that these attitudes and feelings are more highly correlated with how well a student achieves academically than a combination of many of the factors that educators have usually thought crucial, such as class size, salary of teachers, facilities, curriculum.

The pressure to deal more directly with student feelings (increasingly a pressure from students as well as critics) has given rise to dozens of different projects. None of the three examples I will discuss here has yet reached the size or influence of the giant curriculum centers (such as the Educational Development Corporation), which grew up as a result of the post-Sputnik criticism. In the long run they may be much more important, for the post-Sputnik curriculum reforms were essentially attempts to find better ways to teach the traditional disciplines of math, science, or social studies—often with the effect of moving the college curriculum into elementary and secondary schools. The programs I am describing not only operate with different techniques but also begin to define and develop new curriculum subjects and a new school orientation toward practical and applied psychology. If expanded, they will make a profound change in American education—hopefully a change toward a more humane educational process and a more human student.

The project I codirected with Norman Newberg, the Philadelphia School Board's specialist in "affective education," is an example of such a curriculum. It is being developed from within the schools—in this case by a group of urban teachers trying to find a philosophy and method that would work with the students they are asked to teach. The program is based on the assumption that every person handles massive amounts of information and needs to be taught both logical and psychological processes for handling it. Two semester-long courses, one in communications and one in urban affairs, isolate such processes as symbolization, simulation, dreaming, and deescalating pressure, and teach them in an explicit fashion. At the same time the classes are designed to tie these processes to the amorphous undercurrent of student concerns for self-identity, power, and relationship.

I dropped into a high-school communications class one hot day during last summer's field testing, when the teacher was working on "taxonomy of process," or a way of looking at what, why, and how behavior occurs and changes. The purpose of the class was to show the students a simple technique for analyzing their own habitual forms of processing the world around them and then to show them how they could develop new responses if they wanted to. The class was working in groups of two, filling in "What Wheels" for each other. One boy was without a partner, so I joined him; we agreed that I would make a What Wheel for him and he would make one for me. I drew a circle, filled in the spokes, and wrote down my first impressions of him: "strong, quick, Afro, shy, bright."

The teacher asked us to read each other our What Wheels, select one adjective that interested us most, and ask our partner to draw a "Why Wheel" to explain why that adjective was meaningful to him.

Charlie read me his What Wheel—he was perceptive, as students usually are about teachers. Then I read him mine.

"Why'd you write 'shy'? I ain't shy."

"Well, I just met you, so I can't fill out a whole Why Wheel about it. But when I first sat there, I noticed you looked down at your desk instead of up at me. So I just guessed you were shy with strangers—maybe just with strange teachers."

Charlie took his What Wheel from me and looked at it. "You know, that's the truth. I thought nobody, except maybe my mother, knew that about me, but well, it's the truth anyhow."

The murmur of the class's conversation quieted while the teacher told us how to make up "How Wheels" with our partners. We were supposed to write down the range of actions that would either increase or decrease the trait we had been discussing.

"Aw, man, it would be easy to increase being shy," laughed Charlie. "I just wouldn't look at nobody."

"And decreasing it?"

"I'd look at you like I'm looking at you right now," he said, looking me straight in the eye. "And more than that, I'd look at you like that when you first came in here. Teacher, or white man, I wasn't afraid of you; no reason why I should act like I was."

We talked for a while—about my wheels, about the effectiveness of the what, why, how process questions for looking at behavior, and about school. When the bell rang, we shook hands. "See ya around," he said.

"See ya around," I said.

While many teachers have been experimenting with techniques similar to ours, research psychologists usually have been rather disdainful of the messy problems in the schools. Increasingly, however, psychologists such as David McClelland of Harvard are beginning to work on problems of motivation and attitude in schools. The progression of McClelland's study [1953] is a good example of how basic research may be applied to problems in education. McClelland began working on problems of measuring the motivation of rats deprived of food, performed a series of experiments to measure hunger motivation in humans, and then devised a system for measuring "achievement motivation" in men by counting the frequency of its appearance in fantasy images. He defined the need for achievement (*n-Ach*) as a pattern of thought and fantasy about doing things well, and discovered that those people who had such a pattern were characterized by a preference for moderate risk goals, a desire for immediate feedback on their performance, and a liking for personal responsibility. McClelland reasoned that if a society had a great number of such individuals, the society itself should show outstanding achievement. Twenty years were spent in a mammoth research effort to substantiate his claim that achievement research provided a "factual basis for evaluating theories that explain the rise and fall of civilizations." The next step was to devise educational methods for increasing the achievement motive in people who did not have much of it and to test out these methods in this country and abroad.

Dr. Alfred Alschuler, director of the Harvard Achievement Motivation Development Project, which is one result of McClelland's research, is in charge of a federally funded five-year research project to assess what factors lead to effective achievement training. The project has devised many classroom techniques for increasing achievement motivation in students, most of them involving experiential learning that takes place in a game situation. I visited one training program for teachers in a nearby city and sat in on a session that used a contest in making paper airplanes to demonstrate to the teachers how achievement motivation affects their students.

There was a lot of joking around the table, as everyone was a little nervous.

"Now they're going to use the old carrot on us," cracked a little physics teacher sitting on my right.

The head of the math department—an enormous man—smiled broadly, first at the physics teacher and then at me. "Feeling cutthroat?" he asked.

I didn't say so but I was, and he knew it. My "n-Ach" was way up. We eyed each other while we set our own quotas for the number of planes we would make.

Dr. Alschuler gave us the start sign. I was making planes feverishly; out of the corner of my eye, I could see the math department head moving more slowly but doing a better job—the quality-control check at the end of the game might go in his favor. The physics teacher was using mass-production techniques, making one fold at a time.

At the end of five minutes the game was up, and we were all laughing at the tension it had produced. The physics teacher had more planes than any of us, but his mass production assembly had failed—all the planes were missing one wing. I had the second largest number of planes, but several had sloppy folds and were disqualified.

"Nuts to this," said the physics teacher. "I'm not going to get another heart attack over a bunch of paper airplanes. Next time, I'm dropping my quota in half. I'm only going to make six."

I was swearing at myself—I should have been more careful. Next time through the game, I would set a slightly lower quota and do a better job.

The math teacher was smiling broadly. He had won.

Later we all talked about our experience in the game and how our own behavior did or did not reflect the characteristics of a high achiever. Did we set moderate risk goals? Did we utilize information on our success or failure? Then we began to dig into the more fundamental value issues that were involved. Suppose that we could use games like the paper plane construction to teach students the characteristics of a high achiever and through a variety of such exercises could actually train him to think and act as one. Was that a good thing? Did we want to subject our students to the pressure that we had felt? Could we decide that achievement training was good for some students who were not achieving up to our standards and bad for those who were too competitive? On what basis?

Just as researchers are becoming involved in the practical questions of education, so clinical psychotherapy is getting up off its couch and finding ways to add its skill to solving school problems. Dr. Carl Rogers, founder of client-centered therapy, is presently working with Western Behavioral Sciences Institute and a group of Catholic schools to devise ways to use "sensitivity groups" in the schools. (A sensitivity group or T-group is composed of about a dozen people who meet for the purpose of giving feedback on how each person's behavior affects the other people in the group.) The National Training Laboratory, an associate of the National Education Association, is now running a year-round series of T-groups and related experiences for teachers and administrators. And in San Diego, child psychiatrist Dr. Harold Bissell and educator Dr. Uvalo Palomares have set up the Human Development Training Institute, which has written a two-year sequence of lesson plans to improve a primary-school child's self-confidence and awareness and has trained 1000 teachers to use it.

One of the most eclectic approaches in the clinical tradition is the project run by Dr. George Brown of the University of California at Santa Barbara. Brown's project, sponsored by the Ford Foundation through the ebullient Esalen Institution, utilizes many different approaches but particularly the theories of Gestalt therapy that attempt to get youth in touch with how they are feeling in the "here and now." With such theoretical orientations in their background, the teachers in Brown's project are encouraged to devise their own techniques to integrate academic with affective or emotional learning in order to achieve a more "humanistic education."

I joined the teachers at one of the monthly meetings where they learn about new ideas and share with each other the techniques they have developed. Gloria Siemons, a pretty first-grade teacher, was describing an exercise that she had first conducted with the entire class and then used when one child became angry at another. She lined the class up in two rows on the playground, had each child find a partner, put their hands up facing each other, and push.

Push they did, laughing all over the field—especially at their teacher, who was being pushed around in a circle by several of the bigger kids.

Later, when two kids got into an argument at recess, Mrs. Siemons simply asked them: "Are you angry now? Would you like to push?"

"Yes, I'm angry. I'm angry at him."

Both agreed to the contest, pushed for a minute as hard as they could, and then collapsed into each other's arms, giggling. Their anger was worked out, but without hurting each other.

"What would happen," I asked Mrs. Siemons, "if one kid pushed another hard enough to hurt him?"

"We have a rule about that: 'It's OK to be angry with someone and it's OK to push, but it's not OK to push him into the rosebush.' "

Good teachers, particularly good first-grade teachers such as Mrs. Siemons, have always responded to the emotional side of their students' lives, and it is precisely this intuitive gift that Dr. Brown is capitalizing on. By systematizing such techniques and relating them to a general theoretical framework, he and the teachers of his staff have begun to generate hundreds of ways to integrate the feelings of students with the regular curriculum taught from kindergarten to high school.

The techniques being developed, the dozens of programs, and the various theories differ in many respects, but they have several features in common. First, and most important, all of them deal in a very explicit and direct way with the student's feelings, interpersonal relations, or values. That they are so explicit and direct sets them apart from the vague protestations that schools have usually made about this area. While schools were concentrating on math, science, or English, they often ignored or actively suppressed feelings. The new programs make what was covert behavior the subject of overt discussion; they make the implicit explicit. They legitimize feelings, clarify them for the student, and suggest a variety of behaviors that he can use to express them. They do so on the assumption that these feelings exert a powerful effect on a student's behavior. If schools want to influence behavior, then it makes sense to deal directly with its major sources, not just with the binomial theorem, the gerund, or the Seventeenth Amendment.

A factor in the new field that often causes misunderstandings is that most of the programs use nonverbal experiences, either through physical expression and involvement or through art, sculpture, or music. For the most part, this involvement with the nonverbal is not antiverbal or antiintellectual. Nonverbal educational techniques are based on the obvious but little-utilized fact that a child learns most of his emotional response patterns at a very young age— before he can talk. His knowledge of love, rejection, anger, and need does not come through words but through his physical senses—touch, a flushed face, a gnawing in his stomach. Even later, when he begins to talk, the words he learns are *Mama, doggie, see*—words for things and actions, not feelings. Indeed, many children seem entirely unable to give a name to their current feelings—they have been taught how to say "I am bad," but not "I feel bad." Education that deals with feelings is often facilitated by skipping over the verbal labels that have been learned relatively late in life, regaining the other senses, and then reintegrating them with verbal thought and new behaviors.

Another common technique that causes confusion is the reliance of many of the programs on games, dramatic improvisations, and role-playing. Again, though those utilizing the techniques believe in fun and use of games, few of them are simply advocating "fun and games." Their interest stems from an insight into the learning process of small children. By playing games—house, fireman, office, war—little children learn what it will be like to be an adult and begin to develop their own style in that role. But our culture provides few such opportunities for older children or adolescents, even though the society is changing so fast that many of the response patterns they learned as three-year-olds may be no longer relevant, even dangerous. Games and improvisations allow a simulation of the self. While they are real and produce real emotions, their tightly defined limits provide a way to try out new behavior without taking the full consequences that might occur if the same action were performed in ordinary relationships.

There are answers for questions about nonverbal and gaming emphasis, but there are many other questions the programs raise for which there are no answers. At best, solutions will come slowly, and that is bound to produce tremendous strain in a time when events wait for no one. Many of these problems are already developing. Though Dr. Alschuler at Harvard and Dr. Willis Harmon at the Stanford Research Institute are both engaged in large surveys to find out what techniques and philosophies are presently being employed in the field, there is still no common theoretical base for the programs and very little research on their effectiveness. The Achievement Motivation Development Project has by far the most extensive research program, and Dr. Alschuler's experience with it has made him feel strongly about the need for additional evidence before program expansion.

We have very little hard evidence that programs in this new field accomplish much more than natural maturation. We have claims, promises, and fascinating anecdotes. But we should not institute these programs without first using the most sophisticated research techniques we have to improve them and explore their consequences.

In addition to unanswered questions about effectiveness, there are practical limitations to all of the programs. Few have done an adequate job of integrating their material with the usual skills and knowledge that everyone recognizes the schools must continue to teach. No attempt has yet been made to work together with the free-flowing academic programs (such as the Leicestershire movement), which seem natural complements. Though all of the projects I have discussed here stress their responsiveness to student concerns, it is not yet clear how they can do that and yet not be heavily dependent on the skills and personalities of a few teachers like Mrs. Siemons, who can both legitimize anger and make the rosebush out-of-bounds.

Politically, programs with both the potential and the liabilities of these are obvious hot potatoes. It is unclear as yet how projects designed by psychologists will fit in with current efforts toward more community control and what seems to be the resulting concentration on "teaching the basics." Even a mode of politics that is in consonance with the ideals and methods of the new programs is unknown, for the vision they present is often as utopian as that in George Leonard's exciting new book, *Education and Ecstasy.* [1968] How to get from here to there without waiting until 2001 is a complex political problem. Suppose, for instance, that a school district decided to adopt an entirely new curriculum and school organization based on the concepts I have been discussing. Would the teachers be able to change? Great care would have to be taken with their feelings and concerns, for not only are they as human as the children, but . . . they will strike if they feel they are being treated unfairly.

The most fundamental problem, and the one likely to get people the most upset, is the ethical question caused by changing the expectations of what schools are for. At present, students go to school to "learn stuff," and though they may expect schools to provide information, they do not expect schools to change them in any fundamental way or even to offer that opportunity. As long as schools continue to have relatively little explicitly acknowledged impact on the students' values, attitudes, and behaviors, no one is likely to worry much about ethical issues. If schools consciously begin to make important changes in students' lives, people will suddenly become very concerned about what is happening to immature minds that are forced to accept this kind of education for twelve years. They will begin to ask whether there should be compulsory education, or whether students should be free to accept or reject schooling. And they will begin to ask hard questions about what should be taught and how it should be presented.

If, for instance, all children should be motivated, should they also be "achievement motivated?" At what age? Who decides? And who teaches? What is to stop teachers from working out of their own needs rather than for those of their pupils? Should teachers who share an important confidence have the same legal privilege which a lawyer or a minister has? How can parents and children be assured of the privacy that is their right?

The ethical problems are likely to be compounded by the reporting of the mass media. The new field is peculiarly open to parody ("Harvard Prof Teaches Paper Airplane Construction") and to easy association with the exotic and erotic. *Life* . . . stuck a single misleading paragraph on Brown's project into a long article on Esalen Institute. By far the most arresting thing in the article was a two-page picture spread on a nude sensitivity group that had nothing to do with either Brown's project or Esalen.) Sensational publicity is not what the new field needs. It does need the time, the careful research and planning, and the critical reporting that will allow it to grow or decline on its merits. The alternative is a series of fads (created by ignorance and publicity) and death—after a short and enthusiastic life—in disillusionment.

The new programs are too important to allow that to happen. They are delicate, and they are moving into an area that is fundamentally new, so they can be expected to suffer from the attention they attract, to make mistakes, and to run into blind alleys. If it takes the big curriculum-development corporations a million dollars and three years to build a single course in science or social studies, it will be even more difficult to build a fully developed curriculum in a new field. But the effort should be encouraged, for while it may not be novel to assert that a man's feelings are a crucial determinant of his public behavior and private well-being, there is no question about the novelty and significance of school programs that explicitly educate both the feelings and the intellect. Such programs raise many of society's basic questions about purpose and meaning—tough questions, which will not be easy to answer. But they also offer a possibility for building a saner world—a world where people are more open about their feelings, careful in their thinking, and responsible in their actions.

American education is just emerging from a decade of developing a variety of organizational reforms. During this period, educational personnel, time, space, and curricula have all been reorganized. Instructional staffs have been made interdisciplinary teams; "differentiated staffing" has been invented; the usefulness of subgrouping students into small learning teams has been rediscovered. A variety of forms of flexible scheduling have been devised, so that time can be more closely controlled by students and teachers. A variety of previously unavailable instructional spaces have been created—large-group audiovisual spaces, small discussion classrooms, learning laboratories especially designed for individualized instruction, project rooms, workrooms, student–teacher planning rooms, media centers, and open, flexible, carpeted multiuse rooms. The curriculum has provided options for individuals and small "learning teams" to progress at their own rate and make their own choices. The "contract" has been rediscovered. Independent study, the minicourse, and diagnostic and prescriptive teaching have come into their own.

Excellent progress has thus been made in learning how to reorganize schools so that innovation becomes possible. But reorganization—even schoolwide reorganization—is not enough. Many administrators, teachers, and students are discovering that there is little difference in coercing a person in a conventional classroom or in a learning laboratory; that people can be inhumane to one another whether or not the school is on a flexible schedule; that communication gaps can still persist even after organizational barriers to open communications have been removed.

While innovators have been concentrating on organizational innovations, they have been neglecting a significant body of research on the effect of learning climate on the individual. The term *climate,* as I use it, means the aggregate of social and cultural conditions that influence individual behavior in the school—all of the forces to which the individual responds that are present in the school environment.

School Climate Improvement

Eugene R. Howard

When we speak of schools having a warm or cold atmosphere, we are referring to climate. For some time we have felt differences among classrooms and schools, but we have done little to identify characteristics of school climate and even less to modify climate purposely.

"Closed" authoritarian environments, such as exist in many schools and classrooms, condemn learners to continuing criticism, sarcasm, discouragement, and failure; self-confidence, aspiration (for anything but escape), and a healthy self-concept are destroyed. [Watson, 1960-1961] Whitehead called this kind of process *soul murder*.

Learners condemned to such relentless failure learn only that they cannot learn; their anger and distress is frequently vented against the system and the society that has inflicted this inhumane punishment on them. We know how to identify teachers who inflict such environments on their students, but we continue to sentence students to such teachers for a year at a time, often in spite of protests from both students and parents.

We know that an "open," humane climate [Watson, 1960-1961] can stimulate learner initiative and creativity and encourage attitudes of self-confidence, originality, self-reliance, enterprise, and independence. Such a climate appears to be conducive to high academic achievement as well. [Silberman, 1970] Yet most schools do not offer parents and students the alternative of learning in such environments over a period of time. Assignments of pupils to teachers who create such learning environments is typically by chance, not by choice.

We know that the grading and ranking systems in most schools are harmful and irrational. [Kirschenbaum, 1971] We know that success motivates and that a student's self-image is a vital factor in motivating him to learn. Yet we continue to use grading and ranking systems that virtually insure that half the students perceive of themselves as below average and that thousands of the nation's children see themselves as failures by the age of ten.

We know that emotions play an important role in motivation [Watson, 1960-1961], that a warm, secure, loving relationship with others is essential to effective learning. Yet we build schools that physically resemble hospitals, jails, and insane asylums—emotionally sterile environments organized so that the formation of meaningful human relationships within the school environment is difficult or impossible.

We know that people are more likely to be motivated to learn if they have something to say about what and how they will learn. We also know that students vary widely in their ability, range of interest, learning style, energy level, and degree of motivation. Yet we give the same assignment to everyone in a group and expect it to be completed by everyone at the same time.

Learning is a human, personal, emotional process as well as an intellectual one. Our schools must be, in a sense, deinstitutionalized. They must be made safe for creative people—both students and staff members. They must become places where people can communicate with one another across racial, age, sex, and organizational barriers; where people can have progressively more control over what they learn and how they will learn; where each individual, with his beliefs, his feelings, his ambitions, and his hang-ups becomes a part of the curriculum. We must recognize that people who haven't learned about themselves find it difficult or impossible to learn about anything else.

We have not yet learned how to build a humane school—a school for self-actualization—such as is described by Carl Rogers [1969], Arthur Combs [Association for Supervision and Curriculum Development, 1962], and George Leonard [1968], among others. The new frontier for innovation in the seventies is the humane learning environment. We already know from a variety of research sources what some of the characteristics of such an environment should be.

A good place to start might be the launching of a variety of climate-improving projects of limited scope in a variety of settings. A small number of schools are initiating such a project in Denver, Colorado, sponsored by CFK Ltd., a small educational foundation. The foundation has published two papers that offer suggestions to schools desiring to plan climate-improvement projects. [Howard and Jenkins, n.d.; Fox et al., n.d.]

Six (a partial list) of the most important characteristics of an open climate for learning, as defined by CFK Ltd., follow.

1. Open Communication Channels.   The open-climate school is characterized by frequently used communications lines, which cross **age, class, clique, racial,** religious, sex, and hierarchical barriers. Such barriers in closed-climate schools frequently separate the faculty members and the students into competing, hostile camps.

2. Provisions for Widespread Involvement in Decision Making and Problem Solving.   An important characteristic of the open climate is a variety of provisions for widespread participation by students, staff, interested parents, and others in improving the institution. Each within the institution must be involved in shaping the part of the institution that affects him most.

3. Group and Institutional Norms, Beliefs, and Values.   All societies, including school, function on the basis of group and institutional norms, beliefs, and values. Part of this norm-belief-value system may be written as a part of the school's philosophy or as a part of student or staff handbooks. A very important part of this system, however, is unwritten. The unwritten system—typically the more influential—may be inconsistent with the written one. There also may be inconsistencies between the institution's stated norms, beliefs, and value systems and the operating systems within each subgroup. People within an institution behave more positively if the school's norm-belief-value systems are consistent and well understood.

4. Pluralistic Performance Expectations.   Performance expectations of the institution, as expressed by the administrators to other staff members and by teachers to students, constitute an important part of the institution's climate.

In the open-climate school, such expectations are reasonably flexible and consider individual differences; individuals are frequently encouraged to set their own performance goals. The open-climate, humane school does not ask people to do things they are not able to do.

5. Rules and Regulations.   Rules and regulations constitute an important part of a school's climate, affecting, as they must, the behavior of everyone within it. In the humane school, they are clearly stated, and they are viewed as reasonable by those who are affected by them. Some of the institution's rules and regulations are stated, others implied. Ideally, such rules and regulations should be consistent throughout the school—for the institution (as expressed in handbooks and so on) and within both formal and informal subgroups.

6. Pluralistic Reward–Punishment System.   Reward and punishment systems that minimize punishment and emphasize the positive reinforcement of institution-supporting behavior are more likely to foster positive attitudes toward the institution than are systems that primarily emphasize punishment and fear of punishment. An open-climate school provides a wide variety of ways for staff and students to be productive and successful and a wide variety of rewards for successful behavior.

School-improvement projects can be designed to open communications within the school, to encourage widespread involvement in decision making and problem solving, to identify the school's belief and value systems (philosophy), to broaden the school's performance expectations, to clarify the school's stated and unstated rules and regulations, and to humanize the school's reward and punishment systems. These projects differ from organizational innovating; they deal with modifying the basic nature of the institution, not with merely rearranging and reshaping its components. Some of the following projects may stimulate your thinking about how to open up the climate in your school:
1. Deemphasize hierarchy by organizing nonhierarchical teaching teams instead of the hierarchical ones commonly suggested. Further facilitate communications across hierarchical barriers by developing a "flat" organizational plan designed to encourage decentralized decision making.
2. Decrease the amount of staff time presently invested in "snob appeal" activities, which emphasize conformity and competition. Increase the amount of staff time devoted to developing activities for students who are generally considered "out of it." Open membership on the student council to anyone who has an idea for improving the school and is willing to work on it.
3. Develop projects to include students' evaluation of their own work.
4. Replace the present achievement-recognition system with one that emphasizes immediate and widespread rewards for tasks well done.
5. Form a group to rewrite the school's philosophy statement and its book of rules and regulations so that what the school stands for is clearly understood by everyone and so that institutional beliefs are translated into reasonable rules.

6. Revise the school's grading and reporting systems so that everyone experiences some success every day.
7. Form discussion groups designed to foster open communications, mutual respect, and understanding. These can be held either in school or in outside settings.
8. Form a group of students to make a study of the inconsistencies between what the school's philosophy statement says and the manner in which the school's programs operate.
9. Interview a group of the school's "losers" and listen carefully to their description of how school affects their attitudes toward themselves and others. Form a task force to do something about at least one of the concerns expressed by the losers' group.

This list is designed to assist the reader in understanding the kinds of innovative practices I am advocating. These projects are limited in scope, but they would modify, at least to a small extent, the climate of the school. Perhaps if a number of smaller projects can be implemented successfully, the students and staff can begin to value the climate improvement activities and feel confident enough to launch a comprehensive program designed to modify all of the characteristics that keep their school's climate closed.

It is now possible to build a school climate within which students and staff will be happier, more mentally healthy, more positive in their outlook on life, and more productive. Some of our alternative schools have come close to achieving this goal, and a few other schools have started to move vigorously in this direction. Very little, however, has really been done to humanize our schools—this is the challenge of the seventies.

I guess I know more about myself after these two years than ever before. That probably sums it up. With a free atmosphere there's a real chance for knowledge of self and academic subject matter. The only limits are your motivation and interests. Maybe I've heard that before, but I never knew it so well as I do now.

Shirley Geerdes, Teacher

Buena Vista Annex has been called an experimental school, an alternative school, an unusual school. In fact, it is a public school that serves the children of many ethnic minority and poor white families. Traditional means of education have failed increasing numbers of these children in cities each year. We opened Buena Vista Annex on the premise that by using what we knew and what we had available within our school district, we could provide an improved learning environment for these children. We wanted to prove that a school could provide quality education without expensive hardware, packaged programs, and gimmicks so that improved education for city children need not rely upon the random gifts of the federal government. We believed we could prove this because faculty members, parents, the community, and the children wanted it and would work for it. We found quality education simply by using the full potential of the involved human beings.

Buena Vista Annex became a possibility at a time when our school district and the entire city were facing the prospect of court-ordered elementary school desegregation. Ten portable classrooms were to facilitate integration in our district. We saw this as a possibility for providing a fourth- to sixth-grade school dedicated to the principles of integration, teacher excellence and accountability, community participation, personalized instruction, self-motivated learning, remediation in basic skills, differentiated staffing, faculty (rather than administrative) leadership, and new ways of using the traditional school site. We sought teachers who were already committed to these principles; teachers were essential to the success of our school. We wanted

---

Buena Vista Annex

The Process As Product

Beverly Carmody and Cora Meek

teachers who recognize the importance of the uniquely human relationship that exists between children and teachers. We didn't want groovy young teachers with the latest fads to try out. The teachers must be committed to teaching children basic skills without compromising the school's goals. In this way we would make every effort to ensure that children would be able to be themselves, develop at their own rates, and yet still learn.

We knew that the adults as well as the students had to be allowed sufficient freedom in which to work and learn. We believed that teachers must be learners alongside their students, an important variable in ensuring a successful school. Part of the freedom to do this was provided by simply not having an administrator on site. The following quote from our school clerk provides insight into how people feel when this essential idea is implemented:

Your program extends itself to include awareness of staff needs as well as student and teacher needs. In all other school situations where I have worked, a caste system existed, separating teachers from all other personnel. One was made aware of the separation that existed between the credentialed human being and the subhuman, noncredentialed being. Not so at Buena Vista Annex, where all are treated with the same respect.... Since coming to Buena Vista Annex, I've never been tuned out. I personally have not experienced elsewhere such a feeling of fulfillment [before] in a job.

In August 1971 we had ten classroom teachers, two resource teachers, and a part-time district social worker, all committed to the basic philosophy and goals of our school. Each viewed the prospect of a humane school from his own unique perspective. One said:

Buena Vista Annex meant that I would be leaving a very oppressive ghetto school where I was neither happy, or satisfied. The prospect of being responsible for a new school was a lot to handle, but I felt it was much better than what I had known.... This is the first school where an entire faculty seems to believe in the righteousness of children—believe in children, period. At first I had to be sure that this so-called alternative situation was not just a cop-out—I mean, not just a way to contain minority and poor children and then not offer or deliver to them the necessary skills that are needed to function fully and successfully in this society.

Thus, major hopes and concerns were expressed freely from the outset.

We spent our first year painfully establishing human relationships and trust between teachers and children. Our second year began with children and teachers wanting and needing a carefully designed teacher-directed program. In the middle of our second year we found children making it clear that they wanted and expected to be full partners in determining the nature of their learning experience. They were becoming capable of scheduling their days and designing their own academic programs. They were choosing appropriately challenging materials from the learning environment. They began to understand our school environment, because early in the year we stated expectations and requirements for them that they could accept.

Relationships and Trust In the first stage we began to make a workable reality out of our dreams. To do this, we spent a week of intensive discussion, which was not always calm and rational and was often painful. Our discussion was sufficiently honest to establish for us a vehicle for continuing interaction—one that allowed for personal idiosyncrasies, philosophies, moralities, talents, strengths, and weaknesses.

In our first workshop we addressed mainly teacher and child attitudes, centering on the children. We did not want to perpetuate useless traditional rules and methods; we had all experienced their futility in previous teaching assignments. We wanted children to (a) feel good about themselves, (b) know their assets, (c) realize their limitless potentials, (d) make productive use of their energy, (e) be able to make decisions, (f) be aware of self and others, (g) recognize the kinship of all living things, (h) master basic academic skills, and (i) have the ability to adjust to change.

Our discussion on behavior in the school yard illustrates the way we attempted to integrate principle and practice. We tried to develop yard rules that met stated behavioral objectives and emphasized safety and attitude but were not based on moral judgments. We expected each person to acknowledge the rights and freedoms of others while experiencing his own, and to show that in his actions.

We thought that specific yard rules should be determined by the limiting physical circumstances and by the personalities of the children at different school sites. We spent a good deal of time anticipating how we would handle specific crisis behavior situations, such as fights or other activities, that violated our basic standard or threatened physical harm. We envisioned solving these problems through discussions, once we had removed a child from an upsetting situation. Teachers who had previously experienced success at this volunteered their support to teachers who were afraid that they would not be able to break up fights without having an administrator to rely upon. Our concern at this point was to find workable alternatives to suspensions and other punitive measures—the ordinarily accepted means for dealing with problem situations, which do not represent solutions.

We had previously decided to have nongraded classes. This meant that fourth-, fifth-, and sixth-grade children were to be mixed together in all ten classrooms. Realizing that parents and children would need help understanding this important academic difference from other schools, we tried to state clearly our reasons for this decision. Our main reason for considering ungraded classes advantageous was that they forced teachers to look at the individual abilities and needs of each child, regardless of his age or grade. The teacher could then set realistic goals for each child and provide a wide range of necessary learning materials for him.

Since we knew we were going to operate without an on-site administrator, we began the process of running the school as a group through the division of administrative responsibilities. We devised a rotation system for a head teacher to handle monthly administrative duties and crisis situations. We identified ongoing responsibilities and divided them among ourselves on a yearly basis, thus providing the necessary continuity required in many administrative areas, such as in budgets, requisitions, schedules, lunches, Central Office dealings, parent meetings, community services, and so on. In spite of this additional work for teachers, running the school cooperatively provided us enough compensation in personal autonomy that the tasks were handled willingly. It also forced us to face living with our decisions, reevaluating them when necessary.

Thus, we used our workshop to determine cooperatively ways to run a school consonant with our assumptions about the needs of children.

Immediately after this workshop we were challenged with putting our ideas in motion. We opened school for 275 students. Most of our students had come from schools where subtle or nonsubtle threats of punishment were made when children violated the dictates of the adult system. We had all seen and expected various modes of wounded behavior such as open hostility, indifference, and lack of self-discipline. What we had not expected was the intensity of these behaviors and the fact that they seemed to have been catalyzed by our carefully thought-out positions. The frequency of fights overwhelmed us. The blood-thirsty mobs that quickly surrounded the fights became tactical problems we were not prepared to handle. The same children who were fighting in the yard were major problems in our nonauthoritarian classrooms.

We held a crisis meeting. We decided that everyone would be on yard duty at all times, so that enough people were present to handle the situation in keeping with our original goals. We determined to help children understand their motivations through class and individual discussions. We shared our knowledge of children in our classrooms with the rest of the faculty members so all of us could identify effective ways of handling different children consistently. We remained adamant about adhering to our human values.

Most classrooms that first year were close to the open-classroom idea, with lots of materials and choices of activities provided for the children. Many children felt incapable of making decisions for themselves and manifested their resentments at this expectation. They felt uncomfortable making choices and wanted to be told what to do. In spite of these attitudes, with which we had to deal throughout the first year, we held firm to our beliefs that children were to be a part of the decision making that determined their individual curricula.

From Fights to Phonics   The first year was difficult for all of us. It was hard to face the problem of setting limits as fully as was necessary because we didn't want to violate our basic principles. We were timid about asserting our needs as adults functioning in an *institution*; in fact, we resented thinking of our school as one. This had mixed blessings. It kept our human values alive, and it made us available to children and parents as human beings. But it also prevented us from facing some of our legitimate needs and those of the children and the parents.

When we came back for the next year's preschool workshop, we were whole-heartedly ready to face the problem of limit-setting, because we felt good about teaching children; we had changed many self-destructive behavior patterns; and we had successfully worked together to run the school. Since we were building upon the previous year's positive outcomes, we felt strong enough to tackle the problems. We were ready to look critically at the school's program and the ways in which it met or failed to meet the children's apparent needs.

The tremendous input in the domain of human problems that almost exhausted us that first year made feasible the development of a set of behavior rules for the coming year. These were made available to all the children and parents. Our rules made clear the behavior we would not permit at school. We no longer wanted to expend our energies as we had the previous year.

Since we had ungraded classrooms and each teacher knew that he would have many of the same children the following year, we began a school and individual class evaluation. We decided that improvement in reading and math skills needed to be top priority for our second year. Knowing that we would have Title I funds for materials and personnel, we proceeded to develop a total school program based on the specific needs of our students.

The heart of our program was based on setting long-range behavioral objectives for each child in each subject through the use of diagnostic testing. Testing and evaluation of these behavioral objectives would be continued throughout the year. The objectives would be accomplished through individual and small-group instruction, with each child beginning at a level at which he could succeed. In addition, the total staff and auxiliary personnel planned weekly in-service meetings to continuously reevaluate teaching methods, curriculum content, and individual children's needs.

A high degree of one-to-one and small-group work was made possible by carefully designed class-management systems, in which children were to get daily experience in independent work, manipulative activities, and small-group learning. We believed that skills are best learned when approached from many directions. The child might first be exposed to a skill through the use of various games. Then he would work in a small group, receiving formal instruction from the teacher or paraprofessional aide. Next, he might be given independent written work. When the teacher felt the child had mastered a skill, he would administer a brief oral or written evaluative test. If the child showed mastery, a record would be made on a sequential skill-growth chart so that the teacher could know at a glance exactly what each child had mastered. If the child had not mastered the skill at this point, he would try again with new activities and different materials.

To make sure that children were provided with all the materials necessary for this type of program, and in order to allow teachers to plan in depth, six classroom teachers paired in three teams: one teacher taught reading to his class and another class (while the other prepared materials); at those times the other teacher taught math to both classes. To accommodate this system, morning classes ran in two ninety-minute time blocks. The four other classroom teachers had chosen to teach both subjects to their classes.

In the afternoons each teacher covered the remainder of the subjects with his own class—social studies, ethnic studies, science, health, art, music, physical education, and so on. The programs of each classroom depended on the interests and talents of both teachers and students. This program worked efficiently in general operations, in skill teaching, and in classroom discipline, because we knew each other and two-thirds of the children so well.

We believed that to run a child-centered classroom, children should be given what they need. For some it may be traditional workbooks and for others, projects. If a teacher had basic goals that were important enough to work toward, he could be successful only by working from where children were, not where he thought they ought to be. For example, some children need to "play school" because they were not successful at the game before. In a child-centered classroom, they could play the game well because the pressure was removed and the proper materials were available. These children wanted assignments that looked like respectable schoolwork. Success at basic tasks gave them the self-respect that had been denied them through years of failure and frustration. We took pains to provide an abundance of skill-correlated manipulative materials. These children used them to humor us, while they really wanted traditional materials as they began to feel academically successful. So we found that one aspect of true individualization is taking into account the children's concept of what school should be at a given point in their lives.

We observed children enjoying the process of discovering their interests and conquering skill obstacles that were previously insurmountable to them. We are still not at the point where all children are ready to accept that they can be happy at school when they are mastering a skill or pursuing an interest. Some still have to hold on to the position that school is work, not fun—that learning is separate from, not a part of, their growing. They had needed to adopt this position to ensure their personal integrity against an educational system that did not allow for their uniqueness. But some children have been able to let these defenses completely go.

Trust and Learning   About halfway into the semester we started getting messages from the children that they were bored and pressured or simply somewhat dissatisfied with the status quo. Many children were simply arriving at one of the basic goals we had set at the outset—they felt free to communicate their dissatisfactions and question what was happening to them. Some children verbalized their feelings; others let you know that school was losing meaning for them by falling off in their work or by having behavior difficulties. Increasing numbers of our students are now verbalizing their questions.

There need to be several ways to help children when they reach this stage of dissatisfaction. Some children and teachers can use established channels for dialogue. Other children need help getting back in touch with themselves and with parental expectations in order to regain their balance. We try to hold conferences with the child and parents when possible. In other cases, where dissatisfaction is expressed, the teacher and the child work out joint schedules and contracts to increase the child's production level to a point where he can feel good about himself again. Children are often incapacitated by feelings of

Stage Three

guilt and fear of reprisal when they are not working up to expectation. We do a grave injustice to these children when we don't provide them with sufficient structure and alternatives within which to work.

We are convinced that we have an exciting program. We've made many mistakes and learned much in the process. We are still convinced that our vision of collective leadership, classroom options, clear limits, and efficacious skill development can work. We've charted our direction; with continual self-criticism and refinement of our system, we hope to proceed on course.

In regular school the time you think the class is most together is when they're sitting there hating the teacher all at once.

The perceptive student who wrote this was describing the "unite-against-the-common-enemy" syndrome so common to many classrooms where the student feels powerless, in which the curriculum prescribes a course quite apart from the individual needs of the students, and in which teacher knows student and student knows other students only in the most superficial way, roles shrouded in authoritarian or competitive behaviors.

The "togetherness" suggested by our student writer is both negative and illusory. Students in such a classroom jockey for status at the expense of their peers. Their unity is mainly the product of their common alienation and distrust.

Teachers, too, are drawn into a similar bind. Forced to defend their positions of superiority, they isolate themselves from students and colleagues alike lest their power be threatened. In a faculty lunchroom or in a hallway meeting between classes it is not unusual to hear a teacher describe a particularly nonconforming student in angry terms, vowing that the offender will be "put in his place" or "taken down a peg."

All too often the regular school classroom becomes the stage for a power play enacted unwittingly by "we-they" teams on a "win-lose" basis, which in reality is inevitably resolved with a "lose-lose" denouement. The student writer

Community High School

Jay Manley

continues, however:

> But in the Project there was an entirely different feeling. The class felt responsible for what happened.

Another student wrote:

> To me, the most important thing wasn't material. It was a feeling of warmth and, if not always understanding, at the very least acceptance. It's an unusual feeling to find in any fair-sized group, especially one in which all the participants come from such varied backgrounds as we do.

And another:

> There was a feeling that everybody, teachers especially, wanted you to do well. That's the kind of atmosphere in which people can really work.

These students were describing their feelings at the conclusion of the six-week Berkeley Summer Project conducted in 1967. The Project was a humanistically oriented program, providing an integrated curriculum in art, dance, drama, and communication skills, plus broad opportunities for student-initiated project work. Central to it was the development, in each participant, of trust and caring for his fellows. The Project served as a pilot model for what was to become the first alternative school in the Berkeley public system, Community High School.

The contrast between the destructively competitive and isolating atmosphere of the regular school classroom and a dream of what a cooperative and collaborative learning place could be brought me and a group of like-minded teachers together to articulate and activate our visions by trying out a new kind of school. We believed that a school should be the setting only for "win–win" relationships and interactions characterized by continual experimentation, collaboration, and individual growth. The setting in which positive relationships could prevail would need several basic components in terms of size, student population, class offerings, and governance.

The 3000-student Berkeley High School seemed to us an enormous, impersonal structure promoting anonymity, in which flexibility in curriculum, scheduling, and student–teacher interaction was virtually impossible. Therefore, Community High School was designed to operate as a school-within-a-school, an enclave that would primarily develop operational strategies for the cliched (but seldom-realized) concepts of individualization, personalization, and community.

Beginning with 120 tenth-grade students, the program expanded over three years to 300 students, representing grades ten through twelve. The student body was a heterogeneous cross-section of the high-school population in academic ability, race, and sex. Community High School provided a remarkably comprehensive program, yet it permitted students to take highly specialized courses in the regular school. Like the Summer Project, our program had a heavy emphasis on an experiential arts curriculum, as well as provision for wide opportunities for individual and collaborative project work.

Two main principles were established for Community High School: the first was the development of a sense of community and commitment to the needs of the group. The second was the development of individual autonomy and independent thought and action.

In support of the first goal, frequent common activities were offered, including field trips, picnics, and classes oriented in interdependence, such as drama and dance. We paid special attention to the quality of teacher–student, student–student, and teacher–teacher relationships and tried to enrich them by small class sizes, regular student–staff planning and evaluation of all aspects of school operation, a curriculum centered on student interests and concerns, and staff and student discussion and reaction groups. **Community**

Our dual goals were also furthered, as well as tested, by **an interesting system** of "tribes," which were set up within the school when it grew too large for effective town meetings. These tribes—subgroups within our school—offered their members a complete set of classes and were home centers for social activities.

Students were initially assigned to tribes on the basis of having a rich mix of students and thus a tremendous source of energy, ideas, and values—generally lost in the "tracking" of the regular school. But many students and staff determined that the first tribes were too shapeless and lacking in coherent design. Consequently the next tribes were centered on themes, and both students and staff were permitted to choose their own tribe. Thus, the Art and Media Tribe attracted students interested in the arts, film, and photography; the Communications Tribe drew on students concerned with creative writing, drama, and journalism; and so on.

Such subdivisions served individual interests well and created close communication and interaction, but they also limited the broad involvement that was one of the original goals. In this case, individual student needs were not necessarily compatible with broad group needs.

While we envisioned the values of community and autonomy in a nonexclusive relationship, our experience indicated that they generally existed in a sort of natural tension, and a balance between the two was often difficult to maintain. That balance came to be an important dynamic in our program, one that continually demanded our time and energy. At the risk of oversimplification, I would say that the community–autonomy scale is roughly equivalent to a responsibility–freedom scale, responsibility to the group conflicting with freedom to pursue individual interests. So while the dynamic was difficult and frustrating to handle, we were dealing with perhaps the major value conflict of man in a social setting.

When students share in decisions regarding how a class is conducted and how the school is run, a sense of community is fostered. Many classes operated on a contract basis: students and teachers negotiated a study arrangement for a given period of time. The traditional, computerized, grading system soon discontented both staff and students. The grading system implicated many other systems, such as college admissions, transcripts, scholarship application, and so on, as well as tenacious parent and student values. Everyone voiced dislike of grading, but when it came to acting on that concern, few were really prepared to do away with it. Since students and teachers were positively united in their discontent, our solution was to expand grading into a concept of assessment and evaluation in a way that supported our community and "win–win" concerns. We instituted an optional "pass or no credit" system, and we developed a system of student–teacher conferences and written evaluations. We were thus able to deemphasize quantitative grading while stressing qualitative assessment. These processes consumed a huge amount of staff and student time, but nearly all of us felt that this two-way sharing of insights was perhaps the single most valuable instrument for promoting and evaluating student and staff growth.

Parents were involved in the school community also by means of school workshops, opportunities to teach in the school, frequent and well-attended parent meetings, family potlucks, and a regular program newsletter. Parents were so closely involved that significant numbers of them could be mobilized on short notice when the school needed intervention or support in dealings with the high-school administration or the Board of Education.

Autonomy

In support of autonomy, the second goal, we provided highly individualized curricular paths, including student-initiated and student-taught classes, one-to-one tutorials, and independent-study arrangements. For example, one student wanted an oceanography class. Since we had no one able to teach that class, he decided to teach it himself. With a class size of two, he and his student developed a remarkable course. Two other students studied Tai-Chi-Chuan for several semesters with one of our regular staff; they later taught sections of the class themselves. One student with a fierce interest in science and a loathing for literature classes, especially reading, took the dreaded subject as an independent study with one of our staff in whom he had particular trust. Through weekly tutorials on a one-to-one basis he moved from *Scientific American* and other technical journals to a point where he was reading a good deal of literature, including the poetry of Yeats, at the year's end.

Integrating Community and Autonomy

Both community involvement and autonomy were furthered by experimentation with a number of governance and decision-making structures. Ranging from "town meetings" to representative councils, all were designed to bring students and teachers into a partnership in determining priorities and procedures for the school and to help each individual develop confidence and strength within a group. Student–staff committees (nearly always with a majority of students) screened candidates for open staff positions, determined budget allocations, wrote grant proposals, and so forth. Major decisions, such as electing a director for the school, were done by a total community vote on a one-man, one-vote basis. Although on some issues staff technically had the power, students' votes always counted equally. When necessary, they were apprised of the legal limitations under which everyone had to operate.

We learned that readiness and personal development were significant in handling competing interests. Some students were unable to invest in the group; their personal agenda had to be accommodated first. Other students needed to build a security within the group before they could extend themselves as individuals. Still other students possessed, from the outset, the maturity to function effectively both within the group and individually. Finally, all students alternated in their group and individual centeredness.

As their needs and moods changed, so would their interpersonal patterns. One student praised "the flexibility allowing one to work out emotional crises and dead periods. . . . There needs [to be] an all-day, all-year-round growing period for one's education to be complete." We discovered that personal development, like any important learning, does not occur in smooth or predictable patterns. There are spurts and lulls, or "dead periods," and our school legitimized this irregular growth pattern.

If these dimensions of personal growth were cornerstones of our school, it should be noted that from the outset we had seen affective development as prerequisite to cognitive growth and consequently of even greater import, than cognitive mastery. We felt this way because the "win–lose" attitudes seemed rooted in denial and negation of feelings and emotions and appeared to limit and discourage academic and creative achievement as well as social growth. The solution, we thought, was simple: create a warm, supportive learning environment, and students will learn. Some students responses indicated that we were right:

Affect–Cognition: Another Integration

> I have found a new interest this semester—myself. Before I had trouble doing things by myself, without other people. But now I don't mind being alone, as I have really learned to like myself. I can do more things on my own; in short, I feel like I'm gaining my personal independence.
>
> It's a lot easier for me to set up and do big projects and really get involved in them than before. I find myself doing a lot more than I ever thought I could do. I don't have the feeling any more of being afraid that I'll be cut down when I say anything in a group. I can talk freely in a group now and I don't let certain remarks bother me. I have also put more effort into helping people, not only in our class but in the different tribes too.

As we worked through the first semesters, we learned that our assumption of the primacy of affective development was perhaps ill-founded and that, at least for some students, a rigorous although noncompetitive and nonjudgmental emphasis on cognitive growth was necessary for the student to feel good about himself. Our experience suggested that the relationship between affective and cognitive growth was not linear, but rather a circular or cyclical pattern; focus on affect supported effective learning; without increasing cognitive competence, however, significant effective growth was unlikely.

This interrelationship was described clearly and movingly by an evaluation letter written for Elizabeth Avakian, a gifted, creative, and exceedingly patient English teacher. She had worked throughout the year with a Black eleventh-grade male student. His response illuminates the deep-seated frustration and defenses she had to break through, in this case by means of a one-to-one tutorial class. His letter suggests the pain of failure and the avoidance mechanisms utilized to prevent further hurt through exposure. Finally, it reveals the undeniable impotence that results from felt inadequacy in the mastery of skills and competence considered basic to our way of life.

> This is what has happened to me in my time with you in your class. I have learned to read a lot better and write better. I have learned to communicate a lot better than what I had in the past. I have learned not to be ashamed of the way I read. If I read slow, so what? That's the way I read. I also feel that I still cannot spell very well, but I think that if I had a little more help and some more effort I could learn how to spell a lot better. The things that have not happened to me in Community High School: I have not found out who I am yet and I had hoped to find out that in this year, but it will have to come sometime later. I haven't changed at all. I am still me, but that me that I think that I am is not me; it's someone else. There have been some changes, come to think of it. I feel that I am a lot smarter than what I used to be. CHS has done a lot for me. They taught me things that no other school could ever teach me. I have learned how to talk to other people and how to say what I want to say and not have to think that what I say is stupid. I think that there should be more schools like the CHS. CHS made it possible for me to have a teacher for myself with no one else. CHS made it possible for me to learn how to read better than what I was. CHS showed me skills like photography and aikido. CHS has responded to my needs, showing me how to read.
>
> My experience in your class has been a lot of fun and I have enjoyed it but you have done things that lots of people said they could not do. You made the impossible happen for me. It's a really good feeling to come up to something and be able to read it and know that at some time you could not read it. It's a really good feeling.

Our errors and excesses at Community High School were many; our learning was sometimes painfully slow. But we did facilitate a "win–win" kind of interaction as well as significant learning for many students who had been rejected or who had ejected themselves from the regular school system. In addition, we were able to revitalize school life for many otherwise "successful" students who were simply bored in the regular school. We feel proud of that; it is that potential, I think, that in the short period of three years turned the high school around from a monolithic giant to a setting of seven alternative schools—each with a particular focus and style—including, as one alternative, the traditional school.

Our pioneering model acted as a catalyst for change, and it redirected attention to the fundamental resource of a learning place—its human relationships—in which both students and teachers win.

Understanding, acceptance, equality
Brown, Black, Yellow, Red, White
When people are people.

Good energy—satisfaction
Sensitivity, humor and truth
No jive authority.

Involvement
One to one basis
High on love.

good teaching happens when

Darlene Lockwood

Allport, Gordon W. *Becoming: Basic Considerations for a Psychology of Personality.* New Haven, Conn.: Yale University Press, 1955.

————. *The Nature of Prejudice.* Reading, Mass.: Addison-Wesley, 1954.

Alschuler, Alfred, ed. *New Directions in Psychological Education.* Educational Opportunities Forum. Albany, N.Y.: New York State Department of Education, 1969.

Anastasi, A. *Psychological Testing.* New York: Macmillan, 1968.

Appell, M. L. "Selected Student Reactions to Student-Centered Courses." Unpublished manuscript. Terre Haute, Ind.: State University of Indiana, 1959.

Assagioli, R. *Psychosynthesis: A Manual of Principles and Techniques.* New York: Hobbs-Dorman, 1965.

Association for Supervision and Curriculum Development. *Perceiving, Behaving, Becoming.* Edited by Arthur Combs. Washington, D.C.: National Education Association, 1962.

———— (1970 Yearbook Committee). *To Nurture Humaneness: Commitment for the 70s.* Edited by Mary-Margaret Scobey and Grace Graham. Washington, D.C.: National Education Association, 1970.

Axline, Virginia M. *Dibs: In Search of Self.* New York: Ballantine Books, 1964.

Back, K. W. "Stimulus Response: The Group Can Comfort but It Can't Cure." *Psychology Today* (December 1972).

Ballinger, S. "The Social Studies and Social Controversy." *School Review* (April 1963): 97–111.

Baratz, S., and Baratz, J. C. "Negro Ghetto Children and Urban Education: A Cultural Solution." *Social Education* 33 (1969): 401–405.

Baruch, Dorothy W. *One Little Boy.* New York: Dell, 1952.

Bay Area Radical Teachers' Organizing Collective. "No More Teachers' Dirty Looks." San Francisco, 1972.

Bennett, G. L. "Response to Robert Williams." *The Counseling Psychologist* 2 (1970): 88–89.

Berg, Stephen; Marks, S. J.; and Pilz, J. Michael. *Between People: A Reader for Open Learning.* Glenview, Ill.: Scott, Foresman, 1972.

Berne, Eric. *Games People Play: The Psychology of Human Relationships.* New York: Grove Press, 1964.

Bibliography

Bettelheim, Bruno. *Love Is Not Enough*. New York: Free Press, 1950.

Blos, Peter. *On Adolescence: A Psychoanalytic Interpretation*. New York: Free Press, 1962.

Borton, Terry. *Reach, Touch, and Teach*. New York: McGraw-Hill, 1970.

Brown, George Isaac. *Human Teaching for Human Learning: An Introduction to Confluent Education*. New York: Viking Press, 1971.

Brown, Roger. *Social Psychology*. New York: Free Press, 1965.

Bruner, Jerome S. *On Knowing: Essays for the Left Hand*. Cambridge, Mass.: Harvard University Press, 1962; New York: Atheneum, 1965.

———. *Process of Education*. Cambridge, Mass.: Harvard University Press, 1960.

———. *Toward a Theory of Instruction*. Cambridge, Mass.: Harvard University Press, Belknap Press, 1966.

Bull, Patricia. "Student Reactions, Fall 1965." Unpublished manuscript. Cortland, N.Y.: State University College, 1966.

Childs, John L. *Education and Morals*. New York: Appleton-Century-Crofts, 1950.

Clark, Donald H., and Kadis, Asya L. *Humanistic Teaching*. Columbus, Ohio: Charles E. Merrill, 1971.

Clark, Kenneth B. *Prejudice and Your Child*. Boston: Beacon Press, 1963.

Clemans, W. U. "A Note in Response to a Request by the Editor to Comment on R. L. Williams' Article." *The Counseling Psychologist* 2 (1970): 90–92.

Cole, Michelle, and Black, Stuart. *Checking It Out: Some Lower East Side Kids Discover the Rest of America*. New York: Dial Press, 1971.

Coleman, James S. *Equality of Educational Opportunity*. Washington, D.C.: U.S. Government Printing Office, 1966.

———. "How Do the Young Become Adults?" *Review of Educational Research* 42 (1972): 43.

Coles, Robert. *Children of Crisis: A Study of Courage and Fear*. New York: Dell, 1967.

Collins, Alice H. *The Lonely and Afraid: Counseling the Hard to Reach*. New York: Odyssey Press, 1969.

Commission on Tests. *Righting the Balance*. New York: College Entrance Examination Board, 1970.

Committee on Concepts and Values. *A Guide to Content in the Social Studies*. Washington, D.C.: National Council for the Social Studies, 1957.

Coopersmith, Stanley. *The Antecedents of Self-Esteem*. San Francisco: W. H. Freeman, 1967.

Corsini, Raymond I., and Howard, Daniel D., eds. *Critical Incidents in Teaching*. Englewood Cliffs, N.J.: Prentice-Hall, 1964.

Cremin, Lawrence A. *The Transformation of the School: Progressivism in American Education, 1876–1957*. New York: Vintage, 1961.

Cummings, Susan N., and Casney, John J., Jr. *Communication for Education.* Scranton, Pa.: Intext Educational Publishers, 1971.

Dawson, Helaine. *On the Outskirts of Hope: Educating Youth from Poverty Areas.* New York: McGraw-Hill, 1968.

Dennison, George. *The Lives of Children: The Story of the First Street School.* New York: Random House, 1969.

De Ropp, R. S. *The Master Game.* New York: Dell, 1968.

Drews, Elizabeth M. *Learning Together: How to Foster Creativity, Self-Fulfillment, and Social Awareness in Today's Students and Teachers.* Englewood Cliffs, N.J.: Prentice-Hall, 1972.

Egan, Gerard. *Encounter: Group Processes for Interpersonal Growth.* Belmont, Calif.: Wadsworth, Brooks/Cole Division, 1970.

Ellis, R. S. *The Psychology of the Individual.* New York: Appleton-Century-Crofts, 1928.

Erikson, Erik H. *Childhood and Society.* New York: Norton, 1963.

————. *Identity: Youth and Crisis.* New York: Norton, 1968.

————. *Insight and Responsibility: Lectures on the Ethical Implications of Psychoanalytic Insight.* New York: Norton, 1964.

Fader, Daniel. *The Naked Children.* New York: Bantam Books, 1971.

Fantini, Mario D., and Weinstein, Gerald. *The Disadvantaged: Challenge to Education.* New York: Harper and Row, 1968.

————. *Making Urban Schools Work.* New York: Holt, Rinehart and Winston, 1968.

Fenton, Edwin. *Teaching the New Social Studies in Secondary Schools: An Inductive Approach.* New York: Holt, Rinehart and Winston, 1966.

Festinger, Leon. "Behavioral Support for Opinion Change." *Public Opinion Quarterly* 28 (Fall 1964): 404–417.

————. *A Theory of Cognitive Dissonance.* Evanston, Ill.: Row, Peterson, 1957.

Foster, Marcus A. *Making Schools Work: Strategies for Changing Education.* Philadelphia: Westminster Press, 1971.

Fox, Robert S.; Brainard, E.; Carnie, G.; Georgiades, W.; Howard, G.; Kettering II, C. F.; and Olivero, J. *The Principal As Climate Leader.* Englewood, Colo.: CFK Ltd., n.d.

Fraiberg, Selma H. *The Magic Years: Understanding and Handling the Problems of Early Childhood.* New York: Charles Scribner's Sons, 1959.

Friedenberg, Edgar Z. *Coming of Age in America: Growth and Acquiescence.* New York: Vintage Books, 1967.

————. *The Dignity of Youth and Other Atavisms.* Boston: Beacon Press, 1965.

————. *The Vanishing Adolescent.* New York: Dell, 1959.

Gardner, John W. *Excellence: Can We Be Equal and Excellent Too?* New York: Harper and Row, Harper Colophon Books, 1962.

———. *Self-Renewal: The Individual and the Innovative Society*. New York: Harper and Row, Harper Colophon Books, 1965.

Gartner, Alan; Riessman, Frank; and Kohler, Mary C. *Children Teach Children: Learning by Teaching*. New York: Harper and Row, 1971.

Gibson, William. *The Miracle Worker*. New York: Knopf, 1957.

Ginott, H. G. *Between Parent and Teen-ager*. New York: Avon Books, 1969.

Glasser, William. *Schools Without Failure*. New York: Harper and Row, 1969.

Goodman, Paul. *Compulsory Miseducation and the Community of Scholars*. New York: Random House, Vintage Books, 1962.

Gordon, Thomas. *Parent Effectiveness Training: The "No-Lose" Program for Raising Responsible Children*. New York: Peter H. Wyden, 1970.

Gorman, Alfred H. *Teachers and Learners: The Interactive Process in Education*. Boston: Allyn and Bacon, 1969.

Goslin, D. A. *Teachers and Testing*. New York: Russell Sage Foundation, 1967.

Green, Hannah. *I Never Promised You a Rose Garden*. New York: Holt, Rinehart and Winston, 1964.

Halpern, F. C. "Clinicians Must Listen!" *Clinical Child Psychology Newsletter* 9 (Winter 1970-1971): 8.

Hart, Harold H. *Summerhill: For and Against*. New York: Hart, 1970.

Hentoff, Nat. *Our Children Are Dying*. New York: Viking Press, 1966.

Herndon, James. *The Way It Spozed to Be*. New York: Bantam Books, 1969.

Hickerson, Nathaniel. *Education for Alienation*. Englewood Cliffs, N.J.: Prentice-Hall, 1966.

Hilgard, Ernest R. *Theories of Learning*. New York: Appleton-Century-Crofts, 1956.

Hodgkinson, Harold L. *Education, Interaction, and Social Change*. Englewood Cliffs, N.J.: Prentice-Hall, 1967.

Holt, John. *How Children Fail*. New York: Delta, 1966.

———. *How Children Learn*. New York: Delta, 1967.

———. *What Do I Do Monday?* New York: E.P. Dutton, 1970.

Howard, Eugene R., and Jenkens, John M. *Improving Discipline in the Secondary School*. Englewood, Colo.: CFK Ltd., n.d.

Howard, Robert. *Human Psychology: Experiments in Awareness*. Palo Alto, Calif.: Westinghouse Learning Press, 1972.

Humphreys, L. "Letters." *Science* 166 (1969): 167.

Hunt, Maurice P., and Metcalf, Lawrence E. *Teaching High School Social Studies*. New York: Harper and Row, 1968.

James, Muriel, and Jongeward, Dorothy. *Born to Win: Transactional Analysis with Gestalt Experiments*. Reading, Mass.: Addison-Wesley, 1971.

Janowitz, Gayle. *Helping Hands: Volunteer Work in Education*. Chicago: University of Chicago Press, 1965.

Jensen, A. R. "How Much Can We Boost IQ and Scholastic Achievement?" *Harvard Educational Review* 39 (Winter 1969): 1–123.

Jones, Richard M. *Fantasy and Feeling in Education*. New York: New York University Press, 1968.

Jones, Richard M., ed. *Contemporary Educational Psychology: Selected Essays*. New York: Harper Torchbooks, 1967.

Jourard, Sidney. *The Transparent Self*. Princeton, N.J.: Van Nostrand-Reinhold, 1964.

Kagan, Jerome, ed. *Creativity and Learning*. Boston: Beacon Press, 1968.

Kelley, Earl C. *In Defense of Youth*. Englewood Cliffs, N.J.: Prentice-Hall, 1962.

Kimball, Solon T. "Individualism and the Formation of Values." *Journal of Applied Behavioral Science* 2 (1966): 465–482.

Kirschenbaum, Howard. *WAD-JA-GET: The Grading Game in American Education*. New York: Hart, 1971.

Kohl, Herbert. *Math, Writing, and Games in the Open Classroom*. New York: New York Review, 1974.

———. *Methods of Learning and Testing*. New York: E.P. Dutton, 1972.

———. *The Open Classroom*. New York: Vintage Books, 1969.

———. *Reading, How To: A People's Guide to Alternative Methods of Learning and Testing*. New York: E.P. Dutton, 1973.

———. *36 Children*. New York: New American Library, 1967.

Kozol, Jonathan. *Death at an Early Age*. Boston: Houghton Mifflin, 1967.

———. *Free Schools*. Boston: Houghton Mifflin, 1972.

Krathwohl, David R.; Bloom, Benjamin S.; Masia, Bertram B. *Taxonomy of Educational Objectives: The Classification of Educational Goals. Handbook II: Affective Domain*. New York: David McKay, 1964.

Leary, M. E. "Children Who Are Tested in an Alien Language: Mentally Retarded?" *The New Republic* 162 (1970): 17–18

Leonard, George B. *Education and Ecstacy*. New York: Delacorte Press, 1968.

Lewis, H. R., and Streifield, H. S. *Growth Games*. New York: Harcourt Brace Jovanovich, 1970.

Luft, Joseph. *Of Human Interaction*. Palo Alto, Calif.: National Press, 1969.

McClelland, David. *The Achievement Motive*. New York: Appleton-Century-Crofts, 1953.

McClosky, Mildred G., ed. *Teaching Strategies and Classroom Realities*. Englewood Cliffs, N.J.: Prentice-Hall, 1971.

McClosky, Mildred G., and Kleinbard, P. *Youth into Adult*. New York: National Commission on Resources for Youth, 1974.

McDonald, Frederick J. *Educational Psychology*. 2d ed. Belmont, Calif.: Wadsworth, 1965.

McGinnies, Elliott. "Cross-cultural Studies in Persuasion: I. An Attempt to Induce Both Direct and Generalized Attitude Change in Japanese Students." *Journal of Social Psychology* 70 (1966): 69–75.

McGucken, William. "The Philosophy of Catholic Education." In *Philosophies of Education*. Edited by N. B. Henry. Chicago: Society for the Study of Education, 1942.

Maslow, Abraham H. "Some Educational Implications of the Humanistic Psychologies." *Harvard Educational Review* 38 (Fall 1968).

————. *Toward a Psychology of Being*. Princeton: Van Nostrand, 1962.

Mayesoff, Milton. *On Caring*. New York: Harper and Row, 1971.

Mearns, Hughes. *Creative Power: The Education of Youth in the Creative Arts*. New York: Dover, 1958.

Messick, S., and Anderson, S. "Educational Testing, Individual Development, and Social Responsibility." *The Counseling Psychologist* 2 (1970): 80–88.

Moustakas, Clark E. *Teaching As Learning: Becoming Alive and Free in Teaching*. New York: Ballantine Books, 1972.

Moynihan, P. "Benign Neglect for Issue of Race?" *Wall Street Journal* (3 March 1970): 20.

Munday, Leo A. "Measurement for Equal Opportunity." *The Counseling Psychologist* 2 (1970): 93–97.

Mussen, Paul H.; Conger, John J.; and Kagan, Jerome. *Child Development and Personality*. 3d ed. New York: Harper and Row, 1969.

Neill, A. S. *Summerhill*. New York: Hart, 1960.

New Vocations Project. *Working Loose*. San Francisco: American Friends Service Committee, 1971.

Newland, T. E. "Testing Minority-Group Children." *Clinical Child Psychology Newsletter* 9 (1970): 5.

Nyberg, David. *Tough and Tender Learning*. Palo Alto, Calif.: National Press Books, 1971.

Nyquist, Ewald B., and Hawes, Gene R., eds. *Open Education: A Sourcebook for Parents and Teachers*. New York: Bantam Books, 1972.

Oliver, Donald W., and Shaver, James P. *Teaching Public Issues in the High School*. Boston: Houghton Mifflin, 1966.

Otto, H. A. *Group Methods to Actualize Human Potential: A Handbook*. Beverly Hills, Calif.: Holistic Press, 1970.

Passow, A. Harry, ed. *Education in Depressed Areas*. New York: Teachers College Press, Columbia University, 1963.

Pearl, Arthur, and Riessman, Frank. *New Careers for the Poor*. New York: Free Press, 1965.

Pierce, W. D.; West, G. I.; Dent, H. E.; Rawls, J. D.; and Woodson, W. B. *A Reply to San Francisco Unified School District Report on Special Education Classes*. San Francisco: Association of Black Psychologists, 5 May 1970.

Psychosynthesis Research Foundation. *Psychosynthesis in Education*. New York: Psychosynthesis Research Foundation, 1972.

Purkey, William W. *Self-Concept and School Achievement*. Englewood Cliffs, N.J.: Prentice-Hall, 1970.

Ramacharaka. *Raja Yoga or Mental Development*. Chicago: Yogi Publication Society, 1934.

Rasberry, Sally, and Greenway, Robert. *Rasberry Exercises: How to Start Your Own School and Make a Book*. Freestone, Calif.: Freestone, 1971.

Raths, Louis E.; Harmin, Merrill; and Simon, Sidney B. *Values and Teaching: Working with Values in the Classroom*. Columbus, Ohio: Charles E. Merrill, 1966.

Redl, Fritz. *When We Deal with Children: Selected Writings*. New York: Free Press, 1966.

Redl, Fritz, and Wineman, David. *Controls from Within: Techniques for the Treatment of the Aggressive Child*. New York: Free Press, 1952.

Reed, Ishmael. *19 Necro-Mancers From Now*. Edited by Anne Freedgood. New York: Doubleday, 1970.

Riessman, Frank. *Blueprint for the Disadvantaged*. New York: Anti-Defamation League of B'nai B'rith, n.d.

Robinson, Clark. *Making the Most of School and Life*. New York: Macmillan, 1952.

Rogers, Carl R. *Freedom to Learn*. Columbus, Ohio: Charles E. Merrill, 1969.

Rossman, Michael. *On Learning and Social Change: Transcending the Totalitarian Classroom*. New York: Random House, 1969.

Sarason, Seymour B. *The Culture of the School and the Problem of Change*. Boston: Allyn and Bacon, 1971.

Schiffman, Muriel. *Self-Therapy: Techniques for Personal Growth*. Menlo Park, Calif.: Self-Therapy Press, 1967.

Schwebel, Milton. *Who Can Be Educated?* New York: Grove Press, 1968.

Shiel, Barbara J. "Evaluation: A Self-Directed Curriculum, 1965." Unpublished manuscript, 1966.

Silberman, Charles E. *Crisis in the Classroom: The Remaking of American Education*. New York: Random House, Vintage Books, 1970.

Soar, Robert S. "Achieving Humanness: Supporting Research." In *Humanizing the Secondary School*, 55–58. Washington, D.C.: National Education Association, Association for Supervision and Curriculum Development, 1969.

Sommer, J. "Response to Robert Williams." *The Counseling Psychologist* 2 (1970): 92.

Spolin, Viola. *Improvisation for the Theater: A Handbook of Teaching and Directing Techniques*. Evanston, Ill.: Northwestern University Press, 1963.

Stace, W. T. *The Concept of Morals*. New York: Braziller, 1937.

Stevens, John O. *Awareness: Exploring, Experimenting, Experiencing*. Lafayette, Calif.: Real People Press, 1971.

Sutich, Anthony, and Vick, Miles, eds. *Readings in Humanistic Psychology*. New York: Free Press, 1969.

Sykes, A. J. "A Study in Attitude Change." *Occupational Psychology* 40 (1966): 31–41.

Taba, Hilda. *Curriculum Development: Theory and Practice*. New York: Harcourt, Brace and World, 1962.

Today's Education, November 1970.

Watson, Goodwin. "What Psychology Can We Feel Sure About?" *Teachers College Record* 61 (1960–1961): 253–257.

Wechsler, D. *The Measurement of Adult Intelligence*. Baltimore: Williams and Wilkins, 1944.

Weinstein, Gerald, and Fantini, Mario D., eds. *Toward Humanistic Education: A Curriculum of Affect*. New York: Praeger, 1970.

Wesman, A. G. "Intelligent Testing." *American Psychologist* 23 (1968): 267–274.

Wheelis, Allen. "How People Change." *Commentary* (May 1969): 56–66.

———. *The Quest for Identity*. New York: Norton, 1958.

Whitehead, Alfred N. *The Aims of Education*. New York: Macmillan, 1954.

Wigginton, Eliot, ed. *The Foxfire Book*. New York: Doubleday, 1972.

———. *Foxfire 2*. Garden City, N.Y.: Anchor Press, 1973.

Wikoff, R. L. "Danger: Attacks on Testing Unfair." *Clinical Child Psychology Newsletter* 9 (Spring 1970): 3–4.

Williams, H. D. "Experiment in Self-Directed Education." *School and Society* 31 (1930): 715–718.

Williams, R. L. "Black Pride, Academic Relevance, and Individual Achievement." *The Counseling Psychologist* 2 (1970a): 19–22.

———. "Letters." *Science* 167 (1970b): 124.

Wilson, John. *Language and the Pursuit of Truth*. Cambridge, England: Cambridge University Press, 1967.

Witty, P. A., and Jenkins, A. D. "The Case of 'B——,' a Gifted Negro Girl." *Journal of Social Psychology* 6 (1935): 117–124.

Zahn, Jane. *Creativity Research: Its Implications for Adult Education*. Boston: Boston College, Center for the Study of Liberal Education for Adults, 1966.

Marcia Perlstein has extensive academic and practical knowledge in psychology, counseling, and education. She is a marriage, family, and child counselor in Berkeley, California, specializing in individual and group work with adolescents and young adults, and recently in feminist counseling. She is credentialed as a school counselor and has worked mainly with youth in San Francisco, including several years with latino and black teen-agers in a community-operated program. For one year she helped train paraprofessional mental-health aides at Napa State Hospital in a program cosponsored by the University of California at Berkeley and the Center for Community Psychiatry.

She has taught in several public secondary schools, both traditional and alternative, and was instrumental in the design of Opportunity I and Opportunity II High Schools in San Francisco Unified School District. She served as coordinator of Opportunity II during its first year of existence. Marcia Perlstein developed the first high-school women's studies and psychology classes in her district, which she currently teaches. On the college level, she has trained new teachers and taught in the continuing education of certificated teachers. She is currently an instructor at the extension divisions of the University of California at Berkeley and at Santa Cruz. She has also been a part-time instructor at California State University, San Francisco and an adjunct instructor at Antioch College-West. In addition to teaching classes in curriculum, human relations, and social psychology, she has coordinated workshops in thematic problem areas, including ethnic studies, change, and confrontation.

As an educational consultant for school districts, civic organizations, and professional groups, Marcia Perlstein has conducted workshops on personal growth in the human relations and communications fields. She has worked with students, parents, teachers, administrators, and community leaders. Her work has taken her extensively through California and to several cities across the nation. Currently she is an associate for the National Commission on Resources for Youth. In this capacity she has helped develop seminar activities for teen-agers serving as aides in a day-care center, visited innovative youth participatory projects, set up workshops for educators interested in implementing programs where youth have significant decision-making roles, and worked on the production of educational films.

About the Author